Collins

Year 8, Pupil Book 1

NEW MATHS FRAMEWORKING

Matches the revised KS3 Framework

Outcomes not covered in Bk1/2/3:   MNU 3-09a

MNU 3-09b

MTH 3-12a

Outcomes only partially covered in Bk1/2/3:   MNU 3-04a (problems in context)

MTH 3-05b (explanation of prime numbers.

MNU 3-10a (Very little in way of DST questions).

MTH 3-13a (No rule generality)

MTH 3-16a (only covers triangles)

MTH 3-17b (investigate navigation in the world).

MTH 3-17c (include technology).

MTH 3-14a (No single lines of symmetry or diagonal lines of symmetry).

Kevin Evans, Keith Gordon, Trevor Senior, Brian Speed

Contents

Introduction

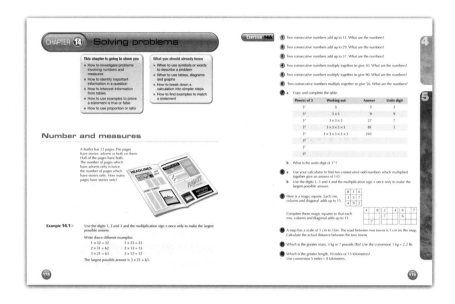

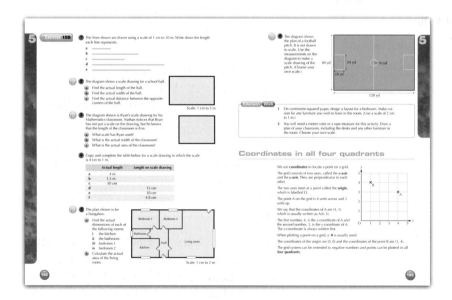

Learning objectives

See what you are going to cover and what you should already know at the start of each chapter. The purple and blue boxes set the topic in context and provide a handy checklist.

National Curriculum levels

Know what level you are working at so you can easily track your progress with the colour-coded levels at the side of the page.

Worked examples

Understand the topic before you start the exercises by reading the examples in blue boxes. These take you through how to answer a question step-by-step.

Functional Maths

Practise your Functional Maths skills to see how people use Maths in everyday life.

Look out for the Functional Maths icon on the page.

Extension activities

Stretch your thinking and investigative skills by working through the extension activities. By tackling these you are working at a higher level.

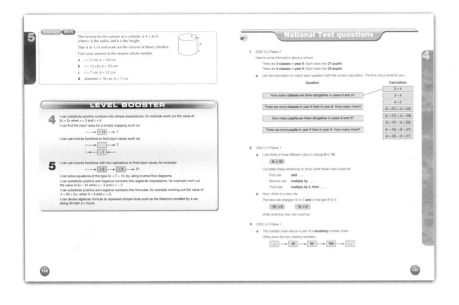

Level booster

Progress to the next level by checking the Level boosters at the end of each chapter. These clearly show you what you need to know at each level and how to improve.

National Test questions

Practise the past paper Test questions to feel confident and prepared for your KS3 National Curriculum Tests. The questions are levelled so you can check what level you are working at.

Extra interactive National Test practice

Watch and listen to the audio/visual National Test questions on the separate Interactive Book CD-ROM to help you revise as a class on a whiteboard.

 Look out for the computer mouse icon on the page and on the screen.

Functional Maths activities

Put Maths into context with these colourful pages showing real-world situations involving Maths. You are practising your Functional Maths skills by analysing data to solve problems.

Extra interactive Functional Maths questions and video clips

Extend your Functional Maths skills by taking part in the interactive questions on the separate Interactive Book CD-ROM. Your teacher can put these on the whiteboard so the class can answer the questions on the board.

See Maths in action by watching the video clips and doing the related Worksheets on the Interactive Book CD-ROM. The videos bring the Functional Maths activities to life and help you see how Maths is used in the real world.

 Look out for the computer mouse icon on the page and on the screen.

CHAPTER 1

Number and Algebra **1**

This chapter is going to show you

- How to multiply and divide negative numbers
- How to find the highest common factor and the lowest common multiple of sets of numbers
- How to find the prime factors of a number
- What square numbers and square roots are
- How to generate and describe number patterns

What you should already know

- How to add and subtract negative integers
- How to generate terms of a simple number sequence
- Recognise the square and triangle number sequences
- How to test numbers for divisibility

See notes pg 1 Book 2

Negative numbers

Example 1.1 *levels*

Work out the answers to: **a** −2 − +4   **b** −6 − −3 + −2

a Rewrite as −2 − 4 and count along a number line −2 − 4 = −6

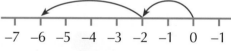

b Rewrite as −6 + 3 − 2 and count along a number line −6 + 3 − 2 = −5

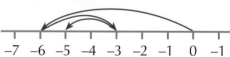

Example 1.2

Work out the answers to: **a** −2 × +4 **b** −6 × −3 **c** −15 ÷ −5 **d** +6 × −4 ÷ −2

a 2 × 4 = 8, and − × + is equivalent to −. So, −2 × +4 = −8

b 6 × 3 = 18, and − × − is equivalent to +. So, −6 × −3 = +18

c 15 ÷ 5 = 3, and − ÷ − is equivalent to +. So, −15 ÷ −5 = +3

d +6 × −4 = −24, −24 ÷ −2 = +12

Example 1.3

Find the missing numbers in: **a** ☐ × 3 = −6   **b** −12 ÷ ☐ = 3

a The inverse problem is ☐ = −6 ÷ +3. So, the missing number is −2.

b The inverse problem is ☐ = −12 ÷ +3. So, the missing number is −4.

1 Copy each of these calculations to show the pattern in each list of answers. Then fill in the missing numbers.

a 3 + +1 = 4
  3 + 0 = 3
  3 + –1 = 2
  3 + –2 = ...
  3 + ... = ...
  3 + ... = ...

b –2 – +1 = –3
  –2 – 0 = –2
  –2 – –1 = –1
  –2 – –2 = ...
  –2 – ... = ...
  –2 – ... = ...

c 4 – +2 = 2
  3 – +1 = 2
  2 – 0   = 2
  1 – –1 = ...
  0 – ... = ...
  ... – ... = ...

2 Work out the answer to each of these.

a +3 – +2
b –4 – –3
c +7 – –6
d –7 + –3
e +7 – +3
f –9 – –5
g –6 + +6
h +6 – –7
i –6 + –6
j –1 + –8
k +5 – +7
l 7 – –5
m –2 – –3 + –4
n – +1 + +1 – +2

3 Find the missing number to make each of these true.

a +2 + –6 = ☐
b +4 + ☐ = +7
c –4 + ☐ = 0
d +5 + ☐ = –1
e +3 + +4 = ☐
f ☐ – –5 = +7
g ☐ – +5 = +2
h +6 + ☐ = 0
i ☐ – –5 = –2
j +2 + –2 = ☐
k ☐ – +2 = – 4
l –2 + –4 = ☐

4 Work out each of these.

a –7 + 8
b –2 – 7
c +6 – 2 + 3
d –6 – 1 + 7
e –3 + 4 – 9
f –3 – 7
g –4 + – 6
h +7 – +6
i –3 – 7 + –8
j –5 + –4 – –7

5 In these 'walls', subtract the number in the right-hand brick from the number in the left-hand brick to find the number in the brick below.

a
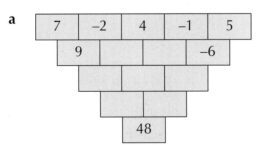

b
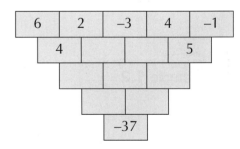

6 Copy and complete each of the following patterns.

a 3 × +3 = 9
  2 × +3 = 6
  1 × +3 = ...
  0 × +3 = ...
  ... × +3 = ...
  ... × +3 = ...

b 3 × –2 = –6
  2 × –2 = –4
  1 × –2 = ...
  0 × –2 = ...
  ... × –2 = ...
  ... × –2 = ...

c –2 × +1 = –2
  –1 × +1 = ...
  ... × +1 = ...
  ... × +1 = ...
  ... × +1 = ...
  ... × +1 = ...

7 Work out the answer to each of these.

a $+2 \times -3$ b $-3 \times +4$ c $-5 \times +2$ d -6×-3

e $-3 \times +8$ f $-4 \times +5$ g -3×-4 h -6×-1

i $+7 \times -2$ j $+2 \times +8$ k $+6 \times -10$ l $+8 \times +4$

m -15×-2 n $-6 \times -3 \times -1$ o $-2 \times +4 \times -2$

8 Work out the answer to each of these.

a $+12 \div -3$ b $-24 \div +4$ c $-6 \div +2$ d $-6 \div -3$

e $-32 \div +8$ f $-40 \div +5$ g $-32 \div -4$ h $-6 \div -1$

i $+7 \div -2$ j $+12 \div +6$ k $+60 \div -10$ l $+8 \div +4$

m $-15 \div -2$ n $-6 \times -3 \div -2$ o $-2 \times +6 \div -3$

9 Find the missing number in each calculation. (Remember: Numbers without a + or −
sign in front are always positive.)

a $2 \times -3 = \boxed{}$ b $-2 \times \boxed{} = -8$ c $3 \times \boxed{} = -9$

d $\boxed{} \div -5 = -15$ e $-4 \times -6 = \boxed{}$ f $-3 \times \boxed{} = -24$

g $-64 \div \boxed{} = 32$ h $\boxed{} \times 6 = 36$ i $-2 \times 3 = \boxed{}$

Level 5

Extension **Work**

This is an algebraic magic square.

1 Find the value in each cell when $a = 7$, $b = 9$, $c = 2$.

2 Find the value in each cell when $a = -1$, $b = -3$, $c = -5$.

$a + c$	$c - a - b$	$b + c$
$b + c - a$	c	$a + c - b$
$c - b$	$a + b + c$	$c - a$

HCF and LCM

MTH 3-05a

HCF stands for Highest Common Factor.
LCM stands for Lowest Common Multiple.

Look at the diagrams below. What do you think they are showing?

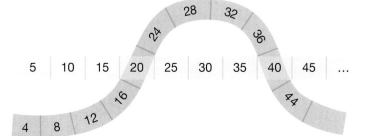

Example 1.4 ▷ Find the lowest common multiple (LCM) of the following pairs of numbers.

   a   3 and 7   **b**   6 and 9

   a   Write out the first few multiples of each number:

        3, 6, 9, 12, 15, 18, ⟨21⟩, 24, 27, ...

        7, 14, ⟨21⟩, 28, 35, ...

     You can see that the LCM of 3 and 7 is 21.

   b   Write out the first few multiples of each number:

        6, 12, ⟨18⟩, 24, ...

        9, ⟨18⟩, 27, 36, ...

     You can see that the LCM of 6 and 9 is 18.

Example 1.5 ▷ Find the highest common factor (HCF) of the following pairs of numbers.

   a   15 and 21   **b**   16 and 24

   a   Write out the factors of each number: 1, ⟨3⟩, 5, 15

                                         1, ⟨3⟩, 7, 21

     You can see that the HCF of 15 and 21 is 3.

   b   Write out the factors of each number: 1, 2, 4, ⟨8⟩, 16

                                         1, 2, 3, 4, 6, ⟨8⟩, 12, 24

     You can see that the HCF of 16 and 24 is 8.

Exercise 1B

1 Write down the numbers in the row below that are multiples of:

   a   2   **b**   3   **c**   5   **d**   10

10	4	23	18	69	81	8	65	33	72	100

2 Write down the first ten multiples of the following numbers.

   a   4   **b**   5   **c**   8   **d**   9   **e**   10

3 Write out all the factors of the following.

   a   15   **b**   20   **c**   32   **d**   12   **e**   25

4 Use your answers to Question 2 to help to find the LCM of the following pairs.

   a   5 and 8   **b**   4 and 10   **c**   4 and 9   **d**   8 and 10

5 Use your answers to Question 3 to help to find the HCF of the following pairs.

   a   15 and 20   **b**   15 and 25   **c**   12 and 20   **d**   20 and 32

6 Find the LCM of the following pairs.

   a   5 and 9   **b**   5 and 25   **c**   3 and 8   **d**   4 and 6

   e   8 and 12   **f**   12 and 15   **g**   9 and 21   **h**   7 and 11

   [*Hint:* Write out the multiples of each number.]

7 Find the HCF of the following pairs.

a	15 and 18	**b**	12 and 32	**c**	12 and 22	**d**	8 and 12
e	2 and 18	**f**	8 and 18	**g**	18 and 27	**h**	7 and 11

[*Hint:* Write out the factors of each number.]

Extension Work

The odd numbers are 1, 3, 5, 7, 9, 11, …

The square numbers are 1, 4, 9, 16, 25, 36, …

The triangle numbers are 1, 3, 6, 10, 15, 21, …

1 Add up the odd numbers consecutively, starting at 1,

i.e. 1, 1 + 3, 1 + 3 + 5, 1 + 3 + 5 + 7, etc.

What do you notice about the answers?

2 Add up consecutive triangle numbers,

i.e. 1, 1 + 3, 3 + 6, 6 + 10, 10 + 15, etc.

What do you notice about the answers?

Square numbers and square roots

You met square numbers in Year 7. For example,
$5^2 = 5 \times 5 = 25$.

The opposite of the square of a number is its square root.
This is shown by the sign $\sqrt{}$. For example, $\sqrt{25} = 5$.

The following table gives the square roots of the square
numbers up to 144.

You will have to learn these.

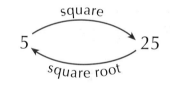

Square number	1	4	9	16	25	36	49	64	81	100	121	144
Square root	1	2	3	4	5	6	7	8	9	10	11	12

Example 1.6 Work out the answer to: **a** $\sqrt{4} \times \sqrt{36}$ **b** $\sqrt{144} \div \sqrt{4}$

a $\sqrt{4} \times \sqrt{36} = 2 \times 6 = 12$

b $\sqrt{144} \div \sqrt{4} = 12 \div 2 = 6$

Example 1.7 Use your calculator to find: **a** $\sqrt{729}$ **b** $\sqrt{1000}$

a Calculators work in different ways. On some calculators, you have to key the
number first and then press the square root key $\sqrt{}$. On others, you have to
press the square root key before pressing the number key.

The answer is 27. Make sure you know how to use your calculator.

b The answer is 31.622 776 6. You may round this to 32 or 31.6.

Exercise 1C

1 $3^2 + 4^2 = 5^2$ is an example of a *special square sum* (made up of only square numbers). There are many to be found. See which of the following pairs of squares will give you a special square sum.

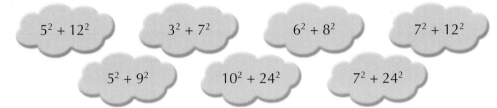

$5^2 + 12^2$ $3^2 + 7^2$ $6^2 + 8^2$ $7^2 + 12^2$

$5^2 + 9^2$ $10^2 + 24^2$ $7^2 + 24^2$

2 Write down the value represented by each of the following. Do not use a calculator.

a $\sqrt{16}$	**b** $\sqrt{36}$	**c** $\sqrt{4}$	**d** $\sqrt{49}$	**e** $\sqrt{1}$
f $\sqrt{9}$	**g** $\sqrt{100}$	**h** $\sqrt{81}$	**i** $\sqrt{25}$	**j** $\sqrt{64}$

3 Work out each of these.

a $\sqrt{4} \times \sqrt{9}$	**b** $\sqrt{64} \div \sqrt{4}$	**c** $\sqrt{81} \div \sqrt{9}$	**d** $\sqrt{100} \times \sqrt{144}$
e $\sqrt{25} \times \sqrt{9}$	**f** $\sqrt{49} \times \sqrt{9}$	**g** $\sqrt{25} \times \sqrt{4} \times \sqrt{81}$	**h** $\sqrt{100} \times \sqrt{81} \div \sqrt{36}$

4 With the aid of a calculator, write down the value represented by each of the following.

a $\sqrt{289}$	**b** $\sqrt{961}$	**c** $\sqrt{529}$	**d** $\sqrt{2500}$	**e** $\sqrt{1296}$
f $\sqrt{729}$	**g** $\sqrt{3249}$	**h** $\sqrt{361}$	**i** $\sqrt{3969}$	**j** $\sqrt{1764}$

5 Make an estimate of each of the following square roots. Then use your calculator to see how many you got right.

a $\sqrt{256}$	**b** $\sqrt{1089}$	**c** $\sqrt{625}$	**d** $\sqrt{2704}$	**e** $\sqrt{1444}$
f $\sqrt{841}$	**g** $\sqrt{3481}$	**h** $\sqrt{441}$	**i** $\sqrt{4096}$	**j** $\sqrt{2025}$

6 Use a calculator to work out each of the following. Round each answer to the nearest whole number.

a $\sqrt{300}$	**b** $\sqrt{500}$	**c** $\sqrt{200}$	**d** $\sqrt{450}$	**e** $\sqrt{10}$

Extension **Work**

How many squares are there on a chessboard?

The answer is not 64!

For example, in this square ⊞ there are five squares:

four this size ☐ and one this size ☐

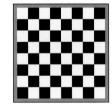

In this square ▦ there are 14 squares:

nine this size ☐, four this size ☐ and one this size ☐

By drawing increasingly larger 'chessboards', work out how many squares there are and see if you can spot the pattern.

A computer spreadsheet is useful for this activity.

MTH 4-06a

MTH 4-13a

Prime factors

What are the prime factors of 120 and 210?

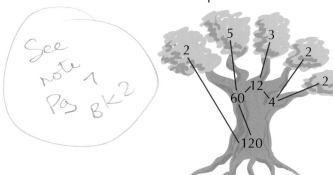

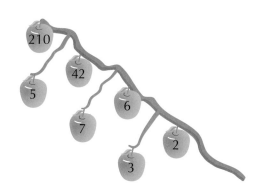

Example 1.8 ▷

Find the prime factors of 18.

Using a prime factor tree, split 18 into 3 × 6 and 6 into 3 × 2.

So, 18 = 2 × 3 × 3.

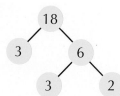

Exercise 1D

① These are the prime factors of some numbers. What are the numbers?

   a 2 × 2 × 3   **b** 2 × 3 × 3 × 5   **c** 2 × 2 × 3 × 3   **d** 2 × 3 × 5   **e** 2 × 2 × 5

② Using a prime factor tree, work out the prime factors of the following.

   a 8   **b** 10   **c** 16   **d** 20   **e** 28
   f 34   **g** 35   **h** 40   **i** 50   **j** 100

③ Use a prime factor tree to work out the prime factors of each of the following. (To help you, a starting multiplication is given.)

   a 42 (6 × 7)   **b** 75 (5 × 15)   **c** 140 (7 × 20)   **d** 250 (5 × 50)
   e 480 (60 × 8)   **f** 72 (8 × 9)   **g** 96 (4 × 24)   **h** 256 (4 × 64)

Extension **Work**

Make a poster showing the prime factors of a large number, such as 400. Draw a picture of a real tree like the one at the start of this section.

Sequences 1

Example 1.9 ▷

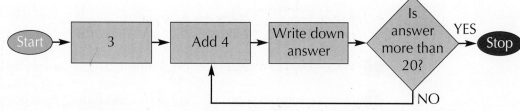

Follow through the above flow diagram and write down the numbers generated.

These are 3, 7, 11, 15, 19, 23.

Example 1.10 ▷

For each of the following sequences: **i** find the term-to-term rule.
ii find the next two terms.

a   2, 6, 10, 14, 18, 22, …

b   1, 3, 27, 81, 243, …

i   4 is added to next term.
So the term-to term-rule is +4.

i   Each term is multiplied by 3 to get the next term. So, the term-to-term rule is × 3.

ii   The next two terms are 26, 30.

ii   The next two terms are 729, 2187.

Exercise 1E

1   Follow each set of instructions to generate a sequence.

a

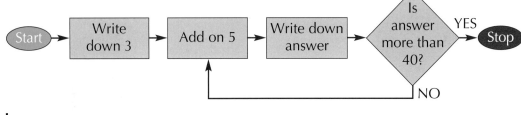

b

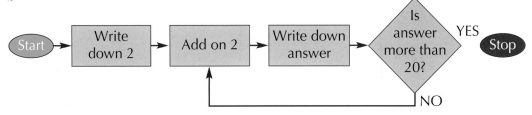

c

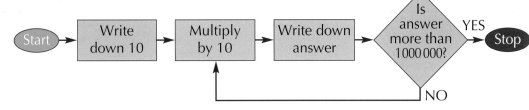

2   What is the name of the sequence of numbers generated by the flow diagram in Question 1, part **b**?

3   Describe the sequence of numbers generated by the flow diagram in Question 1, part **c**.

4   Find the term-to-term rule for each of the sequences below.

   a   1, 4, 7, 10, 13, 16, …   **b**   1, 4, 16, 64, 256, 1024, …
   c   1, 4, 8, 13, 19, 26, …   **d**   1, 4, 9, 16, 25, 36, …

5   Write down four sequences beginning 1, 5, … . Explain how each of them is generated.

6   Find the term-to-term rule for each of the following sequences. Write down the next two terms.

   a   40, 41, 43, 46, 50, 55, …   **b**   90, 89, 87, 84, 80, 75, …
   c   1, 3, 7, 13, 21, 31, …   **d**   2, 6, 12, 20, 30, 42, …

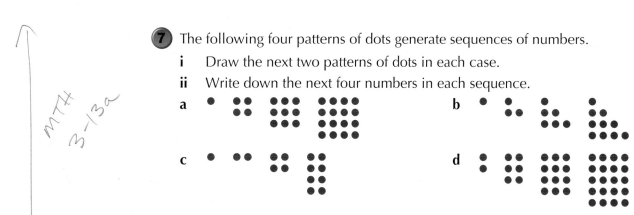

7 The following four patterns of dots generate sequences of numbers.

   i   Draw the next two patterns of dots in each case.

   ii Write down the next four numbers in each sequence.

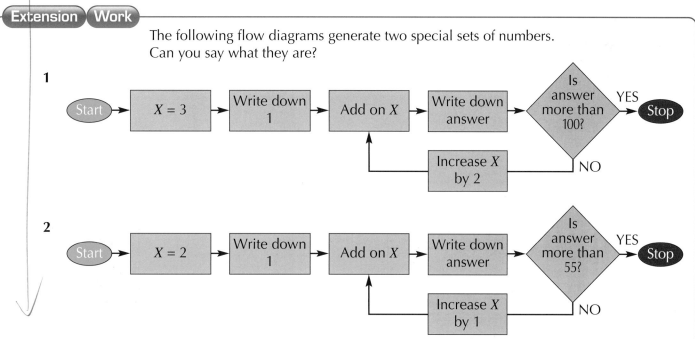

The following flow diagrams generate two special sets of numbers.
Can you say what they are?

1

Start → $X = 3$ → Write down 1 → Add on X → Write down answer → Is answer more than 100? — YES → Stop

Increase X by 2 ← NO

2

Start → $X = 2$ → Write down 1 → Add on X → Write down answer → Is answer more than 55? — YES → Stop

Increase X by 1 ← NO

Sequences 2

Paving slabs, 1 metre square, are used to put borders around square ponds. For example:

  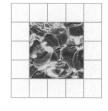 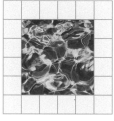

1×1 m² pond
8 slabs

2×2 m² pond
12 slabs

3×3 m² pond
16 slabs

4×4 m² pond
20 slabs

How many slabs would fit around a 5×5 m² pond? What about a 100×100 m² pond?

Example 1.11   For each of these sequences, write down: **i** the first term.   **ii** the constant difference.

   a   3, 7, 11, 15, 19, 23, …   **b** 5, 8, 11, 14, 17, 20, 23, …

   a   The first term is 3. The constant difference is 4.

   b   The first term is 5. The constant difference is 3.

Example 1.12 ▷

Using the term-to-term rules given, generate each of these sequences.

a First term 5, term-to-term rule: + 6

b First term 32, term-to-term rule: $\times \frac{1}{2}$

c First term 3, term-to-term rule: subtract 1 then multiply by 2

a The sequence is 5, 5 + 6 = 11, 11 + 6 = 17, … . This gives 5, 11, 17, 23, 29, 35, … .

b The sequence is $32 \times \frac{1}{2} = 16$, $16 \times \frac{1}{2} = 8$, … . This gives 32, 16, 8, 4, 2, 1, $\frac{1}{2}$, $\frac{1}{4}$, … .

c The sequence is $(3 - 1) \times 2 = 4$, $(4 - 1) \times 2 = 6$, $(6 - 1) \times 2 = 10$, … . This gives 3, 4, 6, 10, 18, 34, 66, … .

Example 1.13 ▷

Write down the first five terms of each of the following sequences.

a 3 × term position number + 4

b $5n - 1$, where n is the term position number

a First term is $3 \times 1 + 4 = 7$, second term is $3 \times 2 + 4 = 10$, third term = $3 \times 3 + 4 = 13$, fourth term is $3 \times 4 + 4 = 16$, fifth term is $3 \times 5 + 4 = 19$.

So, the sequence is 7, 10, 13, 16, 19, … .

b $n = 1$ gives $5 \times 1 - 1 = 4$, $n = 2$ gives $5 \times 2 - 1 = 9$, $n = 3$ gives $5 \times 3 - 1 = 14$, $n = 4$ gives $5 \times 4 - 1 = 19$, $n = 5$ gives $5 \times 5 - 1 = 24$.

So, the sequence is 4, 9, 14, 19, 24, … .

Exercise 1F

1 For each of the following sequences, write down the first term, and the constant difference.

    a 4, 9, 14, 19, 24, 29, …   **b** 1, 3, 5, 7, 9, 11, …

    c 3, 9, 15, 21, 27, 33, …   **d** 5, 3, 1, –1, –3, –5, …

2 Given the first term a and the constant difference d, write down the first six terms of each of these sequences.

    a $a = 1, d = 7$ **b** $a = 3, d = 2$ **c** $a = 5, d = 4$

    d $a = 0.5, d = 1.5$ **e** $a = 4, d = -3$ **f** $a = 2, d = -0.5$

3 Write down the first five terms of each of these sequences.

    a First term 3   Term-to-term rule: Multiply by 2

    b First term 4   Term-to-term rule: Multiply by 3 and add 1

    c First term 5   Term-to-term rule: Subtract 1 and multiply by 2

4 The position-to-term definition of each of four sequences is given below. Use this to write down the first five terms of each sequence.

    a 2 × (term position number) – 1   **b** 3 × (term position number) + 1

    c 4 × (term position number) + 2   **d** 2 × (term position number) + 3

5 The nth term of a sequence is given by a rule below. Use each rule to write down the first five terms of its sequence.

    a $4n + 1$ **b** $3n + 2$ **c** $3n - 2$ **d** $2n + 1$

MTH 4-13a

Fibonacci numbers

You will need a calculator.

The Fibonacci sequence is: 1, 1, 2, 3, 5, 8, 13, 21, …

It is formed by adding together the previous two terms, that is $5 = 3 + 2$, $8 = 5 + 3$, etc.

Write down the next five terms of the sequence.

Now divide each term by the previous term, that is $1 ÷ 1 = 1$, $2 ÷ 1 = 2$, $3 ÷ 2 = 1.5$, $5 ÷ 3 = …$

You should notice something happening.

You may find a computer spreadsheet useful for this activity.

If you have access to the Internet, find out about the Italian mathematician after whom the sequence is named.

Solving problems

An Investigation

At the start of the last section, you were asked to find the number of slabs that would be needed to go round a square pond of a certain size.

1 × 1 m² pond
8 slabs

2 × 2 m² pond
12 slabs

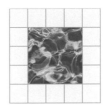

3 × 3 m² pond
16 slabs

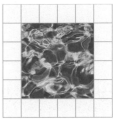

4 × 4 m² pond
20 slabs

To solve this problem you need to:

Step 1: Break down the problem into simple stages.

Step 2: Set up a table of results.

Step 3: Predict and test a rule.

Step 4: Use your rule to answer the question.

Step 1 This has been done already with the diagrams given.

Step 2

Pond size (m²)	Number of slabs
1 × 1	8
2 × 2	12
3 × 3	16
4 × 4	20

Step 3 Use the table to spot how the sequence is growing.

In this case, it is increasing in 4s.

So, a 5 × 5m² pond will need 24 slabs as shown on the right.

You can also see that the number of slabs (S) is 4 times the side length of the pond (P) plus 4. This can be given as:

$$S = 4P + 4$$

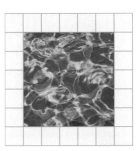

Step 4 Now use the rule for the $100 \times 100m^2$ pond, where $P = 100$:

$$S = 4 \times 100 + 4 = 404$$

So, 404 slabs will be needed.

Exercise 1G

Do the following investigations. Make sure you follow the steps given above and explain clearly what you are doing.

① Write a rule to show how many square slabs it takes to make a border around rectangular ponds.

 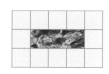 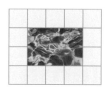

First side	Second side	Slabs
1	2	10
1	3	12
2	3	14

② The final score in a football match was 5–4. How many different half-time scores could there have been?

For a match that ended 0–0, there is only one possible half-time result: (0–0)

For a match that ended 1–2, there are six possible half-time scores: (0–0, 0–1, 0–2, 1–0, 1–1, 1–2)

Take some other low-scoring matches, such as 1–1, 2–1, 2–0, etc., and work out the half-time scores for these.

(*Hint:* Set up a table like the one in Question 1.)

LEVEL BOOSTER

4
I can write down the multiples of any whole number.
I can work out the factors of numbers under 100.

5
I can add and subtract negative numbers, for example $-7 + -3 = -10$.
I can write down and recognise the sequence of square numbers.
I know the squares of all numbers up to 12 and the corresponding square roots.
I can use a calculator to work out powers of numbers.
I can find any term in a sequence given the first term, say 5, and the term-to-term rule such as 'goes up by 6 each time', for example, the 20th term is 119.
I know that the square roots of positive numbers can have two values, one positive and one negative, for example $\sqrt{36} = +6$ or -6.

6
I can multiply and divide negative numbers, for example $-5 \times +3 = -15$.
I can find the lowest common multiple (LCM) for pairs of numbers, for example, the LCM of 24 and 30 is 120.
I can find the highest common factor (HCF) for pairs of numbers, for example, the HCF of 24 and 30 is 6.
I can write a number as the product of its prime factors, for example, $24 = 2 \times 2 \times 2 \times 3 = 2^3 \times 3$.

1 *2000 Paper 2*

    a Write down the next two numbers in the sequence below.

        281, 287, 293, 299, ..., ...

    b Write down the next two numbers in the sequence below.

        1, 4, 9, 16, 25, ..., ...

    c Describe the pattern in part **b** in your own words.

MTH 3-13a

2 *2007 4–6 Paper 1*

    a A **three-digit** number is a **multiple of 4**.

        What could the number be?

        Give an example.

        Now give a **different** example.

    b A **two-digit** number is a **factor of 100**.

        What could the number be?

        Give an example.

        Now give a **different** example.

MTH 3-05a.

3 *2002 Paper 1*

Copy and complete these calculations by filling in the missing numbers in the boxes using only negative numbers.

$$\boxed{} - \boxed{} = 5 \qquad \boxed{} - \boxed{} = -5$$

4 *2007 4–6 Paper 1*

Copy the following and write a number in each box to make the calculations correct.

$$\boxed{} + \boxed{} = -8 \qquad \boxed{} - \boxed{} = -8$$

MNU 3-04a

Blackpool Tower

Blackpool Tower is a tourist attraction in Blackpool, Lancashire, England. It opened to the public on 14 May 1894. Inspired by the Eiffel Tower in Paris, it rises to 518 ft 9 inches.

The foundation stone was laid on 29 September 1891. The total cost for the design and construction of the Tower and buildings was about £290 000. Five million bricks, 2500 tonnes of steel and 93 tonnes of cast steel were used to construct the Tower. The Tower buildings occupy a total of 6040 sq yards.

When the Tower opened, 3000 customers took the first rides to the top. Tourists paid 6 old pence for admission, a further 6 old pence for a ride in the lifts to the top, and a further 6 old pence for the circus.

Inside the Tower there is a circus, an aquarium, a ballroom, restaurants, a children's play area and amusements.

In 1998 a 'Walk of Faith' glass floor panel was opened at the top of the Tower. Made up of two sheets of laminated glass, it weighs half a tonne and is two inches thick. Visitors can stand on the glass panel and look straight down 380 ft to the promenade.

Use the information to help you answer these questions.

1 In what year did the Tower celebrate its centenary (100th birthday)?

2 How many years and months did it take to build the Tower?

3 The Tower is painted continuously. It takes seven years to paint the Tower completely. How many times has it been painted since it opened?

4 The aquarium in the Tower opened 20 years earlier than the Tower. What year did the aquarium celebrate its 100th birthday?

5 The largest tank in the aquarium holds 32 000 litres of water. There are approximately 4.5 litres to a gallon. How many gallons of water does the tank hold?

6 The water in the tropical fish tanks is kept at 75°F. This rule is used to convert from degrees Fahrenheit to degrees Centigrade.

°F → Subtract 32 → Divide by 9 → Multiply by 5 → °C

Use this rule to convert 75°F to °C.

7 The circus in the base of the Tower first opened to the public on 14 May 1894. Admission fee was 6 old pence. Before Britain introduced decimal currency in 1971 there were 240 old pence in a pound.

a What fraction, in its simplest form, is 6 old pence out of 240 old pence?

b What is the equivalent value of 6 old pence in new pence?

c When it first opened, it would have cost 18 old pence to see all the attractions. In 2008 there is a one-off charge of £9.50.

  i How many times more expensive is it in 2008 than when the Tower opened?

  ii In real terms, one old penny when the Tower opened is worth £1.83 in 2008. How much more expensive was it to visit the Tower when it opened in 2008 values?

8 Over 650 000 people visit the Tower every year. The Tower is open every day except Christmas day. Approximately how many people visit the Tower each day on average?

9 a Assuming a brick weighs 3 kg, what was the total weight of bricks used to build the Tower? Answer in tonnes.

b What was the total weight of all building materials?

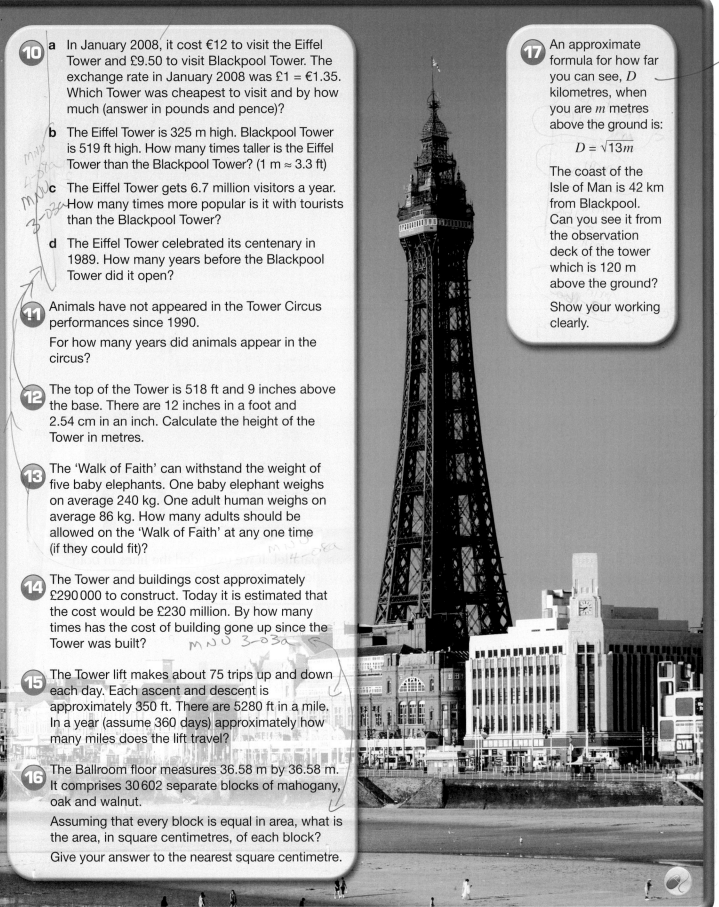

10 a In January 2008, it cost €12 to visit the Eiffel Tower and £9.50 to visit Blackpool Tower. The exchange rate in January 2008 was £1 = €1.35. Which Tower was cheapest to visit and by how much (answer in pounds and pence)?

b The Eiffel Tower is 325 m high. Blackpool Tower is 519 ft high. How many times taller is the Eiffel Tower than the Blackpool Tower? (1 m ≈ 3.3 ft)

c The Eiffel Tower gets 6.7 million visitors a year. How many times more popular is it with tourists than the Blackpool Tower?

d The Eiffel Tower celebrated its centenary in 1989. How many years before the Blackpool Tower did it open?

11 Animals have not appeared in the Tower Circus performances since 1990.

For how many years did animals appear in the circus?

12 The top of the Tower is 518 ft and 9 inches above the base. There are 12 inches in a foot and 2.54 cm in an inch. Calculate the height of the Tower in metres.

13 The 'Walk of Faith' can withstand the weight of five baby elephants. One baby elephant weighs on average 240 kg. One adult human weighs on average 86 kg. How many adults should be allowed on the 'Walk of Faith' at any one time (if they could fit)?

14 The Tower and buildings cost approximately £290 000 to construct. Today it is estimated that the cost would be £230 million. By how many times has the cost of building gone up since the Tower was built?

15 The Tower lift makes about 75 trips up and down each day. Each ascent and descent is approximately 350 ft. There are 5280 ft in a mile. In a year (assume 360 days) approximately how many miles does the lift travel?

16 The Ballroom floor measures 36.58 m by 36.58 m. It comprises 30 602 separate blocks of mahogany, oak and walnut.

Assuming that every block is equal in area, what is the area, in square centimetres, of each block?

Give your answer to the nearest square centimetre.

17 An approximate formula for how far you can see, D kilometres, when you are m metres above the ground is:

$$D = \sqrt{13m}$$

The coast of the Isle of Man is 42 km from Blackpool. Can you see it from the observation deck of the tower which is 120 m above the ground?

Show your working clearly.

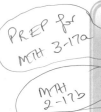

PREP for MTH 3-17a

MTH 2-17b

MTH 2-16a

MTH 2-16a

MTH 3-16a

This chapter is going to show you

- How to identify parallel and perpendicular lines
- How to measure and draw reflex angles
- How to calculate angles in triangles
- How to use the properties of quadrilaterals
- How to draw triangles accurately

What you should already know

- How to draw and measure lines to the nearest millimetre
- How to draw and measure acute and obtuse angles *MTH 2-17b*
- The names of the different types of quadrilateral
- How to recognise shapes that have reflective and rotational symmetry

Parallel and perpendicular lines

MTH 3-17a

IDENTIFYING PARALLEL LINES is not mentioned specifically in cfe but could be included as preparation for *MTH 3-17a*

Example 2.1 ▷   —————— These two lines are parallel. If we extended the lines in both
—————— directions, they would never meet.

We show that two lines are parallel by drawing arrows on them like this:

Example 2.2 ▷   Two lines are perpendicular if the angle between them is 90°. This is
also called a right angle.

90°

We show that two lines are perpendicular by labelling the 90° angle with a square corner.

Exercise 2A

1 Write down which of the following sets of lines are parallel.

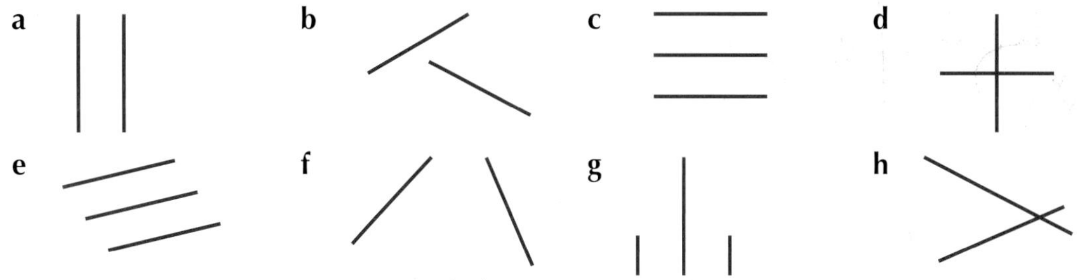

a   b   c  d

e   f  g 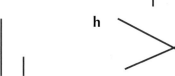 h

2 Copy each of the following diagrams onto square dotted paper.

On each diagram, use your ruler to draw two more lines that are parallel to the first line. Show that the lines are parallel by adding arrows to them.

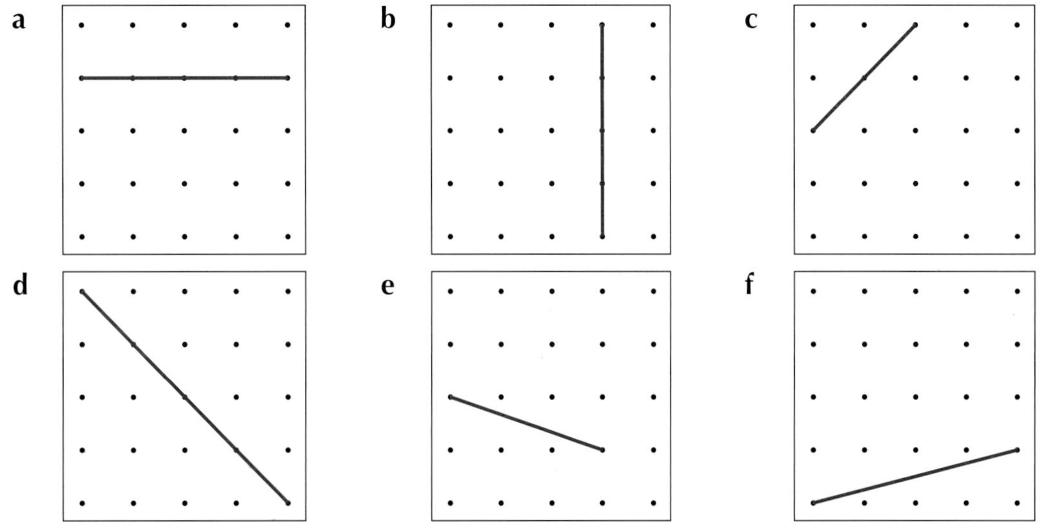

a 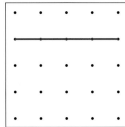 b 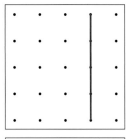 c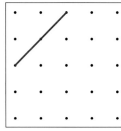

d 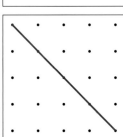 e 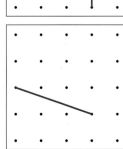 f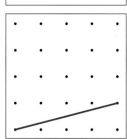

3 Write down which of the following pairs of lines are perpendicular.

a   b   c   d

e   f   g   h

4

The line AB is perpendicular to the line CD.

Copy and complete the following.

a

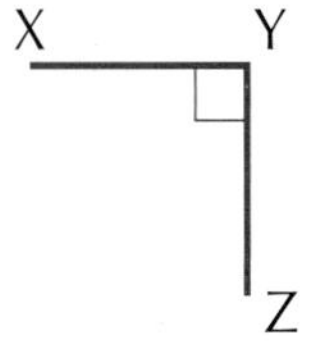

The line XY is perpendicular to the line …

b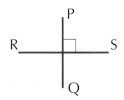

The line … is perpendicular to the line …

MTH 3-17a ?

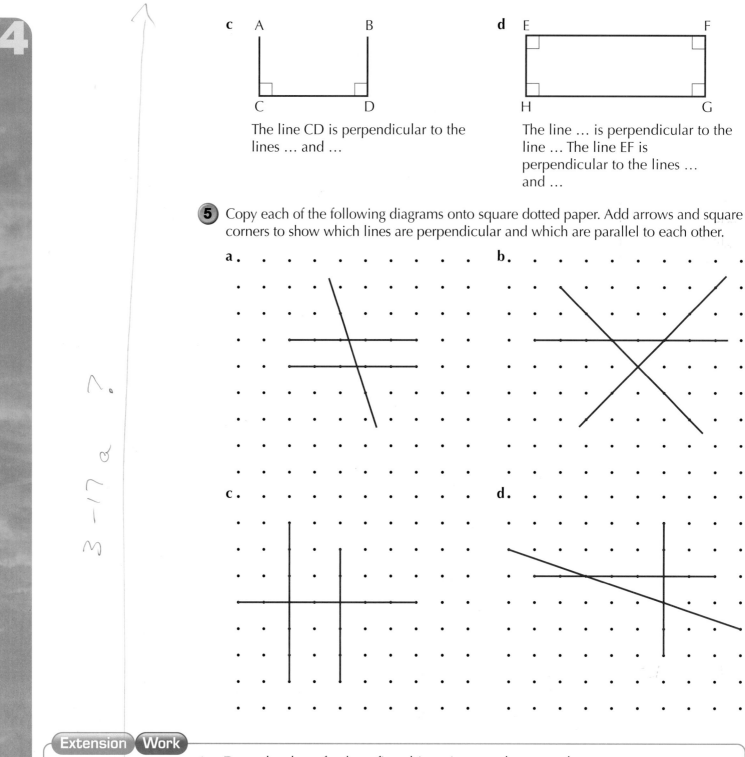

c
A   B

C   D

The line CD is perpendicular to the lines … and …

d
E   F

H   G

The line … is perpendicular to the line … The line EF is perpendicular to the lines … and …

5 Copy each of the following diagrams onto square dotted paper. Add arrows and square corners to show which lines are perpendicular and which are parallel to each other.

a.

b.

c.

d.

1 Draw sketches of at least five objects in your classroom that:

a contain parallel lines.

b contain perpendicular lines.

Label any right angles on your sketches with square corners and any parallel lines with arrows.

2 Use your ruler to draw a straight line of any length.

Now draw two more lines that are both perpendicular to this line.

Write down what you notice about the two new lines.

Measuring and drawing angles

When two lines meet at a point, they form an **angle**. An angle is a measure of rotation and is measured in degrees (°).

Types of angle

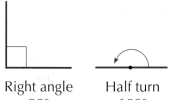

Right angle
90°

Half turn
180°

Full turn
360°

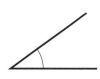

Acute angle
less than 90°

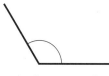

Obtuse angle
between 90° and 180°

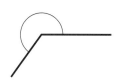

Reflex angle
between 180° and 360°

Notice that on a semicircular protractor there are two scales. Both scales run from 0° to 180°. One goes clockwise and other goes anticlockwise. It is important that you use the correct scale.

When measuring or drawing an angle, always decide first whether it is an acute angle or an obtuse angle.

Example 2.3 ▷

First, decide whether the angle to be measured is acute or obtuse. This is an acute angle (less than 90°).

Place the centre of the protractor at the corner of the angle, as in the diagram.

The two angles shown on the protractor scales are 60° and 120°. Since you are measuring an acute angle, the angle is 60° (to the nearest degree).

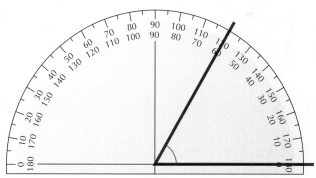

Example 2.4 ▷

Measure the size of this reflex angle.

First, measure the inside or interior angle. This is an obtuse angle.

The two angles shown on the protractor scales are 30° and 150°. Since you are measuring an obtuse angle, the angle is 150°.

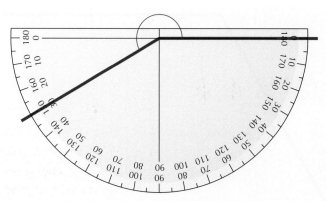

The size of the reflex angle is found by subtracting this angle from 360°. The reflex angle is therefore 360 – 150°, which is 210° (to the nearest degree).

Exercise 2B

1 Write down whether each of the following angles is acute, obtuse, reflex or a right angle.

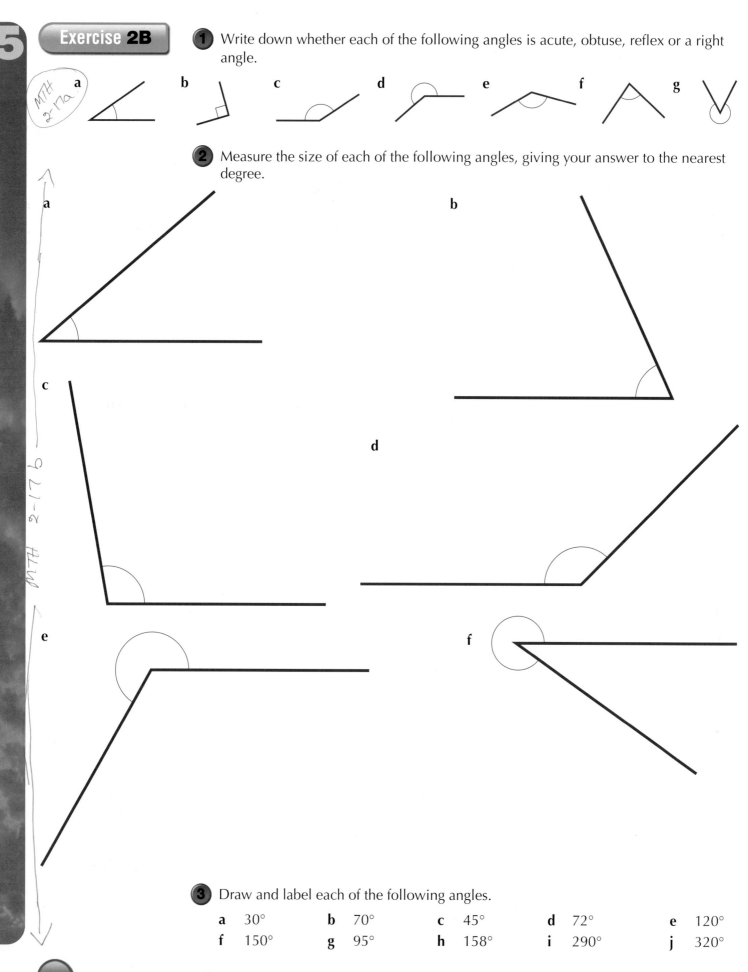

a   b   c   d   e   f   g

2 Measure the size of each of the following angles, giving your answer to the nearest degree.

a

b

c

d

e

f

3 Draw and label each of the following angles.

a	30°	b	70°	c	45°	d	72°	e	120°
f	150°	g	95°	h	158°	i	290°	j	320°

Extension Work

Angles in a triangle

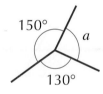

A

B

C

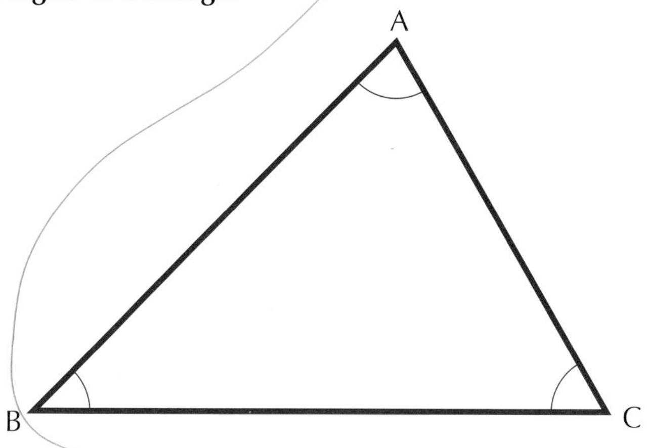

a Measure the three angles in the triangle ABC.
Copy and complete the following.
Angle A = ...°, Angle B = ...°, Angle C = ...°

b Add the three angles together.
Copy and complete the following.
Angle A + Angle B + Angle C = ...°

c Now draw some triangles of your own and repeat the above.

d Write down anything you notice.

Calculating angles

You can calculate the **unknown angles** in a diagram from the information given.
Unknown angles are usually shown by letters, such as *a*, *b*, *c*, ...

Remember: Usually the diagrams are not to scale.

Angles around a point

Angles around a point add up to 360°.

Example 2.5 ▷   Calculate the size of the angle *a*.

150°

130°

a

$a = 360° - 150° - 130°$
$a = 80°$

Angles on a straight line

Angles on a straight line add up to 180°.

Example 2.6 ▷   Calculate the size of the angle *b*.

155°   *b*

$b = 180° - 155°$
$b = 25°$

Angles in a triangle   The angles in a triangle add up to 180°.

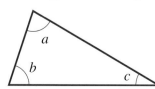

a

b   *c*

$a + b + c = 180°$

Example 2.7 Calculate the size of the angle *c*.

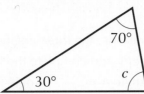

70°
30°
c

$c = 180° - 70° - 30°$

$c = 80°$

MTH 3-17a

Example 2.8 Calculate the size of angle *d*.

d
50°

$d = 180° - 90° - 50°$

$d = 40°$

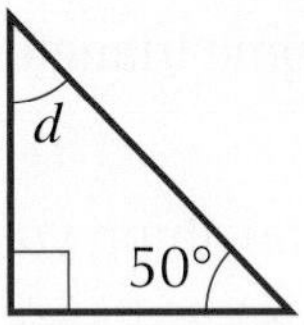

Pg 22 Ex 2C
Q1 + Q2
could be 'included
in MTH 3-17a
though not 'angles
in 2D shapes'

5

Exercise 2C

MTH 3-17a ?

1 Calculate the size of each unknown angle.

a

120°
a
100°

b

130°

c

60°
120°

d

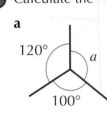

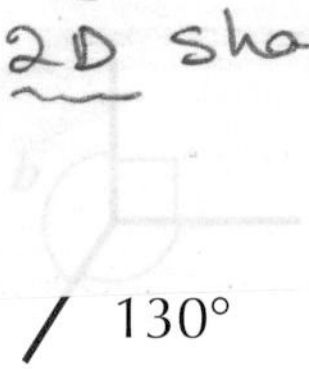

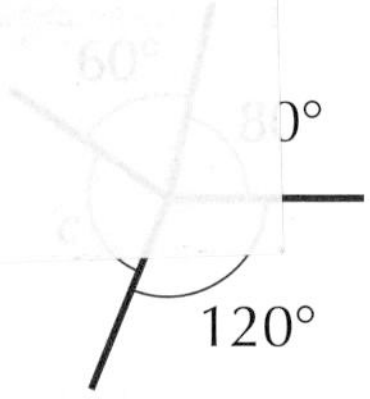

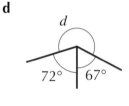

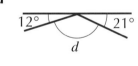

d
72°
67°

2 Calculate the size of each unknown angle.

a

a
120°

b

55°
b

c

c
58°
32°

d

12°
21°
d

MTH 3-17a

3 Calculate the size of each unknown angle.

a

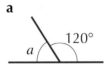

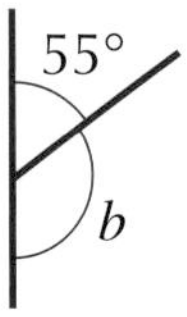

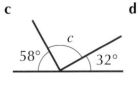

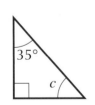

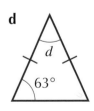

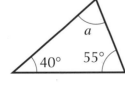

a
40°
55°

b

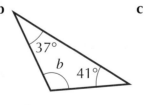

37°
b
41°

c

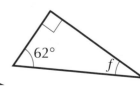

35°
c

d

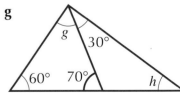

d
63°

e

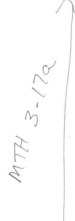

98°
e
25°

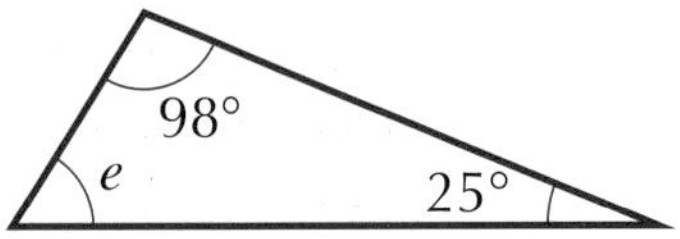

f

62°
f

g

g
30°
60°
70°
h

Extension **Work**

Calculate the size of the unknown angle(s) in each diagram.

1

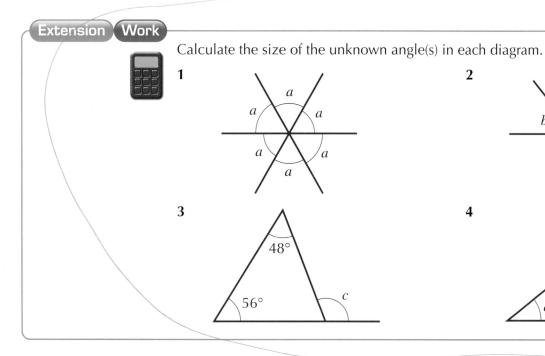

2

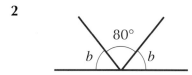

3

4

The geometric properties of quadrilaterals

Read carefully and learn all the properties of the quadrilaterals below.

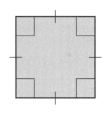

Square
- Four equal sides
- Four right angles
- Opposite sides parallel
- Diagonals bisect each other at right angles
- Four lines of symmetry
- Rotational symmetry of order four

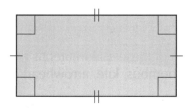

Rectangle
- Two pairs of equal sides
- Four right angles
- Opposite sides parallel
- Diagonals bisect each other
- Two lines of symmetry
- Rotational symmetry of order two

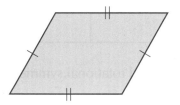

Parallelogram
- Two pairs of equal sides
- Two pairs of equal angles
- Opposite sides parallel
- Diagonals bisect each other
- No lines of symmetry
- Rotational symmetry of order two

MTH
3-17a

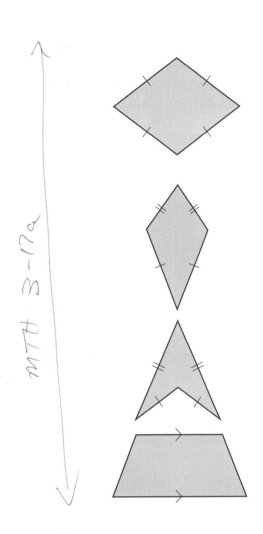

Rhombus

- Four equal sides
- Two pairs of equal angles
- Opposite sides parallel
- Diagonals bisect each other at right angles
- Two lines of symmetry
- Rotational symmetry of order two

Kite

- Two pairs of adjacent sides of equal length
- One pair of equal angles
- Diagonals intersect at right angles
- One line of symmetry

Arrowhead or Delta

- Two pairs of adjacent sides of equal length
- One pair of equal angles
- Diagonals intersect at right angles outside the shape
- One line of symmetry

Trapezium

- One pair of parallel sides
- Some trapezia have one line of symmetry

Exercise 2D

1 Copy the table below and put each of these quadrilaterals in the correct column: square, rectangle, parallelogram, rhombus, kite, arrowhead and trapezium.

No lines of symmetry	One line of symmetry	Two lines of symmetry	Fours lines of symmetry

2 Copy the table below and put each of these quadrilaterals in the correct column: square, rectangle, parallelogram, rhombus, kite, arrowhead and trapezium.

Rotational symmetry of order one	Rotational symmetry of order two	Rotational symmetry of order four

3 A quadrilateral has four right angles and rotational symmetry of order two. What type of quadrilateral is it?

4 A quadrilateral has rotational symmetry of order two and no lines of symmetry. What type of quadrilateral is it?

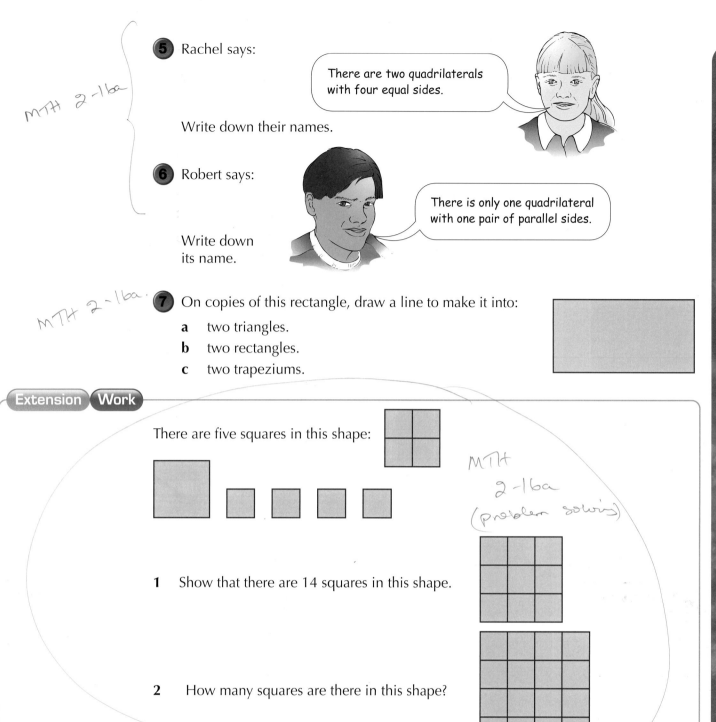

MTH 2-16a

5 Rachel says:

> There are two quadrilaterals with four equal sides.

Write down their names.

6 Robert says:

> There is only one quadrilateral with one pair of parallel sides.

Write down its name.

MTH 2-16a

7 On copies of this rectangle, draw a line to make it into:

a two triangles.

b two rectangles.

c two trapeziums.

Extension Work

There are five squares in this shape:

MTH 2-16a (problem solving)

1 Show that there are 14 squares in this shape.

2 How many squares are there in this shape?

Constructions

Examples 2.9 and 2.10 remind you how to construct triangles with accurate measurements.

When constructing the triangles, you will need to be accurate enough to draw the lines to the nearest millimetre and the angles to the nearest degree.

MTH 3-16a

You will need a sharp pencil, a ruler and a protractor.

Leave any construction lines and marks that you make on the completed diagram.

Example 2.9

Here is a sketch of a triangle ABC. It is not drawn accurately.

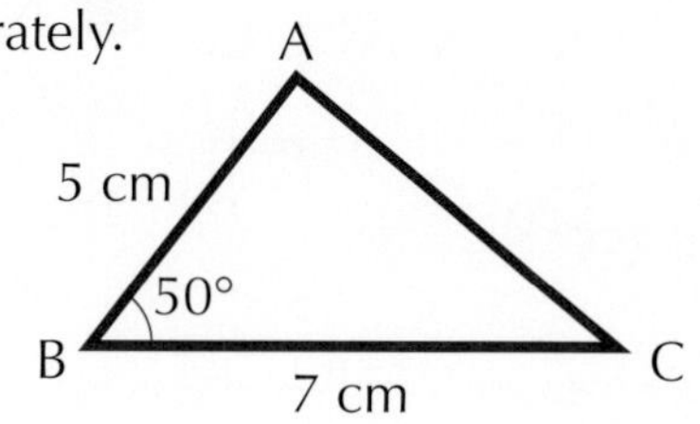

Construct the triangle ABC.
- Draw line BC 7 cm long.
- Draw an angle of 50° at B.
- Draw line AB 5 cm long.
- Join AC to complete the triangle.

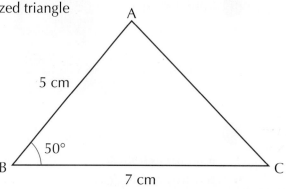

The completed, full-sized triangle is given on the right.

Example 2.10

Here is a sketch of a triangle XYZ. It is not drawn accurately.

Construct the triangle XYZ.
- Draw line YZ 8 cm long.
- Draw an angle of 40° at Y.
- Draw an angle of 50° at Z.
- Extend both angle lines to intersect at X to complete the triangle.

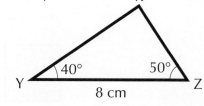

The completed, full-sized triangle is given on the right.

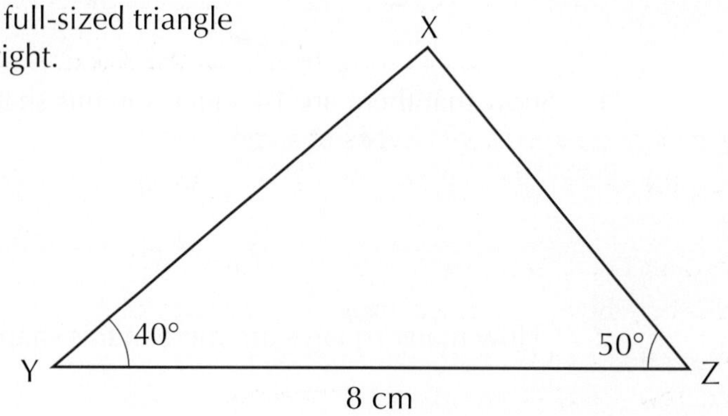

Exercise 2E

1. Construct each of the following triangles. Remember to label all lines and angles.

The triangles are not drawn to scale.

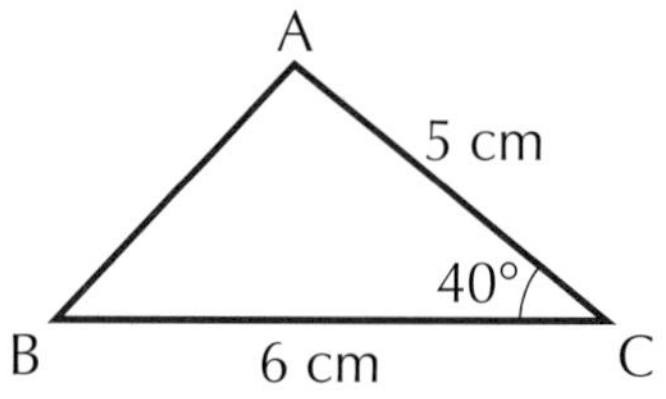

a   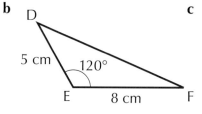   b   c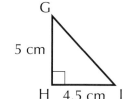

MTH 3-16a

2 Construct each of the following triangles. Remember to label all lines and angles. The triangles are not drawn to scale.

a

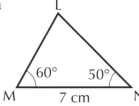

L

60°   50°

M   7 cm   N

b

P

40°   40°

Q   8 cm   R

c

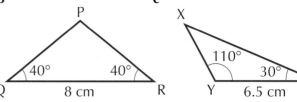

X

110°

30°

Y   6.5 cm   Z

3 Construct the triangle ABC with AB = 5 cm, angle A = 60° and angle B = 50°.

4 Construct the triangle XYZ with XY = 7 cm, XZ = 6 cm and angle X = 45°.

Extension **Work**

1 Make an accurate copy of the parallelogram on the right.

2 Construct some accurate shapes of your own. First decide on the type of shape and draw a sketch of it. Label your sketch with the measurements you want your shape to have. Now make an accurate construction of the shape, using a ruler and protractor.

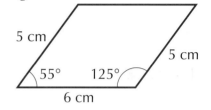

5 cm

5 cm

55°   125°

6 cm

LEVEL BOOSTER

4
I can recognise the different types of angle.
I know the names of the different types of quadrilateral.

5
I can draw and measure angles to the nearest degree.
I know that the angles of a triangle add up to 180°.
I know the symmetry properties of quadrilaterals.
I can draw triangles from given information.
I know the angles around a point add up to 360°.

5

1   *2002 Paper 1*

Two pupils drew angles on square grids.

a   Which word below describes angle A?

acute   obtuse   right-angled   reflex

b   Is angle A bigger than angle B?

Explain your answer.

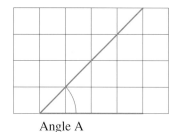   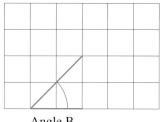

Angle A   Angle B

2   *2006 3–5 Paper 1*

a   The line on the square grid is one side of a **square**.

On a copy of the grid, draw 3 more lines to complete the square.

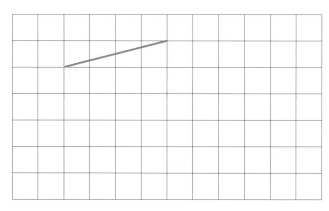

b   The line on the square grid is one side of a **quadrilateral**.

The quadrilateral has only **one pair of parallel sides**.

On a copy of the grid, draw 3 more lines to show what the quadrilateral could be.

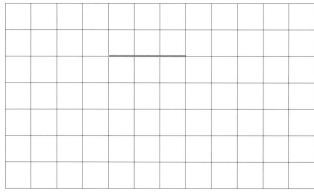

3   *2000 Paper 1*

Look at these angles.

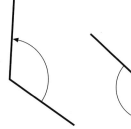         

Angle P   Angle Q   Angle R   Angle S   Angle T

One of the angles measures 120°. Write its letter.

4   2004 3–5 Paper 2

a   A pupil measured the angles in a triangle.

She said:

"The angles are 30°, 60° and 100°."

Could she be correct?

Explain your answer.

b   This diagram is not drawn accurately.

Calculate the size of angle m.

Show your working.

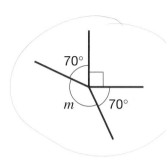

MTH 3-17a

not "a 2D shape" but could be included See Page 22.

5   2005 3–5 Paper 1

The diagram shows triangle PQR.

Work out the sizes of angles a, b and c.

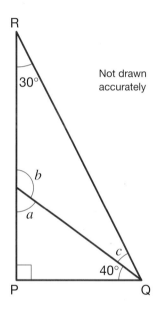

Not drawn accurately

MTH 3-17a

CHAPTER 3

Statistics **1**

This chapter is going to show you

- How to work with a probability scale
- How to work out probabilities in different situations
- How to collect data from a simple experiment and record it in a frequency table

What you should already know

- Some basic ideas about chance and probability
- How to interpret data from line graphs, tables and bar charts

Probability

Look at the pictures. Which one is most likely to happen where you live today?

We use probability to decide how likely it is that different events will happen.

Example 3.1

Here are some words we use when talking about whether something may happen:
very likely, unlikely, certain, impossible, an even chance, very unlikely, likely
Put these words in order.

The two complete opposites here are impossible and certain, with an even chance (evens) in the middle. So, these can be given in the order:

impossible, very unlikely, unlikely, **even chance**, likely, very likely, **certain**

Example 3.2

Mark these four events on the probability scale:

A is the probability that when a dice is rolled, the score is *not* 6.
B is the probability that when a dice is rolled, the score is either 1 or 2.
C is the probability that a coin will land to give either a Head or a Tail.
D is the probability that it will *not* rain at some time this year.

Impossible	Very unlikely	Unlikely	Even chance	Likely	Very likely	Certain
↑		↑			↑	↑

It is *very likely* that the dice will not give a score of 6.

There is less than an even chance that the dice will give a score of 1 or 2. So, it is *unlikely*.

The coin will land to give a Head or a Tail. So, it is *certain*.

It will rain at some time this year. So, not raining is *impossible*.

Impossible	Very unlikely	Unlikely	Even chance	Likely	Very likely	Certain
↑		↑			↑	↑
D		**B**			**A**	**C**

Example 3.3

Which is more likely to happen: flipping a Tail on a coin or rolling a number less than 5 on a dice?

A coin can only land two ways (Head or Tail). So, provided the coin is fair, there is an even chance of landing on a Tail.

On a dice there are four numbers less than 5 and two numbers that are not. So, there is more than an even chance of rolling a number less than 5. So, rolling a number less than 5 is more likely than getting a Tail when a coin is flipped.

Example 3.4

A spinner has five equal sections.

What is the chance of the spinner landing on: **a** 2? **b** 4 or 5?

a There is only one section with the number 2 on it.
So, it is very unlikely that the spinner will land on 2.

b There are two sections with 4 or 5 on them. So, there is less than an even chance of landing on 4 or 5, but this is twice as likely as landing on 2.

Exercise 3A

1

Impossible	Very unlikely	Unlikely	Even chance	Likely	Very likely	Certain

Copy the probability scale above. For each of the following events, write its letter **a**, **b**, **c**, **d** or **e** on the scale.

a Obtaining a Head when spinning a coin.   **b** Winning the lottery with one ticket.
c It snowing in July in England.   **d** The Sun rising tomorrow.
e Rolling a dice and scoring more than 1.

2 Write down an event for which the outcome is:

a certain.   **b** impossible.   **c** even chance.   **d** very unlikely.
e likely.   **f** very likely. **g** unlikely.

3 Below are two grids.

Grid 1　　　　　　　　　Grid 2

■	▲	●	▲
▲	■	▲	■
▲	●	▲	▬

■	▬	●	■
▬	■	■	■
■	●	■	▬

A shape is picked at random. Copy and complete the sentences below.

a Picking a triangle from Grid … is impossible.

b Picking a square from Grid … is likely.

c Picking a square from Grid … is unlikely.

d Picking a rectangle from Grid … is very unlikely.

e Picking a triangle from Grid … is fifty–fifty.

4 Bag A contains two red marbles, one blue marble and one green marble. A marble is picked at random.

Bag A

Copy and complete each of these sentences.

a There is the same chance of picking a …… marble as a …… marble.

b It is twice as likely that a …… marble is picked than a …… marble or a ……. marble.

Bag B contains four red marbles, one blue marble and no green marbles. A marble is picked at random.

Bag B

Copy and complete each of these sentences.

c It is impossible to pick a …… marble.

d It is very likely that a …… marble is picked.

e From which bag is there a better chance of picking a blue marble? Explain your answer.

5 A fair spinner has six sides, as shown. Copy and complete each of these sentences.

a There is an even chance that the spinner will land on the letter …

b It is unlikely that the spinner will land on the letter …

c It is very unlikely that the spinner will land on the letter …

6 A man has six blue shirts, three white shirts and one grey shirt in his wardrobe. He picks a shirt at random.

Copy and complete each of these sentences.

a It is likely that the man will pick a …… shirt.

b It is very unlikely that the man will pick a …… shirt.

c It is …… that the man will pick a green shirt.

1   Think about your school and write down ten events that are:

    a very likely.   **b** evens chance.   **c** very unlikely.

2   Think of yourself, this week and write down ten events that are:

    a impossible.   **b** evens chance.   **b** certain.

Probability scales

The probability of an event is:

$$P(\text{event}) = \frac{\text{Number of outcomes in the event}}{\text{Total number of all possible outcomes}}$$

Probabilities can be written as either fractions or decimals. They always take values between 0 and 1, including 0 and 1. The probability of an event happening can be shown on the probability scale:

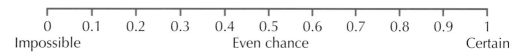

| 0 | 0.1 | 0.2 | 0.3 | 0.4 | 0.5 | 0.6 | 0.7 | 0.8 | 0.9 | 1 |

Impossible   Even chance   Certain

If an event is the complete opposite of another event, such as raining and not raining, then their probabilities add up to 1.

Look at the probability scale and see how many pairs of decimals you can find that add up to 1.

Example 3.5

There are 10 coloured counters in a bag. Three are blue, five are red and the rest are yellow. A counter is picked out at random. Calculate the probability of the counter being:

a blue.   **b** red.   **c** yellow.

a As there are 3 blue counters out of 10 counters altogether, the probability of getting a blue counter is $\frac{3}{10}$.

b As there are 5 red counters out of 10 counters altogether, the probability of getting a red counter is $\frac{5}{10} = \frac{1}{2}$.

c As there are 2 yellow counters out of 10 counters altogether, the probability of getting a yellow counter is $\frac{2}{10} = \frac{1}{5}$.

Example 3.6 Terry has a bag of marbles.

In the bag are:

1 red marble   2 green marbles
3 white marbles   4 blue marbles

Terry took one marble out of the bag at random. What is the probability that it is:

a white?   **b** green?   **c** red?   **d** blue?

There are 1 + 2 + 3 + 4 = 10 marbles in the bag.

a 3 marbles are white, so the probability of taking out a white marble is $\frac{3}{10}$.

b 2 marbles are green, so the probability of taking out a green marble is $\frac{2}{10}$.

c 1 marble is red, so the probability of taking out a red marble is $\frac{1}{10}$.

d 4 marbles are blue, so the probability of taking out a blue marble is $\frac{4}{10}$.

Exercise 3B

1 Tony has a bag of jelly babies. seven are red, two are green and one is black.

    a What colour jelly baby is Tony most likely to pick out?

    b What is the probability of Tony, picking at random:
      i a black jelly baby?   **ii** a green jelly baby?   **iii** a red jelly baby?

2 Mr Bradshaw has a box of 20 calculators. Three of these do not work.

    a How many calculators in Mr Bradshaw's box do work?

    b What is the probability of taking a calculator out, at random, and it:
      i working?   **ii** not working?

3 Ten cards are numbered 0 to 9.   **0 1 2 3 4 5 6 7 8 9**

    A card is picked at random. Work out the probability that it is:

    a 2.   **b** not 2.   **c** odd.   **d** not odd.

    e 7, 8 or 9.   **f** less than 7.   **g** 4 or 5.   **h** not 4 or 5.

4 In a bus station there are 24 red buses, six blue buses and 10 green buses. Calculate the probability that the next bus to arrive at the bus station is:

    a green.   **b** red.   **c** red or blue.   **d** yellow.   **e** not green.

    f not red.   **g** neither red nor blue.   **h** not yellow.

5 The cellar of a café was flooded in the great floods of 2007. All the labels came off the tins of soup and were floating in the water.

    The café owner knew that she had: 17 cans of mushroom soup,
                                       15 cans of tomato soup,
                                       10 cans of vegetable soup,
                                         8 cans of pea soup.

    a How many tins of soup were there in the flooded cellar?

    b After the flood, what is the probability that a tin of soup chosen at random is:
      i mushroom?   **ii** tomato?   **iii** vegetable?   **iv** pea?

1   Look at the numbers in this box:

If a number is chosen at random,
what is the probability that it is:

a   even?

b   a multiple of 5?

c   a factor of 36?

3	4	7	9
10	13	15	16
18	20	21	26
30	35	36	38
41	45	46	50

*MNU
3.22a.*

2   Make up your own box of numbers and your own set of questions.

Then answer them or swap them with classmates.

Collecting data for a frequency table

Handling data is about collecting and organising data. It is also about presenting data using diagrams and being able to interpret diagrams.

Example 3.7

A spinner has five different coloured sections on it: red, green, blue, yellow and black. You want to test whether the spinner is fair by recording which colour the spinner lands on each time you spin it. Here is a table in which to record the results each time the spinner is spun. Each result is recorded with a tick.

Trial number	Red	Green	Blue	Yellow	Black
1					✓
2	✓				
3	✓				
4			✓		
5				✓	
6			✓		
7	✓				
8					✓
9				✓	
10					✓
Total	3	0	2	2	3

One conclusion from these results is that the spinner might be biased (not fair) because it never landed on green.

To be more certain, you would need to carry out many more trials – 50 spins at least!

Example 3.8 ▷ Use the results in Example 3.9 to estimate the probability of the spinner:

    a   landing on red.   **b**   landing on green.   **c**   landing on blue.

    d   landing on yellow.   **e**   landing on black.

    a   There are 3 reds out of 10, so the estimate of P(red) is $\frac{3}{10}$.

    b   There are no greens out of 10 so the estimate of P(green) is 0.

Similarly for blue, yellow and black:

    c P(blue) $= \frac{2}{10} = \frac{1}{5}$ **d** P(yellow) $= \frac{2}{10} = \frac{1}{5}$ **e** P(black) $= \frac{3}{10}$

Exercise 3C

1 Make your own spinner from a piece of card. It can have five sections, as in Example 3.9, or a different number of sections. Label the sections with numbers or colour each in a different colour. Spin the spinner 50 times and record the results in a table. Comment on whether you think that your spinner is biased.

2 Put 20 coloured counters in a bag. Now draw out a counter, note the colour and replace it. Repeat this 50 times. Record the results in a tally chart. Use your results to estimate the probability of choosing each colour. Check your results by emptying the bag.

3 Roll a dice 60 times. Record the results in a table. Use the results to estimate the probability of each score. Comment on whether you think the dice is biased.

Extension Work

When you roll two dice, you have exactly the same chance of rolling a total greater than 8 than you have of rolling a total less than 6.

Roll two dice sufficient times, keeping a record of the results, to see if this is true.

Events

Look at the pictures of the yachts. Can you spot the differences? Some yachts have a flag on the top of the mast. The sails and hulls are different colours.

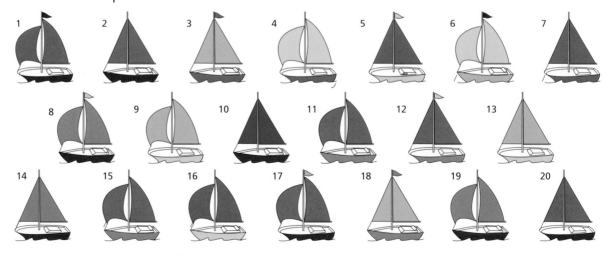

Exercise 3D

Look at the 20 yachts in the picture and answer the questions.

1 How many yachts have each of these features?

   a Round sails   **b** A blue hull

   c Yellow sails   **d** A flag at the top of the mast

   e A pointed hull   **f** Red sails and a curved hull

   g A yellow hull but no flag   **h** Straight green sails

   i A curved red hull

   j A red hull, blue sails and a flag at the top of the mast

2 A sailor takes a yacht at random. What is the probability that it has each of the following?

   a Round sails   **b** A blue hull

   c Yellow sails   **d** A flag at the top of the mast

   e A pointed hull   **f** Red sails and a curved hull

   g A yellow hull but no flag   **h** Straight green sails

   i A curved red hull

   j A red hull, blue sails and a flag at the top of the mast

3 All 20 boats were in a race. Three friends were on the boats.

   Peter was on a boat with green sails.

   Ali was on a boat with a blue hull.

   Andy was on a boat with straight sails.

   a A boat with a blue hull won the race.

      What was the probability that Ali was on the boat that won the race?

   b A boat with green sails was the only boat to capsize.

      What is the probability that Peter was on a boat that capsized?

   c A boat with straight sails came last.

      What is the probability that Andy was on the boat that came last?

Extension **Work**

1 Draw your own set of 10 boats so that:

   a there are more boats with blue hulls than any other colour,

   b there are less boats with red hulls than any other colour,

   c there are the same number of boats with straight sails as curved sails.

2 If one of your boats is chosen at random, what is the probability that it will have:

   a blue sails?

   b a red hull?

   c straight sails?

   d a straight sail and a blue hull?

Experimental probability

Look at the picture. How could you estimate the probability that a train will be late?

Will the train be late again today?

You could keep a record of the number of times that the train arrives late over a period of 10 days. Then use these results to estimate the probability that it will be late in future.

$$\text{Experimental probability} = \frac{\text{Number of events in trials}}{\text{Total number of trials carried out}}$$

Example 3.9 ▷ An electrician wants to estimate the probability that a new light bulb lasts for less than 1 month. He fits 20 new bulbs and 3 of them failed within 1 month. What is his estimate of the probability that a new light bulb will fail?

3 out of 20 bulbs failed within 1 month. So, the experimental probability is $\frac{3}{20}$.

Example 3.10 ▷ A dentist keeps a record of the number of fillings she gives her patients over 2 weeks. Her results are shown in the table.

Number of fillings	None	1	More than 1
Number of patients	80	54	16

Estimate the probability that a patient does not need a filling. (There are 150 records altogether.)

$$\text{Experimental probability} = \frac{80}{150}$$
$$= \frac{8}{15}$$

Example 3.11 ▷ A company manufactures items for computers. The number of faulty items is recorded in this table.

a Copy and complete the table.

Number of items produced	Number of faulty items	Experimental probability
100	8	0.08
200	20	
500	45	
1000	82	

b Which is the best estimate of the probability of an item being faulty? Explain your answer.

a

Number of items produced	Number of faulty items	Experimental probability
100	8	0.08
200	20	20 ÷ 200 = 0.1
500	45	45 ÷ 500 = 0.09
1000	82	82 ÷ 1000 = 0.082

b The last result (0.082), as the experiment is based on more results.

1 A boy decides to carry out an experiment to estimate the probability of a drawing pin landing with the pin pointing up. He drops 50 drawing pins and records the result. He then repeats the experiment several times. His results are shown in the table.

Number of drawing pins	Number pointing up
50	32
100	72
150	106
200	139
250	175

a From the results, would you say that there is a greater chance of a drawing pin landing point up or point down? Explain your answer.

b Which result is the most reliable and why?

c Estimate the probability of a drawing pin landing point up.

d How could the boy improve the experiment?

2 A girl wishes to test whether a dice is biased. She rolls the dice 60 times. The results are shown in the table.

Score	1	2	3	4	5	6
Frequency	6	12	10	9	15	8

a Do you think the dice is biased? Give a reason for your answer.

b How could she improve the experiment?

c From the results, estimate the probability of rolling 1.

d From the results, estimate the probability of rolling 1 or 4.

3 Gary's bus often seemed to arrive late.

He kept a count of how many times it was late each week over a five-week period, as a running total.

After	Days	Number of times late	Probability
1 week	5	3	
2 weeks	10	5	
3 weeks	15	9	
4 weeks	20	10	
5 weeks	25	12	

a Work out the probabilities of the bus being late after each week.

b What would you say is the probability of the bus being late for Gary?

Extension **Work**

Use two dice to see what the following probabilities might be of:

a rolling a double. **b** rolling a total of seven.

4 I understand about chance.

5 I can use a probability scale from 0 to 1.
I can collect data and put it into a frequency table.
I can find experimental probability from a simple experiment.
I understand that different outcomes may result from repeating an experiment.

National Test questions

1 *2006 4–6 Paper 1*

Make three copies of the diagram of a spinner.

On each copy of the spinner, **write five numbers** to make the statements below correct:

a It is **certain** that you will get a number **less than 6**.

b It is **more likely** that you will get an **even** number than an **odd** number.

c It is **impossible** that you will get a **multiple of 3**.

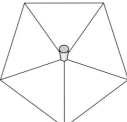

2 *2006 4–6 Paper 2*

I buy **12 packets** of cat food in a box.

The table shows the different varieties in the box.

a I am going to take out a packet at random from the box.

What is the **probability** that it will be cod?

b My cat eats **all** the packets of **cod**.
I am going to take out a packet at random from the ones left in the box.

What is the **probability** that it will be **salmon**?

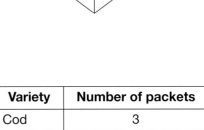

Variety	Number of packets
Cod	3
Salmon	3
Trout	3
Tuna	3

3 *2007 3–5 Paper 1*

Fred has a bag of sweets. Its contents are:

3 yellow sweets
5 green sweets
7 red sweets
4 purple sweets
1 black sweet.

He is going to take a sweet from the bag at random.

a What is the probability that Fred will get a black sweet?

b Write down the missing colour from the sentence below:

The probability that Fred will get a …… sweet is $\frac{1}{4}$.

4 2000 Paper 2

In each box of cereal there is a free gift of a card.

You cannot tell which card will be in a box. Each card is equally likely.

There are four different cards: A, B, C, D

a Zoe needs card A.

Her brother Paul needs cards C and D.

They buy one box of cereal.

What is the probability that the card is one that Zoe needs?

What is the probability that the card is one that Paul needs?

b Then their mother opens the box. She tells them the card is not card A.

Now what is the probability the card is one that Zoe needs?

What is the probability that the card is one that Paul needs?

5 *2005 3–5 Paper 2*

a Aidan puts 2 white counters and 1 black counter in a bag. He is going to take one counter without looking.

What is the **probability** that the counter will be **black**?

b Aidan puts the counter back in the bag and then puts **more black counters** into the bag. He is going to take one without looking.

The **probability** that the counter will be black is now $\frac{2}{3}$.

How many more black counters did Aidan put in the bag?

FM Fun in the fairground

The fair has come to town.

Hoopla

You can buy five hoops for £1.25.

You win a prize by throwing a hoop over that prize, but it must also go over the base that the prize is standing on!

Ben spent some time watching people have a go at this stall and started to count how many goes they had and how many times someone won.

The table below shows his results.

Prize	Number of throws	Number of wins
Watch	320	1
£10 note	240	4
£1 coin	80	2

Hook a duck

This is a game where plastic ducks float around a central stall. They all have numbers stuck to their underside which cannot be seen until hooked up on a stick and presented to the stall holder.

In the game, if the number under the duck is a:

  1 – you win a lollipop   2 – you win a yo-yo
  5 – you win a cuddly toy

Each time a duck is hooked, it is replaced in the water.

Cindy, the stall holder, set up the stall one week with:
● 45 plastic ducks
● Only one of which had the number 5 underneath
● Nine had the number 2 underneath
● All the rest had a number 1 underneath

Cindy charged 40p for one stick, to hook up just one duck.

Use the information on Hoopla to answer these questions.

1 How many sets of 5 hoops thrown did Ben observe?

2 What income would these throws have made for the stall?

3 From the results shown, what is the probability of someone aiming for and winning a:

  a £1 coin?

  b £10 note?

  c watch?

4 What would you say is the chance of someone winning a prize with:

  a one hoop?

  b five hoops?

5 After watching this, Ben decided to try for a £10 note.

He bought 25 hoops and all his throws were aimed at the £10 note.

  a How much did this cost him?

  b What is his probability of winning a £10 note?

Use the information on Hook a duck to answer these questions.

6 What is the probability of hooking the number:
a 1?
b 2?
c 5?

7 What is the probability of winning:
a a cuddly toy?
b a yo-yo?
c a lollipop?

8 What is the probability of winning anything other than a lollipop?

9 Tom spent £1.60 at the stall so that his little sister, Julie, could hook some ducks.
a How many ducks could Julie hook with the £1.60?
b What is the likelihood that, after four goes, Julie has won:
 i a cuddly toy?
 ii a yo-yo?
 iii a lollipop?
 In each case, choose from:
 impossible, very unlikely, unlikely, evens, likely, very likely, certain.

10 Before lunch on Sunday, Cindy took £100 from the stall.
a How many ducks had been hooked that morning?
b How many cuddly toys would you expect Cindy to have given away that morning?
c How many yo-yos would you expect Cindy to have given away that morning?

CHAPTER 4 Number 2

<table>
<tr><td>

This chapter is going to show you

- More about working with fractions, decimals and percentages
- How to calculate simple percentages of quantities
- How to add and subtract fractions with a common denominator

</td><td>

What you should already know

- The equivalences of common fractions, decimals and percentages
- How to add and subtract fractions with denominators 2, 4 and 8
- How to calculate ten per cent of a quantity

</td></tr>
</table>

Fractions and decimals

These diagrams show shapes with various fractions of them shaded. Can you write each of them as a decimal, a fraction and a percentage?

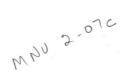

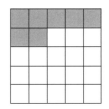 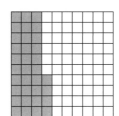 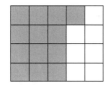 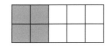

Example 4.1 ▷ Cancel each of the following fractions to its simplest form.

   a $\frac{20}{50}$ **b** $\frac{12}{16}$ **c** $\frac{4}{28}$

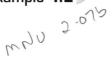

   a $\frac{20}{50} = \frac{2}{5}$ (Cancel by 10)

   b $\frac{12}{16} = \frac{3}{4}$ (Cancel by 4)

   c $\frac{4}{28} = \frac{1}{7}$ (Cancel by 4)

Example 4.2 ▷ Work out the each of these decimals as a fraction.

   a 0.6   **b** 0.45

   a $0.6 = \frac{60}{100} = \frac{3}{5}$ (Cancel by 20)   **b** $0.45 = \frac{45}{100} = \frac{9}{20}$ (Cancel by 5)

Exercise 4A   **1** Cancel each of these fractions to its simplest form.

   a $\frac{4}{12}$ **b** $\frac{6}{9}$ **c** $\frac{14}{21}$ **d** $\frac{15}{20}$ **e** $\frac{18}{20}$ **f** $\frac{20}{50}$

   g $\frac{8}{24}$ **h** $\frac{6}{12}$ **i** $\frac{4}{24}$ **j** $\frac{12}{20}$ **k** $\frac{16}{24}$ **l** $\frac{25}{35}$

5

2 Write each of the following decimals as a fraction with a denominator of 10. Then cancel the fraction to its simplest form, if possible.

    a   0.2   **b**   0.4   **c**   0.1   **d**   0.3

    e   0.6   **f**   0.9   **g**   0.5   **h**   0.8

3 Write each of the following decimals as a fraction with a denominator of 100. Then cancel the fraction to its simplest form, if possible.

    a   0.25   **b**   0.45   **c**   0.12   **d**   0.38

    e   0.66   **f**   0.95   **g**   0.52   **h**   0.84

    i   0.28   **j**   0.65   **k**   0.98   **l**   0.36

    m   0.05   **n**   0.06   **o**   0.48   **p**   0.15

4 Use your answers to Questions 2 and 3 to write down the decimal equivalent to each of these fractions.

    a $\frac{3}{5}$ **b** $\frac{3}{20}$ **c** $\frac{3}{25}$ **d** $\frac{3}{50}$

5 Write down each of the following terminating decimals.

    a $\frac{1}{2}$ **b** $\frac{1}{4}$ **c** $\frac{1}{5}$ **d** $\frac{1}{10}$ **e** $\frac{1}{20}$ **f** $\frac{1}{25}$ **g** $\frac{1}{50}$ **h** $\frac{1}{100}$

Extension **Work**

By dividing the numerator by the denominator, work out the ninths as recurring decimals. They are:

    $\frac{1}{9}$ $\frac{2}{9}$ $\frac{3}{9}$ $\frac{4}{9}$ $\frac{5}{9}$ $\frac{6}{9}$ $\frac{7}{9}$ $\frac{8}{9}$

Describe any patterns that you can see in the digits.

Adding and subtracting fractions

All of the grids below contain 100 squares. Some of the squares have been shaded in. The fraction shaded is shown in its lowest terms.

Use the diagrams to work out $1 - (\frac{1}{5} + \frac{7}{20} + \frac{22}{50} + \frac{1}{25})$.

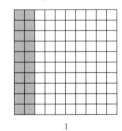 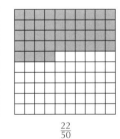 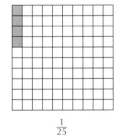

    $\frac{1}{5}$ $\frac{7}{20}$ $\frac{22}{50}$ $\frac{1}{25}$

Example 4.3   Add together:

    a $\frac{1}{5} + \frac{2}{5}$ **b** $\frac{3}{8} + \frac{1}{8}$ **c** $\frac{1}{3} + \frac{1}{3} + \frac{2}{3}$

In each addition, the denominators are the same. So, the numerators are just added.

    a $\frac{1}{5} + \frac{2}{5} = \frac{3}{5}$

    b $\frac{3}{8} + \frac{1}{8} = \frac{4}{8} = \frac{1}{2}$ (The answer here has been cancelled.)

    c $\frac{1}{3} + \frac{1}{3} + \frac{2}{3} = \frac{4}{3} = 1\frac{1}{3}$ (This answer is a top-heavy fraction, so it should be written as a mixed number.)

Example 4.4 ▷ Subtract:

a $\frac{5}{6} - \frac{1}{6}$ b

In each subtraction, the denominators are the same.
So, the numerators are just subtracted.

a $\frac{5}{6} - \frac{1}{6} = \frac{4}{6} = \frac{2}{3}$

b $\frac{5}{8} - \frac{3}{8} = \frac{2}{8} = \frac{1}{4}$

Note that both of these answer

Example 4.5 ▷ Write these improper (top-hea

a $\frac{3}{2}$ b

a $\frac{3}{2} = 3 \div 2 = 1\frac{1}{2}$

b $\frac{9}{5} = 9 \div 5 = 1\frac{4}{5}$

[handwritten note:] Pg 46 Q 3,4,5 is MTH 3-07c

Pg 46 Q 4 + 5 are MTH 3-07b AND MTH 3.07c

Exercise 4B

1 Add each of the following pairs of fractions. Cancel or write as a mixed number as necessary.

a $\frac{1}{3} + \frac{1}{3}$ b $\frac{2}{5} + \frac{1}{5}$ c $\frac{1}{7} + \frac{2}{7}$ d $\frac{1}{4} + \frac{1}{4}$

e $\frac{1}{5} + \frac{3}{5}$ f $\frac{3}{8} + \frac{3}{8}$ g $\frac{5}{6} + \frac{5}{6}$ h $\frac{3}{4} + \frac{3}{4}$

2 Subtract each of the following pairs of fractions. Cancel as necessary.

a $\frac{2}{3} - \frac{1}{3}$ b $\frac{2}{5} - \frac{1}{5}$ c $\frac{2}{7} - \frac{1}{7}$ d $\frac{3}{4} - \frac{1}{4}$

e $\frac{3}{5} - \frac{1}{5}$ f $\frac{5}{8} - \frac{1}{8}$ g $\frac{5}{6} - \frac{1}{6}$ h $\frac{5}{9} - \frac{2}{9}$

3 Write each of the following as a mixed number.

a $\frac{5}{4}$ b $\frac{7}{2}$ c $\frac{11}{6}$ d $\frac{9}{2}$ e $\frac{5}{4}$ f $\frac{10}{7}$ g $\frac{5}{3}$ h $\frac{16}{5}$

4 Work out each of the following, cancelling down or writing as a mixed number as appropriate.

a $\frac{2}{3} + \frac{2}{3}$ b $\frac{5}{8} + \frac{7}{8}$ c $\frac{3}{10} + \frac{1}{10}$ d $\frac{1}{8} + \frac{5}{8}$

e $\frac{4}{15} + \frac{2}{15}$ f $\frac{7}{16} + \frac{1}{16}$ g $\frac{7}{12} + \frac{1}{12}$ h $\frac{3}{4} + \frac{1}{4} + \frac{1}{4}$

5 Work out each of the following, cancelling down or writing as a mixed number as appropriate.

a $\frac{7}{8} - \frac{1}{8}$ b $\frac{5}{12} - \frac{1}{12}$ c $\frac{3}{10} - \frac{1}{10}$ d $\frac{8}{9} - \frac{1}{9}$

e $\frac{4}{15} - \frac{1}{15}$ f $\frac{7}{8} - \frac{5}{8}$ g $\frac{7}{12} - \frac{1}{12}$ h $\frac{3}{4} + \frac{3}{4} - \frac{1}{4}$

Extension Work

Copy the diagram on the right.
Shade in, in separate parts of the diagram, each of these fractions: $\frac{1}{12}, \frac{5}{24}, \frac{1}{8}, \frac{1}{4}, \frac{1}{6}$

Write down the answer to $1 - (\frac{1}{12} + \frac{5}{24} + \frac{1}{8} + \frac{1}{4} + \frac{1}{6})$.

Give your answer in its simplest form.

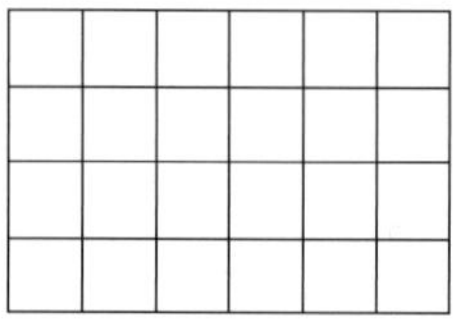

Multiplying fractions

You can use grids to work out fractions of quantities.

This grid shows that $\frac{1}{4}$ of 24 is equal to 6:

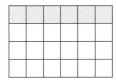

This grid shows that $\frac{2}{3}$ of 24 is equal to 16:

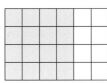

Example 4.6

Use this grid to work out the following.

a $\frac{1}{3}$ of 30 **b** $\frac{3}{10}$ of 30

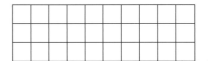

a

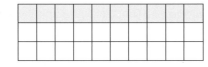

$\frac{1}{3}$ of 30 = 10

b

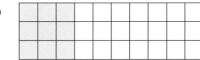

$\frac{3}{10}$ of 30 = 9

Example 4.7

Work out the following.

a $\frac{3}{4}$ of £28 **b** $5 \times \frac{2}{3}$

a $\frac{1}{4}$ of £28 = £7. So, $\frac{3}{4}$ of £28 = $3 \times £7 = £21$

b $5 \times \frac{2}{3} = \frac{10}{3} = 3\frac{1}{3}$

Exercise 4C

1 Use grids to work out the following.

a $\frac{1}{8}$ of 32	**b** $\frac{3}{8}$ of 32	**c** $\frac{1}{4}$ of 32	**d** $\frac{3}{4}$ of 32
e $\frac{1}{5}$ of 25	**f** $\frac{3}{5}$ of 25	**g** $\frac{2}{3}$ of 45	**h** $\frac{5}{6}$ of 120

2 Work out each of these.

a $\frac{5}{8}$ of £32	**b** $\frac{1}{16}$ of 64 kg	**c** $\frac{2}{3}$ of £45	**d** $\frac{5}{6}$ of 240 cm
e $\frac{5}{9}$ of £45	**f** $\frac{2}{7}$ of £28	**g** $\frac{2}{9}$ of £90	**h** $\frac{2}{11}$ of 22 m
i $\frac{6}{7}$ of 28 cm	**j** $\frac{9}{10}$ of 40 grams	**k** $\frac{3}{8}$ of £72	**l** $\frac{3}{4}$ of 48 km

3 Work out each of these, cancelling down or writing as a mixed number as appropriate.

a $5 \times \frac{3}{4}$	**b** $7 \times \frac{4}{5}$	**c** $9 \times \frac{2}{3}$	**d** $4 \times \frac{7}{8}$
e $8 \times \frac{9}{10}$	**f** $6 \times \frac{3}{7}$	**g** $9 \times \frac{5}{6}$	**h** $10 \times \frac{3}{4}$

4 Work out each of these, cancelling down or writing as a mixed number as appropriate.

a $\frac{3}{8} \times 2$ b $\frac{7}{8} \times 8$ c $\frac{2}{3} \times 6$ d $\frac{5}{9} \times 3$

e $\frac{2}{7} \times 5$ f $\frac{8}{9} \times 2$ g $\frac{3}{5} \times 7$ h $\frac{7}{8} \times 6$

Extension **Work**

1 Put these in order of size, smallest to biggest.

$24 \times \frac{5}{8}$ $36 \times \frac{1}{4}$ $35 \times \frac{2}{7}$

2 Put these in order of size smallest to biggest.

$\frac{3}{8} \div 4$ $\frac{1}{4} \div 3$ $\frac{2}{7} \div 5$

Fractions and percentages

Example 4.8 ▷

a Express 8 as a percentage of 25.

b Express 39 as a percentage of 50.

a Write as a fraction: $\frac{8}{25}$
Multiply top and bottom by 4 to get $\frac{32}{100}$. So, 8 is 32% of 25.

b Write as a fraction: $\frac{39}{50}$
Multiply top and bottom by 2 to get $\frac{78}{100}$. So, 39 is 78% of 50.

Example 4.9 ▷

a What percentage of 10 is 8?   b What percentage of 20 is 14?

a Write as a fraction: $\frac{8}{10}$.
Convert to a percentage by multiplying top and bottom by 10 to get 80%.

b Write as a fraction: $\frac{14}{20}$
Convert to a percentage by multiplying top and bottom by 5 to get 70%.

Example 4.10 ▷

Ashram scored 38 out of 50 in a Physics test, 16 out of 20 in a Chemistry test and 18 out of 25 in a Biology test. In which science did he do best?

Convert each mark to a percentage:

Physics: $\frac{38}{50} = \frac{76}{100} = 76\%$

Chemistry: $\frac{16}{20} = \frac{80}{100} = 80\%$

Biology: $\frac{18}{25} = \frac{72}{100} = 72\%$

So Ashram did best in Chemistry.

Exercise 4D

1 Write each of the following fractions as percentages.

a $\frac{1}{2}$ b $\frac{1}{4}$ c $\frac{3}{4}$ d $\frac{1}{10}$

e $\frac{1}{5}$ f $\frac{2}{25}$ g $\frac{7}{20}$ h $\frac{1}{25}$

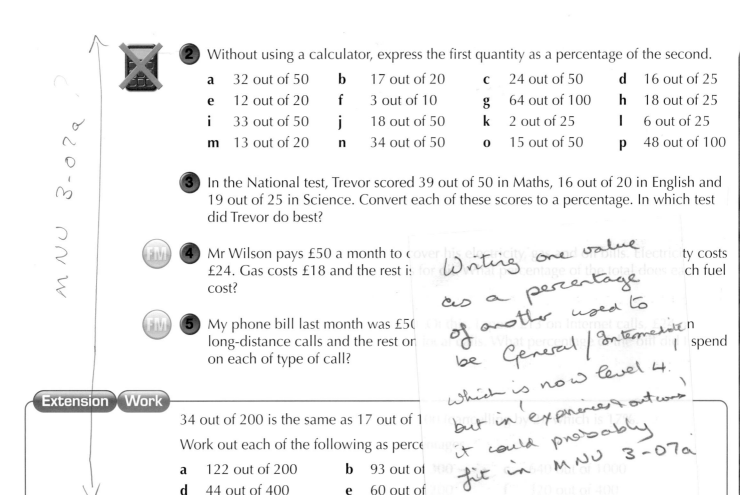

② Without using a calculator, express the first quantity as a percentage of the second.

a	32 out of 50	**b**	17 out of 20	**c**	24 out of 50	**d**	16 out of 25
e	12 out of 20	**f**	3 out of 10	**g**	64 out of 100	**h**	18 out of 25
i	33 out of 50	**j**	18 out of 50	**k**	2 out of 25	**l**	6 out of 25
m	13 out of 20	**n**	34 out of 50	**o**	15 out of 50	**p**	48 out of 100

③ In the National test, Trevor scored 39 out of 50 in Maths, 16 out of 20 in English and 19 out of 25 in Science. Convert each of these scores to a percentage. In which test did Trevor do best?

④ Mr Wilson pays £50 a month to cover his electricity, gas and oil bills. Electricity costs £24. Gas costs £18 and the rest is for oil. What percentage of the total does each fuel cost?

⑤ My phone bill last month was £50. £ __ on long-distance calls and the rest on local calls. What percentage of the bill did I spend on each of type of call?

Extension Work

34 out of 200 is the same as 17 out of 100

Work out each of the following as percentages.

a	122 out of 200	**b**	93 out of ___
d	44 out of 400	**e**	60 out of ___

Percentage increase and decrease

SPORTY SHOES
$\frac{1}{3}$ off all trainers

SHOES-FOR-YOU
30% off all trainers

Which shop gives the best value?

Example 4.11

a A clothes shop has a sale and reduces its prices by 20%. How much is the sale price of each of the following?

   i A jacket originally costing £45.   **ii** A dress originally costing £125.

   i 20% of 45 is 2 × 10% of 45 = 2 × 4.5 = 9. So, the jacket costs:
£45 − £9 = £36

   ii 20% of 125 is 2 × 10% of 125 = 2 × 12.50 = 25. So, the dress costs:
£125 − £25 = £100

Example 4.11
continued

b A company gives all its workers a 5% pay rise. What is the new wage of these employees?

   i Joan, who originally earned £240 per week.

   ii Jack, who originally earned £6.00 per hour.

   i 5% of 240 is $\frac{1}{2} \times 10\%$ of $240 = \frac{1}{2} \times 24 = 12$. So, Joan now earns: £240 + £12 = £252 per week

   ii 5% of 6.00 is $\frac{1}{2} \times 10\%$ of $6.00 = \frac{1}{2} \times 60p = 30p$. So, Jack now earns: £6.00 + 30p = £6.30 per hour

Exercise 4E

Do not use a calculator for these questions.

1 A bat colony has 40 bats. Over the breeding season, the population increases by 30%.
   a How many new bats were born?
   b How many bats are there in the colony after the breeding season?

2 In a wood there are 20 000 midges. During the evening, bats eat 40% of the midges.
   a How many midges were eaten by the bats?
   b How many midges were left after the bats had eaten?
   c What percentage of midges remain?

3 Work out the final amount when:
   a £45 is increased by 10%   **b** £48 is decreased by 10%
   c £120 is increased by 20%   **d** £90 is decreased by 20%
   e £65 is increased by 15%   **f** £110 is decreased by 15%
   g £250 is increased by 25%   **h** £300 is decreased by 20%
   i £6.80 is increased by 10%   **j** £5.40 is decreased by 10%

FM **4 a** In a sale, all prices are reduced by 15%. Give the new price of an item that previously cost:
   i £18   **ii** £26   **iii** £50   **iv** £70

   b An electrical store increases its prices by 5%. Give the new price of an item that previously cost:
   i £200   **ii** £130   **iii** £380   **iv** £100

Extension Work

FM The government charges us VAT at $17\frac{1}{2}$% on most things we buy. Although this seems like an awkward percentage to work out, there is an easy way to do it without a calculator! It is easy to find 10%, which can be used to find 5% (divide the 10% value by 2). This can in turn be used to find $2\frac{1}{2}$% (divide the 5% value by 2). Adding together these three values gives $10\% + 5\% + 2\frac{1}{2}\% = 17\frac{1}{2}\%$.

For example, find the VAT on an item that costs £24 before VAT is added.

10% of £24 = £2.40, 5% of £24 is £1.20, and $2\frac{1}{2}$% of £24 is £0.60.

So, $17\frac{1}{2}$% of £24 = £2.40 + £1.20 + £0.60 = £4.20

Work out the VAT on an item that costs:

a £30   **b** £40   **c** £50   **d** £90   **e** £120   **f** £200

before VAT is addded.

Real-life problems

MNU – 3-07a ?

Percentages occur everyday in many situations. You have already met percentage increase and decrease. Three other examples are buying goods on credit, profit/loss and paying tax.

Example 4.12 ▷

A car costing £6000 can be bought on credit by paying a 25% deposit and followed by 24 monthly payments of £200.

  a   How much will the car cost on credit?

  b   What is the extra cost above the usual price?

  a   Deposit: 25% of £6000 = £1500

       Payments: 24 × £200 = £4800

       Total paid = £1500 + £4800 = £6300

  b   Extra cost = £6300 – £6000 = £300

Example 4.13 ▷

A jeweller makes a brooch for £200 and sells it for £250.
What is the percentage profit?

The profit is £250 – £200 = £50. £50 is one quarter of £200, which is 25%.

Exercise 4F

FM **1** A mountain bike that normally costs £480 can be bought using three different plans as shown below.

Plan	Deposit	Number of payments	Each payment
A	20%	24	£22
B	50%	12	£20
C	10%	36	£18

  a   Work out how much the bike costs using each plan.

  b   Work out the extra cost of each plan.

2 A shop buys a radio for £50 and sells it for £60. Work out the percentage profit made by the shop.

3 A CD costs £14. The shop paid £10 for it. What is the percentage profit?

FM **4** A car that costs £7000 can be bought by paying a 20% deposit, followed by 24 monthly payments of £200 and a final payment of £2000.

  a   How much will the car cost using the credit scheme?

  b   What is the extra cost of the credit scheme?

5 A shop sells a toaster for £20 in a sale. It cost the shop £25. What is the percentage loss?

FM **6** An insurance policy for a motorbike is £300. It can be paid for by a 25% deposit followed by five payments of £50.

  a   How much does the policy cost using the scheme?

  b   What the extra cost of using the scheme?

6

FM **7** **a** Which of these schemes is cheaper to buy a three-piece suite worth £1000?

Scheme A: No deposit followed by 25 payments of £50.

Scheme B: 25% deposit followed by 25 payments of £30.

b Give a reason why someone might prefer scheme A.

LEVEL BOOSTER

4
I know simple fractions and their decimal and percentage equivalents.
I understand what 'per cent' means.
I can add and subtract simple fractions with the same denominator.

5
I can calculate a fraction of a quantity.
I can calculate a percentage of a quantity.
I can multiply a fraction by a whole number (integer).

6
I can change fractions to decimals.
I can add and subtract fractions with different denominators.
I can calculate one quantity as a percentage of another.
I can use percentages to solve real-life problems.

National Test questions

1 *2007 4–6 Paper 1*

Here are six number cards:

    10 12

a Choose two of these six cards to make a fraction that is equivalent to $\frac{1}{3}$.

b Choose two of these six cards to make a fraction that **is greater than $\frac{1}{2}$ but less than 1**.

2 *2004 4–6 Paper 1*

Here are four fractions: $\frac{3}{4}$ $\frac{1}{8}$ $\frac{1}{3}$ $\frac{3}{5}$

Look at (and copy) the number line below. Write each fraction in the correct box.

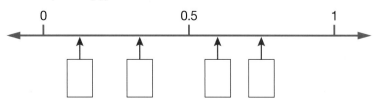

3 *2007 5–7 Paper 1*

a Write down the missing numbers:

50% of 80 = ...

5% of 80 = ...

1% of 80 = ...

MNU 2-07 a.

b Work out 56% of 80.

You can use part **a** to help you.

MNU 2-07 a.

FM **4** *2006 5–7 Paper 1*

a Work out the missing values:

10% of 84 = ...

5% of 84 = ...

$2\frac{1}{2}$% of 84 = ...

MNU 2-07 a.

b The cost of a CD player is £84 **plus** $17\frac{1}{2}$% tax.

What is the **total** cost of the CD player?

You can use part **a** to help you.

MNU 2-07a

Going on holiday

 Calculator allowed

1 This table shows the outgoing flights from Leeds to Tenerife.

Flight	Mon	Tue	Wed	Thu	Fri	Sat	Sun	Departs	Arrives
LS223		✈			✈	✈		13:55	18:30
LS225					✈			07:45	12:30

This table shows the return flights from Tenerife to Leeds.

Flight	Mon	Tue	Wed	Thu	Fri	Sat	Sun	Departs	Arrives
LS224		✈			✈	✈		19:15	23:50
LS226					✈			13:30	18:05

Mr and Mrs Brown and their two children are planning a week's holiday to Tenerife.

Mr Brown goes on the Internet to find the flight times of the planes from Leeds to Tenerife.

a On which days can they fly out to Tenerife?

b The family decides to fly out on Friday morning and return on the latest flight on the following Friday. What are the flight numbers for the two flights?

c How long are these two flights?

d When Mr Brown books the flights, he is informed that he needs to check in at Leeds airport at least 2 hours before the departure time of the flight. What is the latest time the family can arrive at the airport?

e The return ticket costs £280 for an adult and £210 for a child. What is the total cost of the tickets for the family?

f Each member of the family also has to pay a fuel supplement tax at £6, a baggage allowance at £5.50 and £3 to book a seat. Find the total cost for the family.

2 Mr Brown decides to take some euros (€) for the holiday. The exchange rate at the bank is £1 = €1.20.

a Mr Brown changes £500 at the bank. How many euros will he receive?

b Mr Brown also has 100 dollars ($) from a previous holiday to change into euros at the bank. The exchange rate at the bank is $1 = £0.60. How many euros will he receive?

c Mr Brown returns from the holiday with €60. How much is this in pounds?

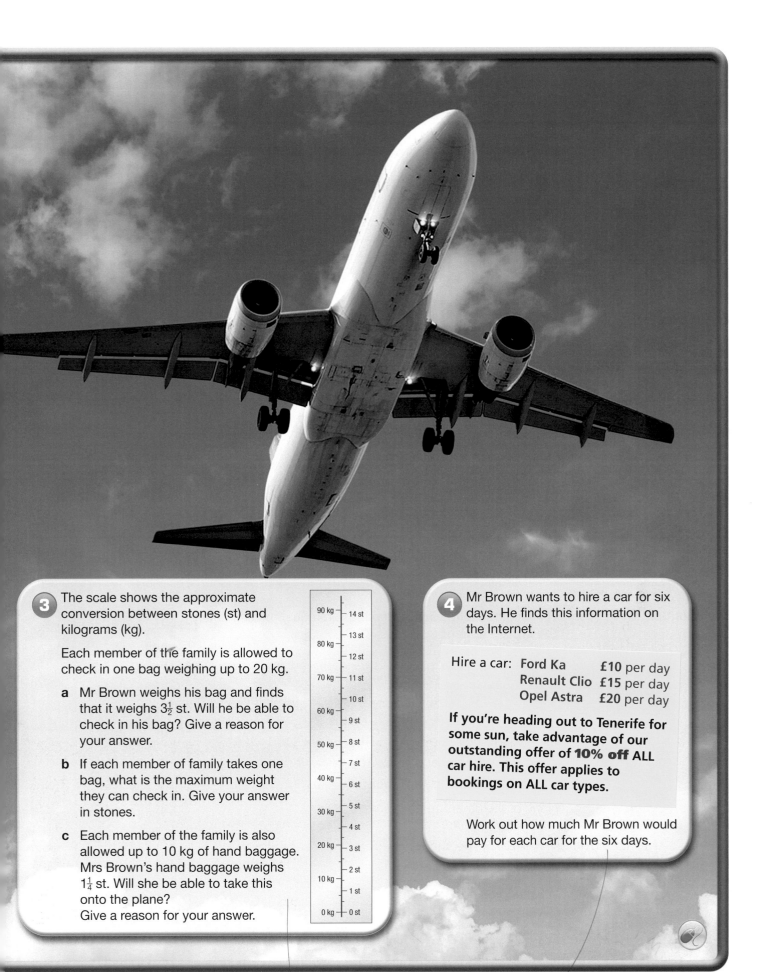

3 The scale shows the approximate conversion between stones (st) and kilograms (kg).

Each member of the family is allowed to check in one bag weighing up to 20 kg.

a Mr Brown weighs his bag and finds that it weighs $3\frac{1}{2}$ st. Will he be able to check in his bag? Give a reason for your answer.

b If each member of family takes one bag, what is the maximum weight they can check in. Give your answer in stones.

c Each member of the family is also allowed up to 10 kg of hand baggage. Mrs Brown's hand baggage weighs $1\frac{1}{4}$ st. Will she be able to take this onto the plane?
Give a reason for your answer.

(scale markings)
90 kg — 14 st
— 13 st
80 kg — 12 st
70 kg — 11 st
— 10 st
60 kg — 9 st
50 kg — 8 st
— 7 st
40 kg — 6 st
— 5 st
30 kg — 4 st
20 kg — 3 st
— 2 st
10 kg — 1 st
0 kg — 0 st

4 Mr Brown wants to hire a car for six days. He finds this information on the Internet.

Hire a car: Ford Ka   £10 per day
             Renault Clio £15 per day
             Opel Astra   £20 per day

If you're heading out to Tenerife for some sun, take advantage of our outstanding offer of 10% off ALL car hire. This offer applies to bookings on ALL car types.

Work out how much Mr Brown would pay for each car for the six days.

MNU 3-03a

> **This chapter is going to show you**
> - How to simplify expressions
> - How to expand brackets
> - How to use index notation

> **What you should already know**
> - How to substitute into algebraic expressions
> - How to add, subtract and multiply with negative numbers

Algebraic shorthand

In algebra, avoid using the × sign whenever you can, because it is easily confused with the variable x. Use instead the shorthand form of multiplication. For example:

$3m$ for $3 \times m$ ab for $a \times b$ $4cd$ for $d \times 4c$

Also, the ÷ sign is often not used. So, for example:

$\frac{a}{b}$ is written instead of $a \div b$

Use of the equals sign

Each side of the = sign must have the same value. The two sides may look different, but are still equal.

Example 5.1 ▷   Which of the following expressions are equal to each other?

$$2 + 3 \quad 4 \times 3 \quad 5 - 2 \quad 3 + 2 \quad a + b \quad b - a \quad ab \quad \frac{b}{a} \quad ba$$

$$\frac{a}{b} \quad b + a \quad a - b \quad 3 \times 4 \quad 3 + 3 \quad 10 \div 2 \quad 2 \div 10 \quad 2 - 5$$

Write correct mathematical statements for those that are equal.

$2 + 3$ is the same as $3 + 2$. That is: $2 + 3 = 3 + 2$

4×3 is the same as 3×4. That is: $4 \times 3 = 3 \times 4$

$a + b$ is the same as $b + a$. That is: $a + b = b + a$

ab is the same as ba. That is: $ab = ba$

None of the others are the same.

Example 5.2 ▷   Solve the equation $x + 2 = 7$

What do you add to 2 to get 7?

You know that $5 + 2 = 7$

So, $x = 5$

Example 5.3 ▷ Solve the equation $x - 3 = 5$.

From what do you take 3 and end up with 5?

You know that $8 - 3 = 5$

So, $x = 8$

MTH
3-15a

Exercise 5A

1 Copy and complete each of these.

    a $6 + 2 = 2 + \square$ **b** $3 + 7 = 7 + \square$ **c** $m + n = n + \square$

    d $3 + 4 = \square + 3$ **e** $5 + 8 = \square + 5$ **f** $k + h = \square + k$

    g $5 + \square = 7 + 5$ **h** $6 + \square = 4 + 6$ **i** $x + \square = y + x$

    j $\square + 9 = 9 + 1$ **k** $\square + 2 = 2 + 7$ **l** $\square + t = t + w$

    m Explain what the answers above show you about addition.

MTH
2-15a

2 Copy and complete each of these.

    a $3 \times 2 = \square \times 3$ **b** $4 \times 5 = \square \times 4$ **c** $m \times n = \square \times m$

    d $6 \times 5 = 5 \times \square$ **e** $7 \times 8 = 8 \times \square$ **f** $k \times h = h \times \square$

    g $\square \times 9 = 9 \times 7$ **h** $\square \times 4 = 4 \times 6$ **i** $\square \times y = y \times x$

    j $4 \times \square = 6 \times 4$ **k** $2 \times \square = 8 \times 2$ **l** $t \times \square = w \times t$

    m Explain what the answers above show you about multiplication.

3 Write each of these expressions using algebraic shorthand.

    a $3 \times n$ **b** $5 \times n$ **c** $7 \times m$ **d** $8 \times t$

    e $a \times b$ **f** $m \times n$ **g** $p \times 5$ **h** $q \times 4$

    i $m \div 3$ **j** $5 \div n$ **k** $7 \times w$ **l** $k \times d$

    m $t \times 3$ **n** $8 \div k$ **o** $9 \times m$ **p** $g \times h$

MTH
3-14a

4 Copy and complete each of these.

    a $mp = m \times \square$ **b** $tv = \square \times v$ **c** $qr = \square \times \square$

    d $\square = k \times g$ **e** $ab = \square \times b$ **f** $hp = h \times \square$

    g $\square = t \times f$ **h** $pt = \square \times \square$

5 Solve each of the following equations, making correct use of the equals sign.

    a $x + 1 = 11$ **b** $x - 3 = 5$ **c** $x + 4 = 19$ **d** $x - 1 = 13$

    e $x + 3 = 9$ **f** $x - 3 = 12$ **g** $x + 7 = 12$ **h** $x - 5 = 10$

    i $x - 12 = 33$ **j** $x + 3 = 80$ **k** $x + 8 = 73$ **l** $x - 7 = 65$

MTH
3-15a

6 In each box, find the pairs of expressions that are equal to each other and write them down. For example:

2 + 3
3 + 2
2 × 3

$2 + 3 = 3 + 2$

a
2 × 7
7 + 2
7 × 2

b
m × n
m + n
mn

c
p × q
q + p
pq

d
4 ÷ 2
2 ÷ 4
$\frac{2}{4}$

e
a − b
a ÷ b
$\frac{a}{b}$

f
4 × 19
19 + 4
19 × 4

g
6 + x
6x
x + 6

h
3y
3 + y
3 × y

7 Calculate each of the following. (Remember, for example, that $3 - 7 = -4$.)

a $5 - 2 = \boxed{}$

$2 - 5 = \boxed{}$

b $9 - 4 = \boxed{}$

$4 - 9 = \boxed{}$

c $10 - 2 = \boxed{}$

$2 - 10 = \boxed{}$

d Write down values for m and t which make:

$m \ - \ t \ = \ t \ - \ m$

$\boxed{} - \boxed{} = \boxed{} - \boxed{}$

e Write down *two* more sets of values for m and t which make:

$m \ - \ t \ = \ t \ - \ m$

$\boxed{} - \boxed{} = \boxed{} - \boxed{}$

$\boxed{} - \boxed{} = \boxed{} - \boxed{}$

f What must be special about m and t for $m - t$ to equal $t - m$?

Extension Work

Only some of these statements are true. Write in a list those which are true.

(*Hint:* Use numbers in place of letters and test the statement.)

1 $b + c = d + e$ is the same as $d + e = b + c$

2 $a - b = 6$ is the same as $6 = a - b$

3 $5x = x + 3$ is the same as $x = 5x + 3$

4 $5 - 2x = 8$ is the same as $8 = 2x - 5$

5 $ab - ba = T$ is the same as $T = ba - ab$

Two rules of algebra

Addition of terms

When you have, for example, $5 + 5 + 5$, you can write it simply as 3×5. Likewise in algebra, terms which use the same letter can be added together in the same way. For example:

$$m + m + m + m = 4 \times m = 4m$$
$$p + p + p = 3 \times p = 3p$$

Example 5.4 ▷ Simplify both of these.

a $\quad d + d + d + d + d$ **b** $\quad pq + pq + pq + pq + pq + pq$

a There are five ds, which simplify to $5 \times d = 5d$.

b There are six pqs, which simplify to $6 \times pq = 6pq$.

Raising a term to a power

A **power** or **index** tells you how many times to multiply a number or a term by itself. For example, 4^3 is a short way of writing $4 \times 4 \times 4$ to give the answer 64.

A term or number raised to a power is said to be in its **index form**.

Example 5.5 ▷ Write $m \times m \times m \times m$ in index form.

In index form, m multiplied by itself four times is written as m^4.

That is, m to the power of four.

Example 5.6 ▷ Write, as simply as possible, $m \times m \times m \times m \times m$.

There are five of the ms multiplied together.

The simplest way of writing this is m^5.

Exercise 5B

1 Simplify each of the following expressions.

a $m + m$	**b** $k + k + k$	**c** $a + a + a + a$	**d** $d + d + d$
e $q + q + q + q$	**f** $t + t$	**g** $n + n + n + n$	**h** $g + g + g$
i $p + p + p$	**j** $w + w + w + w$	**k** $i + i + i + i + i$	**l** $a + a + a + a$

2 Copy and complete each of the following. For example:

$$t + t + t + t = 4 \times t = 4t$$

a $p + p + p = 3 \times p = \boxed{}$

b $m + m + m + m = 4 \times m = \boxed{}$

c $k + k + k = \boxed{} = \boxed{}$

d $h + h + h + h + h = \boxed{} = \boxed{}$

e $\boxed{} = 6 \times m = 6m$

f $\boxed{} = 5 \times p = \boxed{}$

g $\boxed{} = 3 \times g = \boxed{}$

h $\boxed{} = \boxed{} = 7n$

i $\boxed{} = \boxed{} = 5y$

3 Write each of the following expressions in index form.

a	$n \times n \times n$	**b**	$m \times m$	**c**	$p \times p \times p \times p$	**d**	$w \times w \times w$
e	$m \times m \times m$	**f**	$t \times t \times t \times t$	**g**	$k \times k \times k \times k$	**h**	$y \times y \times y$
i	$v \times v \times v \times v$	**j**	$d \times d \times d \times d \times d$	**k**	$t \times t \times t \times t \times t$	**l**	$m \times m \times m$

4 Calculate each of the following powers.

a	3^3	**b**	4^2	**c**	2^4	**d**	4^3
e	5^3	**f**	2^3	**g**	3^4	**h**	10^2
i	10^3	**j**	2^5				

5 Write each of the following as simply as possible.

a	$n \times n$	**b**	$m + m$	**c**	$p \times p \times p$	**d**	$w + w + w$
e	$q \times q \times q \times q$	**f**	$r + r + r + r$	**g**	$k + k$	**h**	$f \times f \times f$
i	$v + v + v + v$	**j**	$d \times d \times d \times d \times d$	**k**	$q + q + q$	**l**	$t \times t \times t \times t$

6 Copy each of these and write out in full.

a	$3t = \dots$	$t^3 = \dots$		**b**	$4m = \dots$	$m^4 = \dots$
c	$2k = \dots$	$k^2 = \dots$		**d**	$5w = \dots$	$w^5 = \dots$
e	$3d = \dots$	$d^3 = \dots$				

Extension **Work**

1 Explain why two consecutive integers multiplied together always give an even number.

2 Show that any three consecutive integers multiplied together always give a number in the six times table.

Like terms and simplification

Like terms are those terms which are multiples of the same letter or of the same combination of letters or of powers of the same letter or combination of letters.
For example, a, $3a$, $\frac{1}{4}a$ and $-5a$ are all like terms. So are $2xy$, $7xy$ and $-8xy$ and x^2, $6x^2$ and $-3x^2$.

The multiples are called **coefficients**. So, in the above examples, 3, $\frac{1}{4}$, -5, 2, 7, -8, 6 and -3 are coefficients.

Only like terms can be added or subtracted to simplify an expression. For example:

$2xy + 7xy - 8xy$ simplifies to xy

$x^2 + 6x^2 - 3x^2$ simplifies to $4x^2$

Unlike terms cannot be combined.

Simplifying an expression means making it shorter by combining its terms where possible. This involves two steps:

- Collect like terms into groups.
- Combine the like terms in each group.

Example 5.7 Simplify $8p + 2q + 3p + 7s + 4q + 9$.

Write out the expression: $8p + 2q + 3p + 7s + 4q + 9$

Then collect like terms: $8p + 3p + 2q + 4q + 7s + 9$

Next, combine them: $11p + 6q + 7s + 9$

So, the expression in its simplest form is:

$11p + 6q + 7s + 9$

Example 5.8 Simplify $7x^2 + y^2 + 2x^2 - 3y^2 + 3z - 5$

Write out the expression: $7x^2 + y^2 + 2x^2 - 3y^2 + 3z - 5$

Then collect like terms: $7x^2 + 2x^2 + y^2 - 3y^2 + 3z - 5$

Next, combine them: $9x^2 - 2y^2 + 3z - 5$

So, the expression in its simplest form is:

$9x^2 - 2y^2 + 3z - 5$

Exercise 5C

1 Simplify each of these.

a	$2b + 3b$	**b**	$5x + 2x$	**c**	$6m + m$	**d**	$3m + m + 2m$
e	$7d - 3d$	**f**	$8g - 3g$	**g**	$4k - k$	**h**	$3t + 2t - t$

2 Simplify each of these.

a	$5g + g - 2g$	**b**	$3x + 5x - 6x$	**c**	$4h + 3h - 5h$	**d**	$4q + 7q - 3q$
e	$5h - 2h + 4h$	**f**	$6x - 4x + 3x$	**g**	$3y - y + 4y$	**h**	$5d - 4d + 6d$
i	$8x - 2x - 3x$	**j**	$5m - m - 2m$	**k**	$8k - 3k - 2k$	**l**	$6n - 3n - n$

3 From each cloud, group together the like terms. For example:

a $3b$ $2a$
$4b$ $5a$ b $\longrightarrow$ $a, 2a, 5a$
$b, 3b, 4b$

a $3t$ g $5t$
$8g$ $9t$ $7g$

b m $7p$ $4m$
$9p$ $10m$
$3p$

c $4k$ $3m$
$5w$ $8m$
$7w$ $7m$ k

d x^2 t $5x^2$
$3t$ $3x^2$ $4t$

e y^2 $2y$ $8y$
$7y^2$ $4y^2$
$3y$

f $7w$ $7g$ $3h$
$3g$ $9h$ $4w$
$3w$ $10g$

4 Simplify each of these expressions.

a	$3b + 5 + 2b$	**b**	$2x + 7 + 3x$	**c**	$m + 2 + 5m$	**d**	$4k + 3k + 8$
e	$3x + 7 - x$	**f**	$5k + 4 - 2k$	**g**	$6p + 3 - 2p$	**h**	$5d + 1 - 4d$
i	$5m - 3 - 2m$	**j**	$6t - 4 - 2t$	**k**	$4w - 8 - 3w$	**l**	$5g - 1 - g$
m	$t + k + 4t$	**n**	$3x + 2y + 4x$	**o**	$2k + 3g + 5k$	**p**	$3h + 2w + w$
q	$5t - 2p - 3t$	**r**	$6n - 2t - 5n$	**s**	$p + 4q - 2q$	**t**	$3n + 2p - 3n$

5 Simplify each of these expressions.

a	$2t + 3g + 5t + 2g$	**b**	$4x + y + 2x + 3y$	**c**	$2m + k + 3m + 2k$
d	$5x + 3y - 2x + y$	**e**	$6m + 2p - 4m + 3p$	**f**	$3n + 4t - n + 3t$
g	$6k + 3g - 2k - g$	**h**	$7d + 4b - 5d - 3b$	**i**	$4q + 3p - 3q - p$
j	$4g - k + 2g - 3k$	**k**	$2x - 3y + 5x - 2y$	**l**	$4d - 3e - 3d - 2e$

6 Simplify each of these expressions.

a	$5x^2 + x^2$	**b**	$6k^2 + 2k^2$	**c**	$4m^2 + 3m^2$	**d**	$6d^2 - 2d^2$
e	$5g^2 - 3g^2$	**f**	$7a^2 - 5a^2$	**g**	$5f^2 + 2f^2$	**h**	$3y^2 - y^2$
i	$t^2 + 3t^2$	**j**	$5h^2 - 2h^2$	**k**	$6k^2 + k^2$	**l**	$7m^2 - 3m^2$

7 Simplify each of these expressions.

a	$8x + 3 + 2x + 5$	**b**	$5p + 2k + p + 3k$	**c**	$9t + 3m + 2t + m$
d	$7k + 3t + 2t - 3k$	**e**	$5m + 4p + p - 3m$	**f**	$8w + 2d + 3d - 2w$
g	$6x + 2y + 4y + 2x$	**h**	$8p + 3q + 4q - 3p$	**i**	$3m + 2t + 3t - m$

Extension Work

When an odd number is added to an even number the answer is always odd, for example, $3 + 4 = 7$.

Copy and complete the two tables below.

+	Even	Odd
Even		Odd
Odd		

×	Even	Odd
Even		
Odd		

Using algebra with shapes

Example 5.9

Find **a** the perimeter and **b** the area of this rectangle.

k

p

a Perimeter $= 2(k + p) = 2k + 2p$

b Area $= k \times p = kp$

Example 5.10

State the area of the shape as simply as possible.

First, split the shape into two parts A and B, as shown.

Shape A has the area $8x$ cm^2.

Shape B has the area $2y$ cm^2.

Total area is $(8x + 2y)$ cm^2.

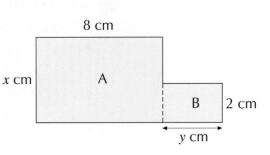

Exercise 5D

1 Write down, as simply as possible, the perimeter of each of these shapes.

a
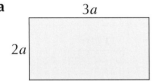
3a

2a

b
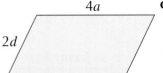
4a

2d

c
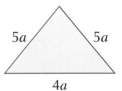
5a   5a

4a

d
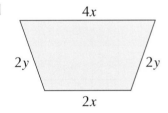
4x

2y   2y

2x

e
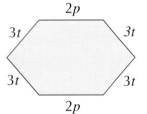
2p

3t   3t

3t   3t

2p

f
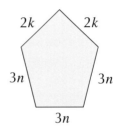
2k   2k

3n   3n

3n

2 What is the area of each rectangle?

a
t cm

2 cm

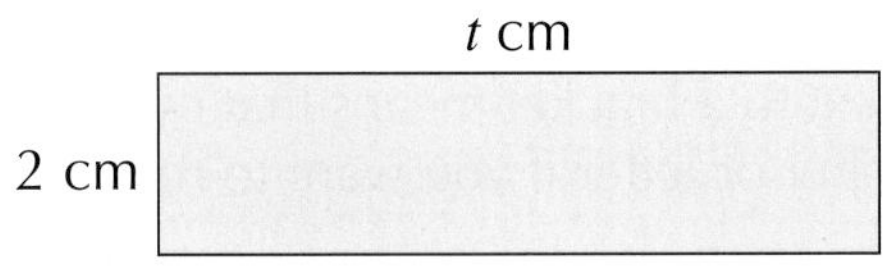

b
5 cm

g cm

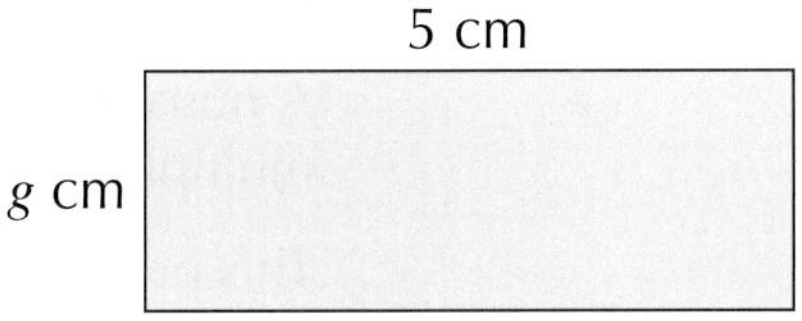

c
k cm

3 cm

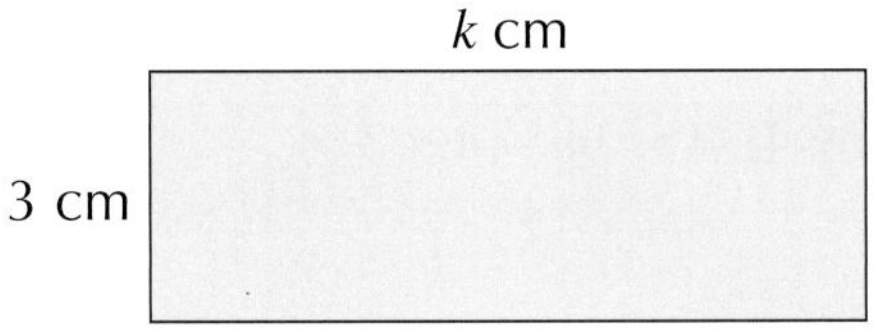

d
7 cm

x cm

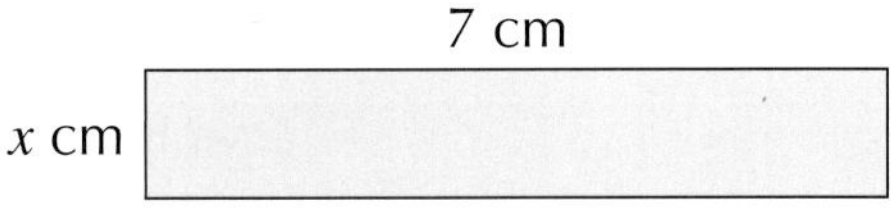

3 Write down, as simply as possible, the perimeter of each of these shapes.

a
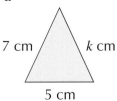
7 cm k cm

5 cm

b
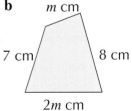
m cm

7 cm   8 cm

2m cm

c
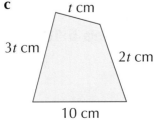
t cm

3t cm   2t cm

10 cm

MTH 3-15b

4 The expression in each box is made by adding the expressions in the two boxes it stands on. Copy the diagrams and fill in the missing expressions.

a

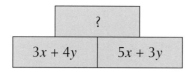

	?	
$3x + 4y$		$5x + 3y$

b

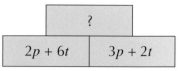

	?	
$2p + 6t$		$3p + 2t$

c

	$3n + 5c$	
$2n + c$		?

d

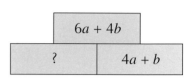

	$6a + 4b$	
?		$4a + b$

Extension Work

The compound shapes below have been split into rectangles.
Work out the area of each rectangle and then add these to get the total area.
Simplify your answer.

a

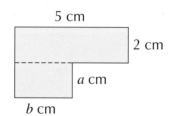

5 cm, 2 cm, a cm, b cm

b

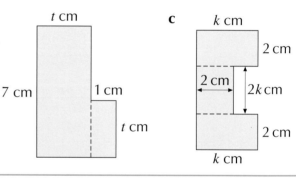

t cm, 7 cm, 1 cm, t cm

c

k cm, 2 cm, 2 cm, $2k$ cm, 2 cm, k cm

Expanding brackets

A number or a letter next to a bracket means that everything in the bracket must be multiplied by that number or letter if you want to remove the bracket.

This process is called **expanding** or **multiplying** out a bracket.

Example 5.11   Expand $4(2m + 3)$.

Multiply each term by 4: $4 \times 2m + 4 \times 3$
This gives: $8m + 12$

Example 5.12   Expand $3(5t - 2w - 3)$.

Multiply each term by 3: $3 \times 5t - 3 \times 2w - 3 \times 3$
This gives: $15t - 6w - 9$

Example 5.13   Expand and simplify $7x - 2(4y - x) - y$.

First, multiply each term in the bracket by -2: $7x - 8y + 2x - y$
Then collect like terms: $7x + 2x - 8y - y$
Finally, combine them: $9x - 9y$
So, the expression in its simplest form is: $9x - 9y$

1 Calculate each of the following by: **i** expanding the bracket.   **ii** calculating the bracket first. See the example below.

  i $2(5 + 3) = 2 \times 5 + 2 \times 3 = 10 + 6 = 16$

  ii $2(5 + 3) = 2 \times 8 = 16$

  a $3(4 + 2)$ **b** $5(3 + 1)$ **c** $4(2 + 3)$

  d $6(3 + 4)$ **e** $8(5 - 2)$ **f** $10(5 - 2)$

2 Multiply out each of the following expressions.

  a $2(x + 3)$ **b** $4(2m + 1)$ **c** $3(3k + 5)$ **d** $2(5n + 2)$

  e $4(5 + 3t)$ **f** $3(2 + 5g)$ **g** $6(1 + 3h)$ **h** $5(3 + 2d)$

  i $3(3a - 1)$ **j** $2(2 - 5c)$ **k** $8(1 - 2f)$ **l** $3(4 - 3b)$

  m $2(3d + 2a)$ **n** $5(4e + 2)$ **o** $2(3x + 2y)$ **p** $7(2q + 5p)$

  q $2(3q - 4p)$ **r** $3(5t - 3s)$ **s** $4(7w - 3k)$ **t** $5(4n - 3d)$

3 Expand and simplify each of the following expressions.

  a $10m + 2(3m + 4)$ **b** $8t + 3(4t + 2)$ **c** $5k + 4(2k + 7)$

  d $9g + 3(5 + 2g)$ **e** $7q + 4(3 + q)$ **f** $9h + 2(4 + 3h)$

  g $8f + 2(4 + 3f)$ **h** $9k + 2(5 + k)$ **i** $10t + 3(1 + 5t)$

4 Expand and simplify each of the following expressions.

  a $5(2h + 3) - 4h$ **b** $3(4t + 2p) - 5t$ **c** $4(3k + m) - 2m$

  d $9g + 2(3g - 4)$ **e** $10t + 3(4g - t)$ **f** $7m + 2(5m - 4g)$

  g $8m + 3(5m - k)$ **h** $12p + 2(3p - 4m)$ **i** $9h + 4(3h - 2p)$

5 Expand and simplify each of the following expressions.

  a $2(2x + 3y) + 3(4x + 2y)$ **b** $3(3p + 2m) + 2(2p + 5m)$

  c $4(5k + 4g) + 2(2k + 3g)$ **d** $3(3e + 2d) + 2(2d + 5e)$

  e $5(5n + 2p) + 3(3n - 4p)$ **f** $4(5t + 3f) + 3(3t - 2f)$

  g $3(p + 6d) + 5(2p - 3d)$ **h** $3(5x - 3y) + 2(4y - x)$

Extension **Work**

1 Show, by taking a few examples, that the sum of any three consecutive integers is a multiple of 3.

2 Do you think that the sum of any three consecutive integers is *always* a multiple of 3? Explain why.

3 Show that the sum of four consecutive integers is never a multiple of 4.

4 Is the sum of the five consecutive integers always a multiple of 5? Explain why.

3 I can solve simple missing number problems such as ☐ + 3 = 7, ☐ = 4.

4 I can simplify algebraic expressions such as $3 \times 2n = 6n$.

I can solve simple equations such as $4x = 32$.

I can simplify algebraic expressions by collecting like terms such as
$3x + 4y + 2x - y = 5x + 3y$.

5 I know the equivalence of algebraic expressions such as $a + b = b + a$.

I can expand a bracket such as $4(2x - 1) = 8x - 4$.

I can write algebraic expressions in a simpler form using index notation such as
$n \times n \times n \times n \times n = n^5$.

National Test questions

1 *2004 3–5 Paper 2*

a Anna says:

> Multiply any number by three.
>
> The answer **must** be an **odd** number.

Give an example to show that Anna is **wrong**.

b Jay says:

> Divide any **even** number by two.
>
> The answer **must** be an **odd** number.

Give an example to show that Jay is **wrong**.

MTH 3-14a

2 *2006 3–5 Paper 1*

A ruler costs k pence.
A pen costs m pence.

Match each statement with the correct expression for the amount in pence.

The first one is done for you.

Statement

| The total cost of 5 rulers |

| The total cost of 5 rulers and 5 pens |

| How much more 5 pens cost than 5 rulers |

| The change from £5, in pence, when you buy 5 pens |

Expression

| $5k$ |

| $5m$ |

| $5 - 5m$ |

| $500 - 5m$ |

| $5k + m$ |

| $5(k + m)$ |

| $5m - 5k$ |

| $5k - 5m$ |

3 *2004 4–6 Paper 1*

One way to make a magic square is to substitute numbers into this algebra grid.

$a + b$	$a - b + c$	$a - c$
$a - b - c$	a	$a + b + c$
$a + c$	$a + b - c$	$a - b$

a Copy the magic square opposite and complete it using the values:

$a = 10$ $b = 3$ $c = 5$

		5
	10	
15		

b Starting with the same algebra grid, I used **different values** for a, b and c to complete the magic square as follows:

What values for a, b and c did I use?

20	21	7
3	16	29
25	11	12

4 *2004 4–6 Paper 2*

a The square and the rectangle below have the **same area**.

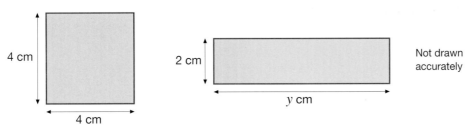

Not drawn accurately

Work out the value of y.

b The triangle and the rectangle below have the **same area**.

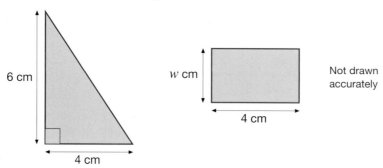

6 cm

4 cm

w cm

4 cm

Not drawn
accurately

Work out the value of *w*.

Show your working.

5 *2005 3–5 Paper 2*

Look at this algebra grid:

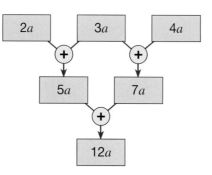

2*a*   3*a*   4*a*

+   +

5*a*   7*a*

+

12*a*

Copy and complete the algebra grids below, simplifying each expression.

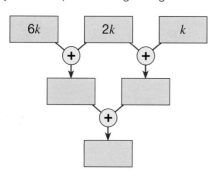

6*k*   2*k*   *k*

+   +

+

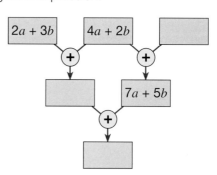

2*a* + 3*b*   4*a* + 2*b*

+   +

7*a* + 5*b*

+

6 *2007 3–5 Paper 2*

a Here is an expression:

2*a* + 3 + 2*a*

Which of the expressions below shows this written as simply as possible?

7*a*   7 + *a*   2*a* + 5

4*a* + 3   4(*a* + 3)

b Here is a different expression:

3*b* + 4 + 5*b* − 1

Write this expression as simply as possible.

This chapter is going to show you	**What you should already know**
● How to find the perimeter and area of a rectangle ● How to find the perimeter and area of a compound shape ● How to read scales ● How to find the surface area of a cuboid ● How to convert from one metric unit to another	● How to find the perimeter of a shape ● How to find the area of a shape by counting squares ● The metric units for length, capacity and mass

Perimeter and area of rectangles

length (*l*)

width (*w*)

The perimeter of a rectangle is the total distance around the shape.

> Perimeter = 2 lengths + 2 widths

This can be written as a formula:

> $P = 2l + 2w$

The units used to measure perimeter are mm, cm or m.

The area of the rectangle is the amount of space inside the shape.

> Area = length × width

This can be written as a formula:

> $A = l \times w$ or $A = lw$

The units used to measure area are mm², cm² or m².

MNU
2-11c

Example 6.1

5 cm

4 cm

Find the perimeter and area of the rectangle.

$P = 2l + 2w = 2 \times 5 + 2 \times 4 = 10 + 8 = 18$ cm

$A = lw = 5 \times 4 = 20$ cm²

Exercise 6A

1 By measuring the length of the sides of the following rectangles, find:
   i   the perimeter.   **ii**   the area.

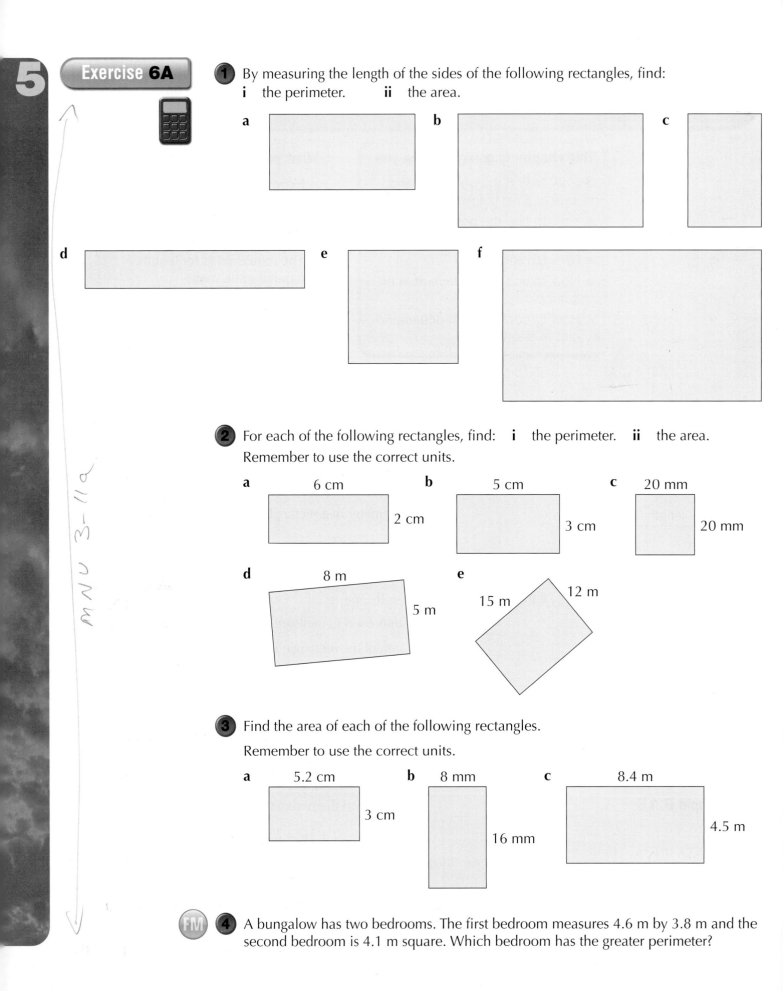

a

b

c

d

e

f

2 For each of the following rectangles, find: **i**   the perimeter.   **ii**   the area.
   Remember to use the correct units.

a   6 cm   2 cm

b   5 cm   3 cm

c   20 mm   20 mm

d   8 m   5 m

e   15 m   12 m

3 Find the area of each of the following rectangles.

   Remember to use the correct units.

a   5.2 cm   3 cm

b   8 mm   16 mm

c   8.4 m   4.5 m

FM   4 A bungalow has two bedrooms. The first bedroom measures 4.6 m by 3.8 m and the
second bedroom is 4.1 m square. Which bedroom has the greater perimeter?

FM **5** A room is 6 m long and 4 m wide. A carpet measuring 5 m by 3 m is placed on the floor of the room. Find the area of the floor not covered by carpet.

Extension **Work**

Estimate the area of each of the irregular shapes drawn on the centimetre square grid below.

To do this, mark with a dot each square that is at least half-covered by the shape, and then count how many squares contain a dot.

For example: dots have been marked on each square that is at least half-covered by shape 1. There are 15 dots in total, so the estimate of the area of shape 1 is 15 cm².

You may wish to start by tracing the shapes on to centimetre-squared paper.

1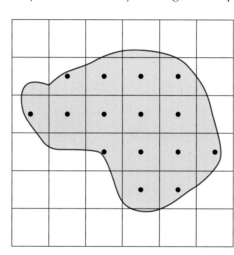

2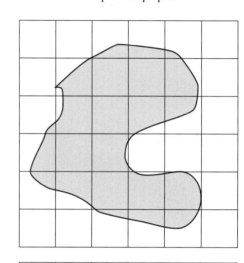

3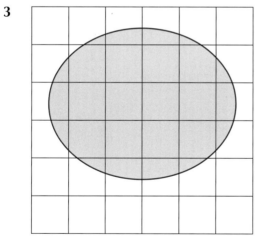

4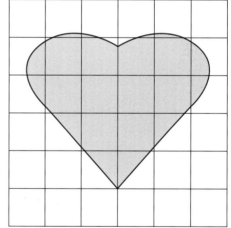

Perimeter and area of compound shapes

A compound shape is a shape that is made by combining other simple shapes, such as squares, rectangles and triangles.

The example shows you how to find the perimeter and area of a compound shape made from two rectangles.

Example 6.2 ▷ Find the perimeter and area of the following compound shape.

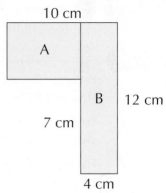

First copy the shape, then find and label the lengths of any sides which are not already shown.

Now the perimeter and area of the compound shape can be worked out as follows:

$P = 10 + 12 + 4 + 7 + 6 + 5$
$= 44$ cm

Total area = Area of A + Area of B
$= 6 \times 5 + 12 \times 4$
$= 30 + 48$
$= 78$ cm^2

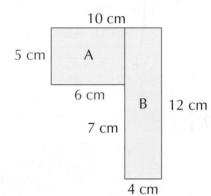

5

Exercise 6B

1 For each of the compound shapes, find: **i** the perimeter. **ii** the area.
Start by copying the diagrams and splitting them up into rectangles as shown.

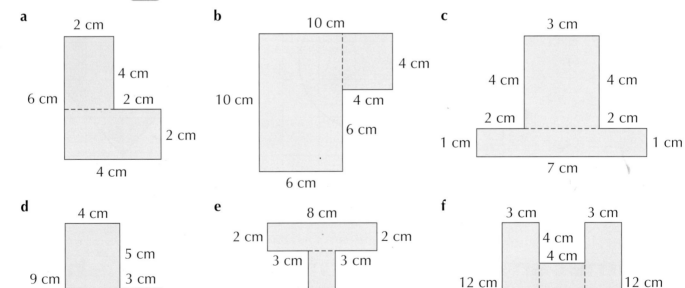

2 Sandra makes a picture frame from a rectangular piece of card for a photograph of her favourite group.

   a Find the area of the photograph.

   b Find the area of the card she uses.

   c Find the area of the border.

     (*Hint:* subtract the two areas.)

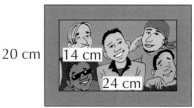

20 cm   14 cm   24 cm   30 cm

(FM) 3 A garden is in the shape of a rectangle measuring 16 m by 12 m.

   a Find the area of the garden.

   b Find the area of the path.

   c Find the area of the flower bed.

   d Find the area of the grass in the garden.

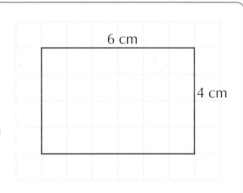

Path   2 m   12 m   Grass   Flower bed   3 m   6 m   16 m

Extension Work

How many rectangles can you draw with a fixed perimeter of 20 cm, but each one having a different area? You may use centimetre-squared paper to draw any diagrams.

Here is an example:

Perimeter = 6 cm + 4 cm + 6 cm + 4 cm = 20 cm

Area = 6 cm × 4 cm = 24 cm^2

6 cm   4 cm

Reading scales

It is important in subjects such as Science and Technology to be able to read scales accurately.

When reading a scale always make sure that you first work out the size of each division on the scale.

Example 6.3 ▷   What length is each arrow pointing to on the ruler shown below?

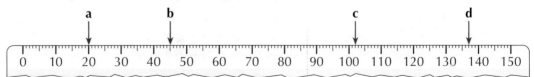

a   b   c   d

0   10   20   30   40   50   60   70   80   90   100   110   120   130   140   150

Each small division on the ruler is 1 mm or 0.1 cm.

So, the arrows are pointing to the following lengths:

a   20 mm = 2 cm   **b**   45 mm = 4.5 cm

c   102 mm = 10.2 cm   **d**   137 mm = 13.7 cm

1 Write down the number that each arrow is pointing to on each of the number lines below.

a
0   10

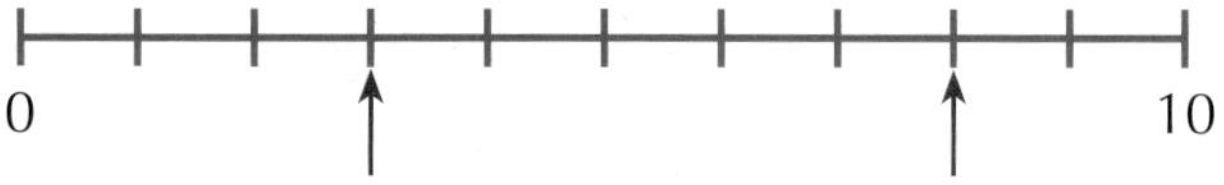

b
0   20

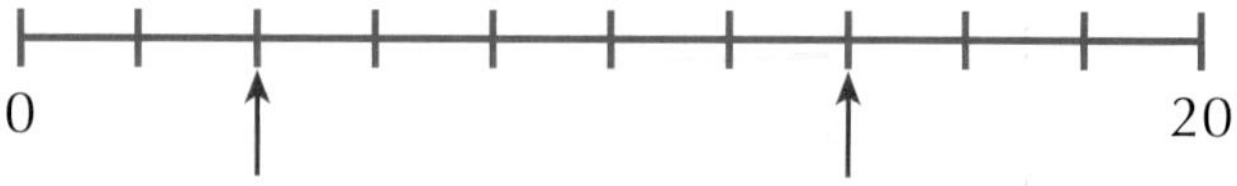

c
0   50

d
0   5

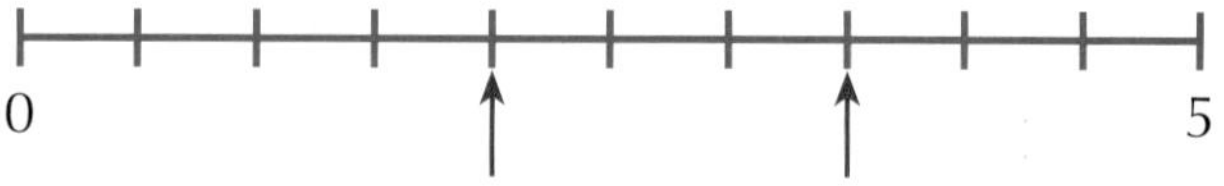

2 Write down the length of each of the following nails. Give your answer in:
i centimetres.   **ii** millimetres.

Each division on the rulers is 1 mm.

a
0   10   20   30   40   50   60   70   80

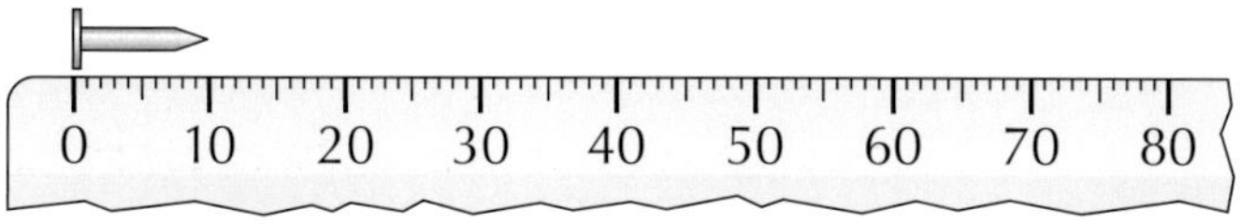

b
0   10   20   30   40   50   60   70   80

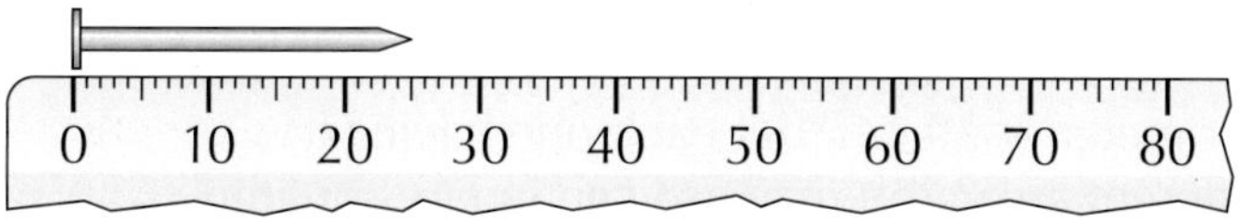

c
0   10   20   30   40   50   60   70   80

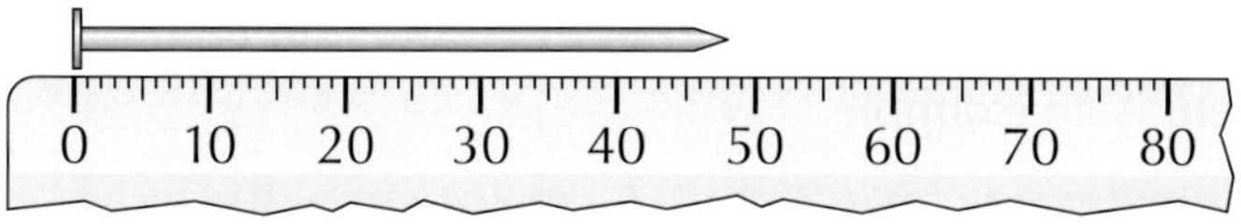

d
0   10   20   30   40   50   60   70   80

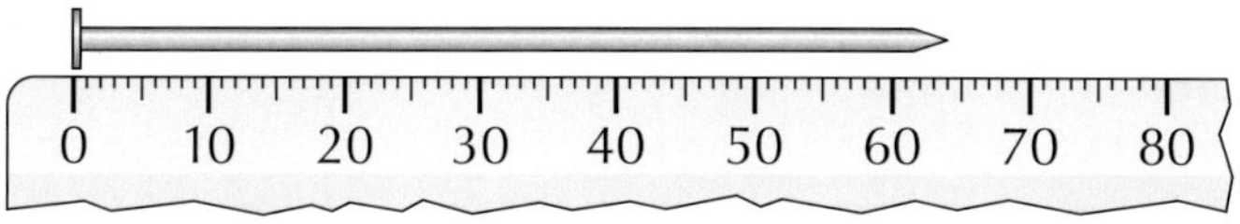

3 Write down the mass shown on each of the following scales.

a
0   50   100   150   200
grams

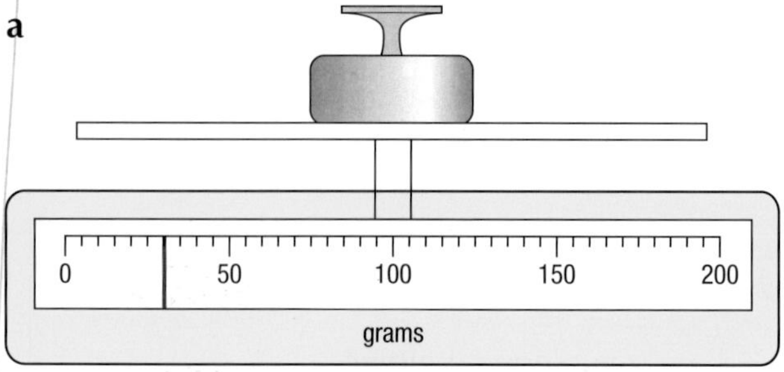

b
0   50   100   150   200
grams

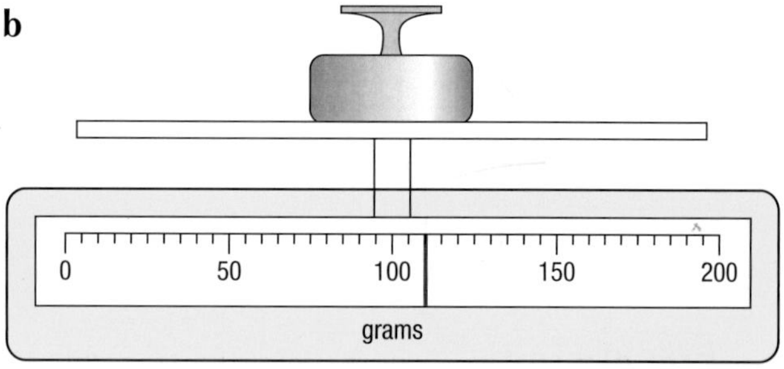

c
0   50   100   150   200
grams

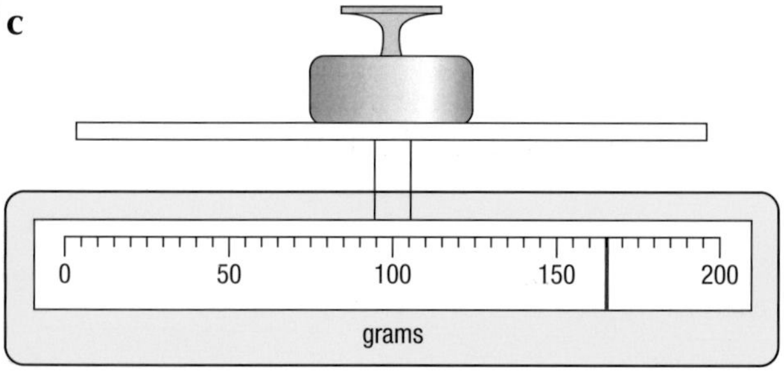

d
2 kg   3 kg
1 kg   4 kg
0 kg   5 kg

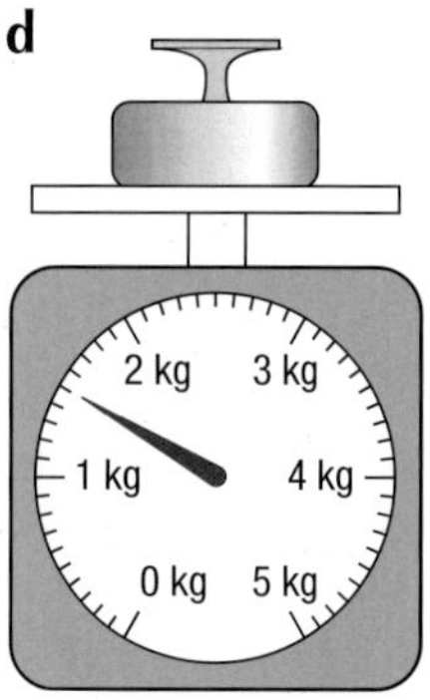

e
2 kg   3 kg
1 kg   4 kg
0 kg   5 kg

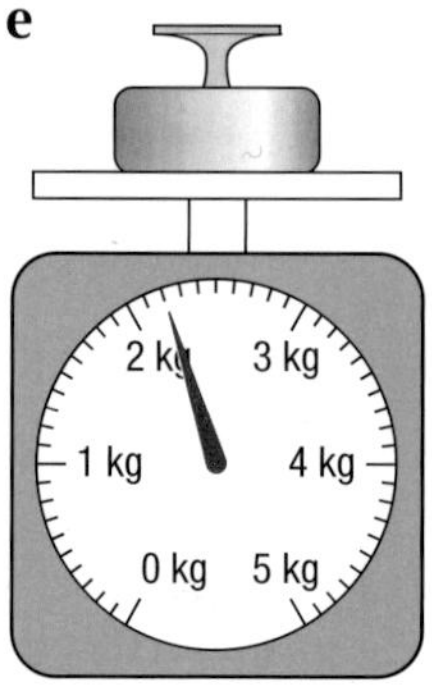

f
2 kg   3 kg
1 kg   4 kg
0 kg   5 kg

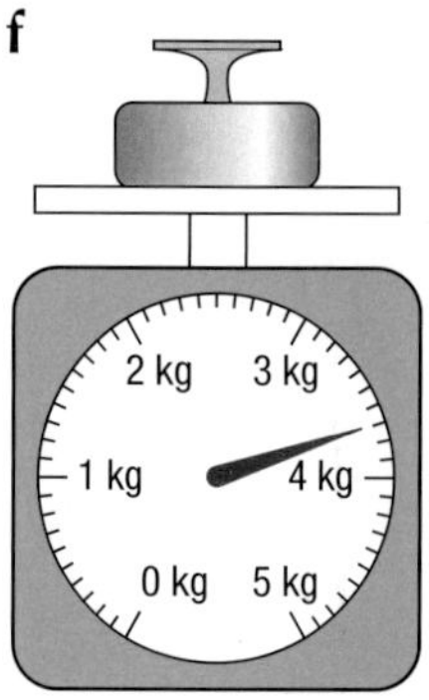

4 Write down the volume of water in each of the following jugs.

a

b

c

d
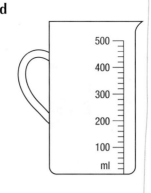

5 Each thermometer below shows the temperature in °C.

i

ii

iii

iv

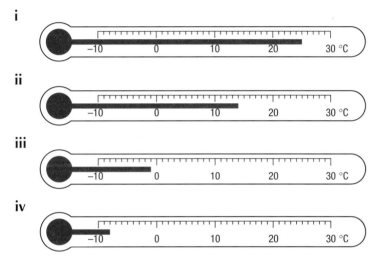

a   Write down the temperatures marked in **i** to **iv** above.

b   What temperature is 5 degrees higher than 2°C?

c   What temperature is 5 degrees higher than –2°C?

d   What temperature is 5 degrees lower than –2°C?

e   The temperature changes from 10°C to –5°C.
    By how many degrees has the temperature changed?

<Extension> <Work>

1   A box contains the following:
    four 10 g weights
    four 20 g weights
    four 50 g weights
    four 100 g weights

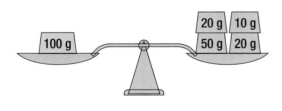

One combination of weights that will balance the scales is shown.

How many other ways to balance the scales can you find?

2   For this activity you will need some weighing scales.

    Weigh some objects in the classroom, giving your answer as accurately
    as possible.

Surface area of cubes and cuboids

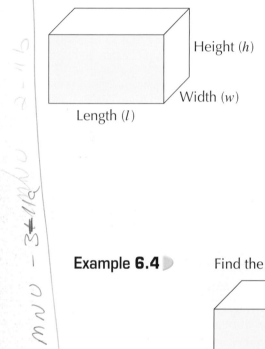

The surface area of a cuboid is found by calculating the total area of its six faces.

Area of top face = length × width = lw

Area of bottom face = lw

Area of front face = length × height = lh

Area of back face = lh

Area of right end face = width × height = wh

Area of left end face = wh

So, the surface area of the cuboid is:

$$S = lw + lw + lh + lh + wh + wh$$
$$S = 2lw + 2lh + 2wh$$

Example 6.4 ▷ Find the surface area of this cuboid.

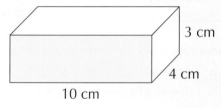

$$S = (2 \times 10 \times 4) + (2 \times 10 \times 3) + (2 \times 4 \times 3)$$
$$= 80 + 60 + 24$$
$$= 164 \text{ cm}^2$$

Exercise 6D

1 Find the surface area of this unit cube.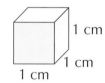

2 Find the surface area for cubes with the following edge lengths.

   a 2 cm   **b** 5 cm   **c** 10 cm   **d** 8 m

3 Six unit (centimetre) cubes are placed together to make the following 3-D shapes.

a   **b**   **c**

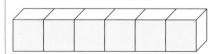      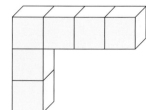

Find the surface area of each shape.

4 Find the surface area for each of the following cuboids.

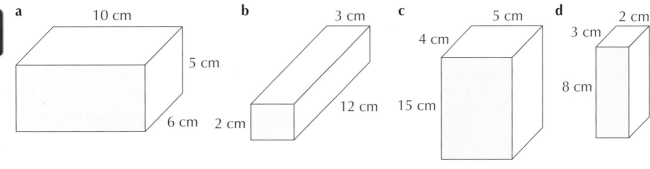

a 10 cm 5 cm 6 cm 2 cm

b 3 cm 12 cm 2 cm

c 5 cm 4 cm 15 cm

d 2 cm 3 cm 8 cm

6

Extension Work

MNU 3-11a

1 Find the surface area of the cereal packet on the left.

Crunchie Loops 23 cm 18 cm 5 cm

2 Find the surface area of the outside of this open water tank.
(A cuboid without a top.)

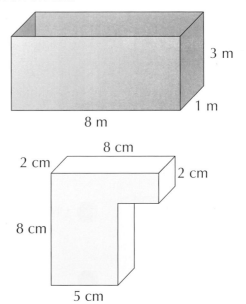

3 m 1 m 8 m

MNU 3-11b

3 Find the total surface area of this 3-D shape. Start by drawing each face separately and finding the lengths of any unknown sides. Then work out the area of each face and add them together to get the total surface area.

8 cm 2 cm 2 cm 8 cm 5 cm

Converting one metric unit to another

Below are the common metric units which you need to know. Also given are the relationships between these units.

Length	Capacity	Weight
Larger unit *Smaller unit*	*Larger unit* *Smaller unit*	*Larger unit* *Smaller unit*
1 kilometre (km) = 1000 metres (m) 1 metre (m) = 100 centimetres (cm) 1 centimetre (cm) = 10 millimetres (mm)	1 litre (l) = 100 centilitres (l) 1 litre (l) = 1000 millilitres (ml)	1 kilogram (kg) = 1000 grams (g)

To convert a smaller unit into a larger unit you need to *divide* by the amount given in the table above.

To convert a larger unit to a smaller unit you need to *multiply* by the amount given in the table above.

Example 6.5 ▷   **a**   Change 7 cm to mm.

10 mm = 1 cm and you are changing a larger unit to a smaller unit, so you need to multiply by 10.

7 × 10 = 70, so 7 cm = 70 mm

     b   Convert 2500 g to kg.

1000 g = 1 kg and you are changing a smaller unit to a larger unit, so you need to divide by 1000.

2500 ÷ 1000 = 2.5, so 2500 g = 2.5 kg

When you are adding or subtracting two metric quantities in different units, you must change them both to the same unit first. It is usually easier to change them both to the smaller unit.

Example 6.6 ▷   What is 800 m + 2 km?

2 km = 2000 m, so 800 m + 2 km = 800 m + 2000 m = 2800 m

If you were asked for the answer in kilometres, you could then convert this as normal:

2800 ÷ 1000 = 2.8 km

Exercise 6E

1 Change each of the following lengths to centimetres.

   a   80 mm   **b**   120 mm   **c**   55 mm   **d**   136 mm   **e**   9 mm

2 Change each of the following lengths to centimetres.

   a   2 m   **b**   10 m   **c**   4.5 m   **d**   3.8 m   **e**   0.4 m

3 Change each of the following lengths to kilometres.

   a   3000 m   **b**   10000 m   **c**   3500 m   **d**   6700 m   **e**   800 m

4 Change each of the following capacities to centilitres.

   a   4 l   **b**   7 l   **c**   1.5 l   **d**   8.2 l   **e**   0.3 l

5 Change each of the following weights to grams.

   a   5 kg   **b**   9 kg   **c**   2.5 kg   **d**   3.2 kg   **e**   0.2 kg

6 Work out each of the following. Give your answer in the smaller unit.

   a   2 cm + 7 mm   **b**   3 km – 800 m   **c**   2.5 l + 70 cl   **d**   1.4 kg – 300 g

5

MWU 2–11 6

7 The two carpets below are joined together to make a longer carpet. How long will the carpet be? Give your answer in metres.

2.5 m   160 cm

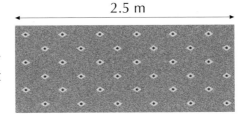 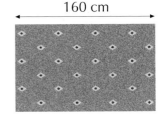

8 Jenny carries home the shopping shown below. Find the total weight that she has to carry. Give your answer in kilograms.

2.5 kg   1 kg   750 g   540 g

9 Simon pours four glasses of lemonade from a 2 litre bottle. If each glass holds 20 cl, how much lemonade is left in the bottle? Give your answer in centilitres.

10 The distance round a school running track is 600 m. During a PE lesson, Hardeep completes 8 circuits. How far does he run altogether? Give your answer in kilometres.

MNU 2-11b

Extension Work

How big is a million?

1 Change one million millimetres into kilometres.

2 Change one million grams into kilograms.

3 How long is one million seconds? Give your answer in days, hours, minutes and seconds.

MNU 2-11b

LEVEL BOOSTER

4 I can read measurements from different types of scales.

I can find the perimeter of 2-D shapes.

I know the names and abbreviations of metric units in everyday use and how to solve problems using these.

5 I can use the formula for the area of a rectangle.

I can find the area of a simple compound 2-D shape.

I can find the surface area of a cube.

I can change from one metric unit to another.

6 I can find the surface area of a cuboid.

National Test questions

1 *2002 Paper 1*

a What is the area of this rectangle?

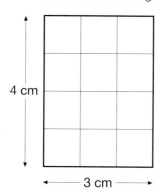

4 cm
3 cm

b I use the rectangle to make four triangles.

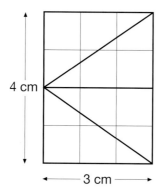

4 cm
3 cm

Each triangle is the same size.

What is the area of **one** of the triangles?

MNU 3-11a

2 *2003 3–5 Paper 1*

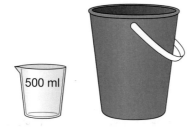

500 ml

Steve needs to put **1 litre** of water in a bucket.

He has a **500 ml** jug.

Explain how he can measure 1 litre of water.

MNU 2-11b

3   *2001 Paper 2*

a   Which rectangles below have an area of 12 cm²?

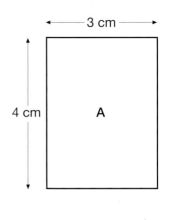

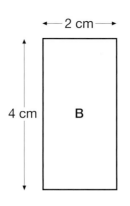

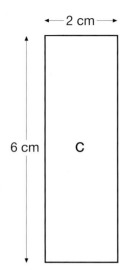

b   A square has an area of 100 cm².

What is its perimeter?

Show your working.

4   *2007 3–5 Paper 1*

A rectangle has an **area** of **24 cm²**.

How long could the sides of the rectangle be?

Give three **different** examples.

5   *2006 3–5 Paper 2*

Find the missing numbers from the statements below:

120 mm is the same as ...... cm.

120 mm is the same as ...... m.

120 mm is the same as ...... km.

CHAPTER 7 Algebra 3

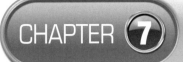

This chapter is going to show you

- How to draw mapping diagrams from functions
- How to identify a function from its inputs and outputs
- How to spot patterns in sets of coordinates
- How to draw distance–time graphs

What you should already know

- How to use a function
- How to plot coordinates

Linear functions

A linear function is a simple rule that involves any of the following:

Addition	Subtraction	Multiplication	Division

Mapping diagrams can illustrate these functions, as shown in Example 7.1.

Example 7.1

Draw a mapping diagram to illustrate:

→ multiply by 2 →

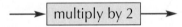

First, draw two number lines. The top line is for the inputs and the bottom line shows the place to which each input maps with the function (see top of next page). Both number lines in this example are shown from 0 to 7.

So, for the function:

→ multiply by 2 →

$0 \rightarrow 0$

$1 \rightarrow 2$

$2 \rightarrow 4$

$3 \rightarrow 6$

and so on.

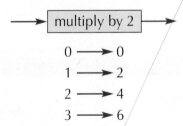

Now draw arrows between the two number lines to show the place to which each number maps:

Input

```
0       1       2       3       4       5       6       7
```

Output

```
0       1       2       3       4       5       6       7
```

Of course, both number lines go on for ever, and each contains hundreds of numbers. But only a small part is needed to show the pattern of mapping.

1 a Copy the mapping diagram for the function 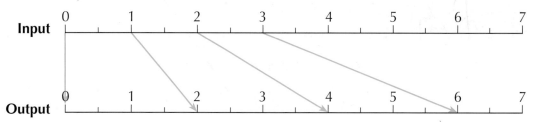 ⟶ | add 3 | ⟶

Input

```
0       1       2       3       4       5       6       7
```

Output

```
0       1       2       3       4       5       6       7
```

b On the diagram map the input values 3 and 4.

c Now map the following values.

    i   0.5   **ii**   1.5   **iii**   2.5   **iv**   3.5

2 a Using two number lines from 0 to 10, draw a mapping diagram to illustrate each of these functions (map each whole number).

    i ⟶ | add 2 | ⟶   **ii** ⟶ | multiply by 3 | ⟶

    iii ⟶ | divide by 2 | ⟶   **iv** ⟶ | subtract 2 | ⟶

b In your mapping diagrams from part **ai** and **aii**, draw the lines from the inputs 0.5, 1.5 and 2.5.

3 a Using two number lines from 0 to 15, draw a mapping diagram to illustrate each of these functions.

    i ⟶ | multiply by 4 | ⟶   **ii** ⟶ | add 5 | ⟶

    iii ⟶ | multiply by 5 | ⟶   **iv** ⟶ | add 6 | ⟶

b In each of your mapping diagrams from part **a**, map the input values 0.5, 1.5 and 2.5.

1   Using number lines from 0 to 10, draw a mapping diagram of the function

$\longrightarrow$ multiply by 2 $\longrightarrow$

2   For each of the arrows drawn on your mapping diagram, extend the arrow line backwards towards the line that joins both zeros. All the arrow lines should meet at the same point on this line.

3   Repeat the above for the function

$\longrightarrow$ multiply by 3 $\longrightarrow$

Do these arrows also join at a point on the line joining the zeros?

4   Do you think all similar functions such as

$\longrightarrow$ multiply by 4 $\longrightarrow$

have this property?

Finding a function from its inputs and outputs

Any function will have a set of outputs for a particular set of inputs. When you can identify the outputs for particular inputs, then you can identify the function.

Example 7.2

State the function that maps the inputs {0, 1, 2, 3} to {0, 5, 10, 15}.

The input 0 maps to 0. Hence the function uses no addition.

Notice that each time the input increases by 1, the output increases by 5. This suggests that the function is: multiply by 5

A check that 1 does map to 5 and 2 to 10 shows that this function is the correct one.

Exercise 7B

1   State the function that maps the following inputs with their respective outputs.
   a   {0, 1, 2, 3} $\longrightarrow$ {4, 5, 6, 7}
   b   {0, 1, 2, 3} $\longrightarrow$ {0, 4, 8, 12}
   c   {0, 1, 2, 3} $\longrightarrow$ {0, 7, 14, 21}
   d   {0, 1, 2, 3} $\longrightarrow$ {7, 8, 9, 10}
   e   {0, 1, 2, 3} $\longrightarrow$ {0, 10, 20, 30}

2   State the function that maps the following inputs with their respective outputs.
   a   {0, 1, 3, 5} $\longrightarrow$ {9, 10, 12, 14}
   b   {0, 3, 4, 5} $\longrightarrow$ {0, 9, 12, 15}
   c   {1, 3, 4, 5} $\longrightarrow$ {9, 11, 12, 13}
   d   {0, 1, 2, 3} $\longrightarrow$ {10, 11, 12, 13}

3 State which function maps the inputs {2, 4, 7, 8} to:

   a   {6, 12, 21, 24}   **b**   {7, 9, 12, 13}   **c**   {16, 32, 56, 64}

4 State which function maps each of the following inputs to {8, 16, 24}.

   i   {0, 8, 16}   **ii**   {1, 2, 3}   **iii**   {10, 18, 26}

5 What are the functions that generate the following mixed outputs from the given mixed inputs? [*Hint*: First put each set of numbers in sequence.]

   a   {2, 4, 1, 3} ⟶ {8, 10, 11, 9}
   b   {4, 2, 3, 5} ⟶ {20, 16, 8, 12}
   c   {6, 3, 5, 4} ⟶ {10, 9, 11, 8}
   d   {8, 10, 7, 9} ⟶ {7, 6, 8, 5}
   e   {3, 2, 1, 0} ⟶ {6, 0, 9, 3}

> **Extension** **Work**
>
> Look at these simple functions:
>
>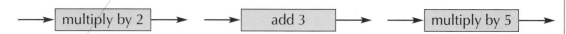
> ⟶ [multiply by 2] ⟶   ⟶ [add 3] ⟶   ⟶ [multiply by 5] ⟶
>
> By using any two of them, you can create six different combined functions, such as:
>
>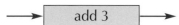
> {2, 3, 4, 5} ⟶ [multiply by 2] ⟶   ⟶ [add 3] ⟶ {7, 9, 11, 13}
>
> Draw a diagram like the one above for the other five possible combined functions.

Graphs from functions

There are different ways to write functions down. For example, the function:

⟶ [add 3] ⟶

can also be written as:

$$y = x + 3$$

where the inputs are x and the outputs are y.

The second way of writing a function makes it easier to draw a graph of the function.

Every function produces a graph. This is drawn by working out from the function a set of **coordinates** for its graph.

Note: The graph of every linear function is a straight line.

Example 7.3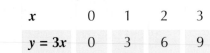

Draw a graph of the function ──→ **multiply by 3** ──→ or $y = 3x$.

First, draw up a table of simple values for x.

x	0	1	2	3
$y = 3x$	0	3	6	9

So, the coordinate pairs are:

$(0, 0)$ $(1, 3)$ $(2, 6)$ $(3, 9)$

Next, plot each point on a grid, join up all the points, and finally, label the line.

Note: This straight line graph has hundreds of other coordinates, *all* of which obey the same rule of the function: that is, $y = 3x$. Choose any points on the line that have not been plotted and you will see that this is true.

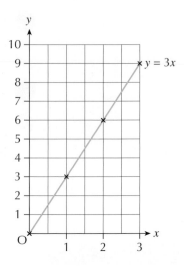

5

Exercise 7C

1 a Copy and complete the table below for the function ──→ **add 3** ──→ or $y = x + 3$.

x	0	1	2	3
$y = x + 3$	3			

b Draw a grid with its x-axis from 0 to 3 and its y-axis from 0 to 7.

c Use the table to help you to draw, on the grid, the graph of the function $y = x + 3$.

2 a Copy and complete the table below for the function ──→ **multiply by 2** ──→ or $y = 2x$.

x	0	1	2	3
$y = 2x$	0			

b Draw a grid with its x-axis from 0 to 3 and its y-axis from 0 to 7.

c Use the table to help you to draw, on the grid, the graph of the function $y = 2x$.

3 a Copy and complete the table below for the function ──→ **subtract 1** ──→ or $y = x - 1$.

x	0	1	2	3	4
$y = x - 1$	-1				

b Draw a grid with its x-axis from 0 to 4 and its y-axis from −1 to 4.

c Use the table to help you to draw, on the grid, the graph of the function $y = x - 1$.

4 **a** Copy and complete the table below for the function ⟶ divide by 2 ⟶ or

$y = \frac{1}{2}x$.

x	0	1	2	3	4
$y = \frac{1}{2}x$	0	0.5			

b Draw a grid with its x-axis from 0 to 4 and its y-axis from 0 to 4.

c Use the table to help you to draw, on the grid, the graph of the function $y = \frac{1}{2}x$.

5 **a** Copy and complete the table below for the functions shown.

x	0	1	2	3	4
$y = x + 5$				8	
$y = x + 3$			5		
$y = x + 1$	1	2			
$y = x - 1$	−1	0			
$y = x - 3$	−3		−1		

b Draw a grid with its x-axis from 0 to 4 and its y-axis from −4 to 10.

c Draw the graph for each function in the table above on the grid.

d What two properties do you notice about each line?

e Use the properties you have noticed to draw the graphs of these functions.

i $y = x + 2.5$ **ii** $y = x - 1.5$

6 **a** Copy and complete the table below for the functions shown.

x	0	1	2	3	4
$y = x$				3	
$y = 2x$			4		
$y = 3x$	0	3			
$y = 4x$					16
$y = 5x$			10		

b Draw a grid with its x-axis from 0 to 4 and y-axis from 0 to 20.

c Draw the graph for each function in the table above on the grid.

d What do you notice about each line?

e Use the properties you have noticed to draw the graphs of these functions.

i $y = 1.5x$ **ii** $y = 3.5x$

Extension **Work**

Here are the equations of 6 graphs.

A: $y = 2x + 1$ B: $y = 3x + 4$ C: $y = x + 2$

D: $y = 3x + 1$ E: $y = 2x + 2$ F: $y = x + 4$

1 Write down three pairs of graphs that are parallel.

2 Write down three pairs of graphs that pass through the same point on the y-axis.

Rules with coordinates

Number puzzles and sequences can be made in coordinates as well as ordinary numbers.

Example 7.4 ▷

There is a dot in each of the rectangles in the diagram. The dots are in the corners that are defined by the coordinates (2, 1), (4, 1), (6, 1), (8, 1).

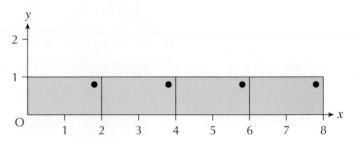

a If the pattern of rectangles continues, write down the coordinates of the next four corners with dots.

b Explain how you can tell that there will be no dot at the coordinate (35, 1).

Looking at the *x*-coordinates (the left-hand numbers), you will notice that the numbers go up in the sequence 2, 4, 6, 8 (even numbers). So, the next four will be 10, 12, 14 and 16.

Looking at the *y*-coordinates (the right-hand numbers), you will notice that the numbers are all 1.

a So, the next four coordinates will be (10, 1), (12, 1), (14, 1), (16, 1).

b Since 35 is not an even number, (35, 1) cannot be the coordinates of a corner with a dot.

Exercise 7D

① Joy has 20 rectangular tiles like the one shown.

She places all these tiles in a row.
She starts her row like this:

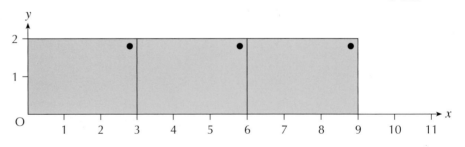

For each rectangular tile, Joy writes down the coordinates of the corner which has a dot. The coordinates of the first corner are (3, 2).

a Write down the coordinates of the next six corners which have a dot.

b Look at the numbers in the coordinates. Describe two things you notice.

c Joy thinks that (41, 2) are the coordinates of one of the corners with a dot. Explain why she is wrong.

d What are the coordinates of the dotted corner in the 20th tile?

2 Joy now places her tiles in a pattern like this:

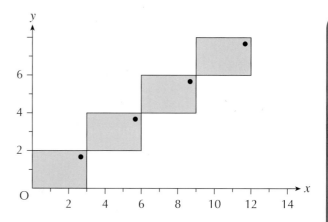

a Write down the coordinates of the first six corners which have a dot.

b Look at the numbers in the coordinates. Describe two things you notice.

c Joy thinks that that (24, 16) are the coordinates of one of the corners with a dot. Explain why she is right.

d What are the coordinates of the dotted corner in the 20th tile?

3 Alan has 20 square tiles like the one shown on the left.

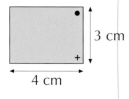

He places all these tiles in a row. He starts his row like this:

For each square tile, Alan writes down the coordinates of the corner with a dot. The coordinates of the first corner are (2, 2).

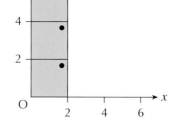

a Write down the coordinates of the next six corners which have a dot.

b Look at the numbers in the coordinates. Describe two things you notice.

c Alan thinks that (2, 22) are the coordinates of one of the corners with a dot. Explain why he is right.

d What are the coordinates of the dotted corner in the 20th tile?

4 Ben has 20 rectangular tiles like the one shown on the left.

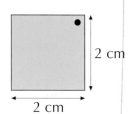

He places all these tiles in a pattern. He starts his pattern like this:

For each rectangular tile, Ben writes down the coordinates of the corner which has a dot. The coordinates of the first corner are (4, 3).

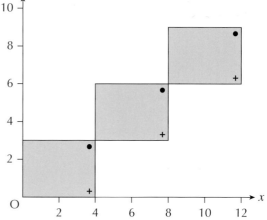

a Write down the coordinates of the next six corners which have a dot.

b Look at the numbers in the coordinates. Describe two things you notice.

c Ben thinks that (24, 10) are the coordinates of one of the corners which has a dot. Explain why he is wrong.

d What are the coordinates of the dotted corner in the 20th tile?

For each rectangular tile, Ben now writes down the coordinates of the corner which has a +. The coordinates of the first corner are (4, 0).

e Write down the coordinates of the next six corners which have a +.

f Look at the numbers in the coordinates. Describe two things you notice.

g Ben thinks that (28, 16) are the coordinates of one of the corners which has a +. Explain why he is wrong.

h What are the coordinates of the corner with a + in the 20th tile?

Extension Work

You are given three coordinates and three graphs. Only one of the relationships is true for all three coordinates. Identify which graph is true for all three.

1 (3, 5), (5, 7), (9, 11) $y = 2x + 1, y = x + 2, y = 2x - 3$

2 (4, 8), (6, 12), (8, 16) $y = x + 4, y = 3x - 4, y = 2x$

3 (2, 3), (5, 9), (7, 13) $y = 2x - 1, y = x + 1, y = x + 6$

4 (1, 4), (3, 10), (4, 13) $y = x + 3, y = 3x + 1, y = 2x + 4$

Distance-time graphs

A distance–time graph gives information about how someone or something has travelled.

Distance–time graphs are often used to describe journeys, as in Example 7.5.

Example 7.5

Mohammed set off from home at 8.00 am to pick up a parcel from the post office. At 8.30 am he arrived at the post office, having walked 4 km. He waited 15 minutes, got his parcel and then walked back home in 20 minutes.

Draw a distance time graph of Mohammed's journey. Estimate how far from home he was at:

a   8.10 am   **b**   9.00 am

The key coordinates (time and distance from home) are:
- Starting out (8.00 am, 0 km).
- Arrival at the post office (8.30 am, 4 km).
- Leaving the post office (8.45 am, 4 km).
- Return home (9.05 am, 0 km)

Using the information above, plot the points and draw the graph.

Note: The axes are clearly and accurately labelled, with precisely placed divisions. It is important to do this when you are drawing graphs.

You can now use your graph to answer the questions.

a   At 8.10 am, Mohammed was 1.3 km from home.

b   At 9.00 am, Mohammed was 1 km from home.

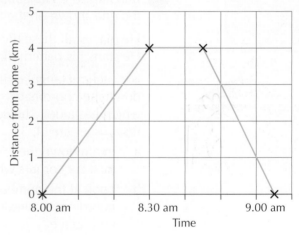

Exercise 7E

1 **a**   Draw a grid with the following scales.

Horizontal axis: Time, from 10.00 am to 11.30 am, with 1 cm to 10 minutes.
Vertical axis: Distance from home, from 0 to 8 km, with 1 cm to 1 km.

b   Draw on your grid the travel graph which shows the following journey.

Gemma left home at 10.00 am, cycled 3 km to a friend's house, arriving there at 10.15 am. She was not at home, so Gemma cycled another 4 km in the same direction to another friend's house, arriving there at 10.35 am. Gemma's friend was in. Gemma stayed there for 15 minutes. Then she went back home, arriving at 11.30 am.

c Approximately how far from home was Gemma at the following times?
  i 10.20 am   **ii** 11.15 am

 2 a Draw a grid with the following scales.
  Horizontal axis: Time, from 8.00 am to 10.30 am, with 1 cm to 10 minutes.
  Vertical axis: Distance, from 0 to 20 km. With 1 cm to 2 km.

b Draw on your grid the travel graph which shows the following journey.
  Anne started her sponsored walk at 8.00 am.
  She walked the first 5 km in 20 minutes.
  She walked the next 5 km in 30 minutes, then stopped to rest for 10 minutes.
  She walked the next 5 km in 25 minutes, then stopped for 15 minutes.
  She walked the last 5 km in 40 minutes.

c At about what time had she walked the following distances?
  i 3 km   **ii** 8 km   **iii** 17 km

 3 a Draw a grid with the following scales.
  Horizontal axis: Time, from 7.00 am to 1.00 pm, with 2 cm to 1 hour.
  Vertical axis: Distance from home, from 0 to 600 km, with 1 cm to 50 km.

b Draw on your grid the travel graph which shows the following journey.
  A bus set off from Sheffield at 7.00 am, travelling to Cornwall.
  At 9.00 am the bus had travelled 150 km. It then stopped for 30 minutes.
  At 11.00 am the bus had travelled a further 250 km. It again stopped for 30 minutes.
  The bus arrived at its destination at 1.00 pm, after a journey of 600 km.

c Approximately how far from Sheffield was the bus at these times?
  i 8.00 am   **ii** 10.30 am   **iii** 12 noon

4 a Draw a grid with the following scales.
  Horizontal axis: Time, from 2.00 pm to 5.00 pm, with 1 cm to 30 minutes.
  Vertical axis: Distance from home, showing 0 to 60 km, with 1 cm to 10 km.

b Draw on your grid the travel graph which shows the following journey.
  A seagull left its nest at 2.00 pm, flying out to sea.
  After 30 minutes, the bird had flown 10 km. It then stopped on the top of a lighthouse for 30 minutes.
  The bird then kept flying out to sea and at 4.00 pm landed on an anchored boat mast, 25 km from its nest.
  The wind picked up and the bird flew again out to sea, stopping at 5.00 pm, 60 km from its nest.

c How far was the bird from its nest at the following times?
  i 3.30 pm   **ii** 4.45 pm

At 10.00 am, Joy set off from her home to walk towards Nicola's home, 500 metres away. At the same time, Nicola set off from her home to walk towards Joy's home.

Both girls were walking with their eyes down and did not see each other as they passed. Joy arrived at Nicola's house at ten past ten. Nicola arrived at Joy's house at six minutes past ten.

1 At what time did they pass each other?

2 For how long were they within 100 metres of each other?

4 I can complete a mapping diagram to represent a simple linear function, for example $x \to 2x$.

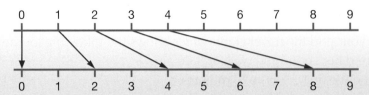

5 I can find the linear function that connect two sets of data, for example $x = \{1, 2, 3, 4, 5\} \to y = \{3, 4, 5, 6, 7\}$ is $y = x + 2$.

I can complete a table of value for a simple linear relationship and use this to draw a graph of the relationship.

I can spot patterns in coordinate diagrams.

I can draw and interpret distance–time graphs that describe real-life situations.

National Test questions

1 *2005 3–5 Paper 2*

A survey showed these results about the number of mobile phones used in the UK:

Use the graph to find the missing numbers from the sentences below:

In **1992**, there were about …… million mobile phones.

Ten years later, there were about …… million mobile phones.

From **1998** to **1999**, the number of mobile phones **increased** by about …… million.

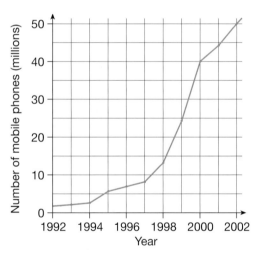

2 *2007 3–5 Paper 2*

I put square tiles on a large grid so that the tiles touch at the corners.

The diagram shows part of my diagonal pattern:

a The **bottom right-hand** corner of **tile 2** is marked with a ●.

Write the coordinates of this point.

b **Tile 4** touches two other tiles.

Write the coordinates of the points where tile 4 touches two other tiles.

c Write the coordinates of the points where **tile 17** touches two other tiles.

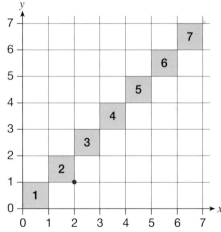

MNU 4-20a

MTH 2-13a

3 *2000 Paper 2*

The graph shows my journey in a lift.

I got in the lift at floor number 10.

a The lift stopped at two different floors before I got to floor number 22. Which floors were these?

b For how long was I in the lift while it was moving?

c After I got out of the lift at floor number 22, the lift went directly to the ground floor.

It took 45 seconds.

Which of the graphs below shows the rest of the lift's journey correctly?

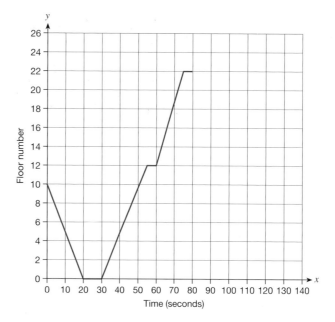

i

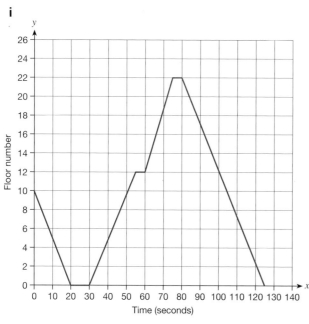

ii

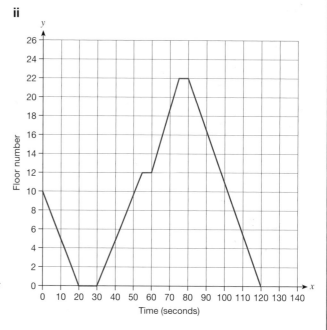

4 *2005 3–5 Paper 1*

P is the **midpoint** of line AB.

What are the coordinates of point P?

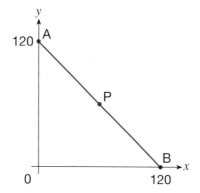

level 5.

FM The M25

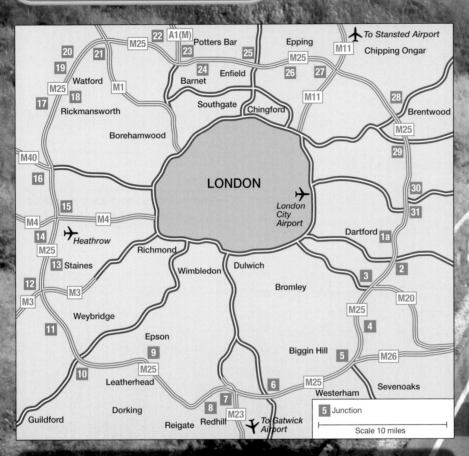

The M25 motorway is an orbital motorway, 117 miles long, that encircles London.

Construction of the first section began in 1973. Construction of the M25 continued in stages until its completion in 1986.

For most of its length, the motorway has six lanes (three in each direction), although there are a few short stretches which are four-lane and perhaps one-sixth is eight-lane, around the south-western corner. The motorway was widened to 10 lanes between junctions 12 and 14, and 12 lanes between junctions 14 and 15, in November 2005. The Highways Agency has plans to widen almost all of the remaining stretches of the M25 to eight lanes.

It is one of Europe's busiest motorways, with 205 000 vehicles a day recorded in 2006 between junctions 13 and 14 near London Heathrow Airport. This is, however, significantly fewer than the 257 000 vehicles a day recorded in 2002 on the A4 motorway at Saint-Maurice, in the suburbs of Paris, or the 216 000 vehicles a day recorded in 1998 on the A 100 motorway near the Funkturm in Berlin.

The road passes through several counties. Junctions 1–5 are in Kent, 6–14 in Surrey, 15–16 are in Buckinghamshire, 17–24 are in Hertfordshire, 25 in Greater London, 26–28 in Essex, 29 in Greater London and 30–31 in Essex.

1. How long is the M25?

2. How many years altogether did it take to build the M25?

3. Look at the map of the M25. How many other motorways intersect with the M25?

4. How many junctions are on the M25?

5. a How many junctions are in Kent?
   b Which county has the most junctions?

6. a Which A road heads into central London in an easterly direction?
   b The A3 crosses the M25 at junction 10. As it goes into London, in which direction is it heading?

7. Use the scale shown.
   a The nearest point that the M25 is to the centre of London is Potters Bar. Approximately how far from the centre of London is this?
   b The furthest point that the M25 is from the centre of London is near junction 10. Approximately how far from the centre of London is this?

8. The original design capacity of the M25 was 65,000 vehicles a day.
   a By how many vehicles per day does the busiest stretch exceed the design capacity?
   b Approximately how many vehicles a year use the M25 at its busiest point?
   c The current annual use of the M25 is approximately 40 million vehicles per year. This is 1.8 times the original estimate. To the nearest thousand, how many vehicles per day were expected to use the M25?

9. There are three airports near to the M25. Heathrow, Gatwick and Stansted. From Stansted to Heathrow via the M25 (anti-clockwise) is 67 miles. From Heathrow to Gatwick (anti-clockwise) is 43 miles. From Gatwick to Stansted (anti-clockwise) is 73 miles. A shuttle bus drives from Stansted and calls at Heathrow and Gatwick then returns to Stansted. It does this 4 times a day. How far does it travel altogether?

10. In 2008 approximately $\frac{2}{5}$ of the M25 was illuminated at night. How many miles is this?

11. About one-sixth of the M25 is eight-lane. Approximately how many miles is this?

12. One of the busiest motorway in the world is the 401 in Toronto, Canada with over 500 000 vehicles per day using the road. Approximately how many times greater is the volume of traffic on the 401 than the M25 at its busiest stretch?

13. Near to Heathrow Airport what is the average number of vehicles using the M25 per hour each day? Give your answer to the nearest 100 vehicles.

14. The legal speed limit on the M25 is 70 mph. Assuming no hold ups, how long would it take to drive around the M25 at the legal speed limit? Answer in hours and minutes.

Distance = speed × time

MTH 2-17c

MTH 3-17c

MNU 3-01a

MNU 3-03a

MNU 3-07a

MNU 3-03a

MTH 4-20b

MNU 3-10a

This chapter is going to show you

- How to multiply and divide by 10, 100 and 1000
- How to round numbers to one decimal place
- How to use a calculator efficiently

What you should already know

- How to multiply and divide by 10
- How to round to the nearest 10 and 100
- How to use standard column methods for the four operations

Powers of 10

The nearest star, Proxima Centauri, is 40 653 234 200 000 kilometres from Earth. An atom is 0.000 000 0001 metres wide. When dealing with very large and very small numbers it is easier to round them and to work with powers of 10. You will meet this later when you do work on Standard Form. In this section you will multiply and divide by powers of 10 and round numbers to whole numbers and to one decimal place.

Example 8.1 ▷ Multiply these numbers by: **i** 10 **ii** 100 **iii** 1000

    a 0.937   **b** 2.363

  a **i** $0.937 \times 10 = 9.37$
      ii $0.937 \times 100 = 93.7$
     iii $0.937 \times 1000 = 937$

  b **i** $2.363 \times 10 = 23.63$
      ii $2.363 \times 100 = 236.3$
     iii $2.363 \times 1000 = 2363$

Example 8.2 ▷ Divide these numbers by: **i** 10 **ii** 100

    a 6   **b** 50

  a **i** $6 \div 10 = 0.6$
      ii $6 \div 100 = 0.06$

  b **i** $50 \div 10 = 5$
      ii $50 \div 100 = 0.5$

Example 8.3 Round each of these numbers to one decimal place (1 dp).

a 9.35 b 4.323 c 5.99

a 9.35 is 9.4 to 1 dp b 4.323 is 4.3 to 1 dp c 5.99 is 6.0 to 1 dp

Exercise 8A

1. Multiply each of these numbers by: i 10 ii 100 iii 1000

   a 5.3 b 0.79 c 24 d 5.063 e 0.003

2. Divide each of these numbers by: i 10 and ii 100

   a 83 b 4.1 c 457 d 6.04 e 34 781

3. Write down the answers to each of these.

   a 3.1 × 10 b 6.78 × 100 c 0.56 × 1000 d 34 ÷ 100
   e 823 ÷ 100 f 9.06 ÷ 10 g 57.89 × 100 h 57.89 ÷ 100
   i 0.038 × 1000 j 0.038 ÷ 10 k 0.05 × 1000 l 543 ÷ 100

4. Round each of these numbers to one decimal place.

   a 4.722 b 3.097 c 2.634 d 1.932 e 0.784
   f 0.992 g 3.999 h 2.604 i 3.185 j 3.475

5. Round each of these numbers to: i the nearest whole number. ii one decimal place.

   a 4.72 b 3.07 c 2.634 d 1.932 e 0.78 f 0.92
   g 3.92 h 2.64 i 3.18 j 3.475 k 1.45 l 1.863

6. Multiply each of these numbers by: i 10 ii 100

   a 0.4717 b 2.6345 c 0.0482

   Round each answer to one decimal place.

7. Divide each of these numbers by: i 10 ii 100

   a 12.34 b 136.71 c 10.05

   Round each answer to one decimal place.

Extension Work

Sometimes we need to round numbers to two decimal places. An obvious case is when we work with money. Here are two examples of rounding to two decimal places (2 dp):

5.642 becomes 5.64 to 2 dp; 8.776 becomes 8.78 to 2 dp.

Round each of these numbers to two decimal places.

a 4.722 b 3.097 c 2.634 d 1.932 e 0.784
f 0.992 g 3.999 h 2.604 i 3.185 j 3.475

Large numbers

Example 8.4 ▷

	10^6	10^5	10^4	10^3	10^2	10	1
a			5	8	7	0	2
b	1	7	0	0	0	5	6

Write down the two numbers shown in the diagram on the left in words. Consider each number in blocks of three digits, that is:

58 702
1 700 056

a 58 702 = Fifty-eight thousand, seven hundred and two.

b 1 700 056 = One million, seven-hundred thousand, and fifty-six.

Example 8.5 ▷

a The bar chart shows the annual profits for a large company over the previous five years. Estimate the profit for each year.

b The company chairman says: 'Profit in 2008 was nearly 50 million pounds.' Is the chairman correct?

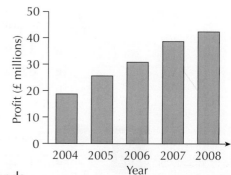

a In 2004 the profit was about 19 million pounds.
In 2005 it was about 25 million pounds.
In 2006 it was about 31 million pounds.
In 2007 it was about 39 million pounds.
In 2008 it was about 43 million pounds.

b The chairman is wrong, as in 2008 the profit is nearer 40 million pounds.

Exercise 8B

(1) Write each of the following numbers in words.

a	4561	**b**	8009	**c**	56 430	**d**	22 108
e	60 092	**f**	302 999	**g**	306 708	**h**	213 045
i	3 452 763	**j**	2 047 809	**k**	12 008 907	**l**	3 006 098

(2) Write each of the following numbers using figures.

a Six thousand, seven hundred and three

b Twenty-one thousand and forty five

c Two hundred and three thousand, four hundred and seventeen

d Four million, forty-three thousand, two hundred and seven

e Nineteen million, five hundred and two thousand and thirty-seven

f One million, three hundred and two thousand and seven

5

3 The bar chart shows the population of some countries in the European Community. Estimate the population of each country.

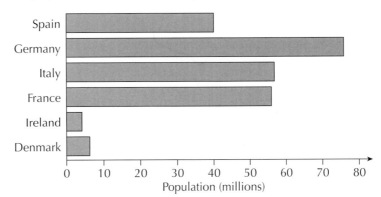

Population (millions)

4 Round each of the following numbers to: **i** the nearest thousand. **ii** the nearest ten thousand. **iii** the nearest million.

   a 3 547 812   **b** 9 722 106   **c** 3 042 309   **d** 15 698 999

(FM) **5** There are 2 452 800 people out of work. The government says: 'Unemployment is just over two million'. The opposition says: 'Unemployment is still nearly three million'. Who is correct and why?

Extension **Work**

A calculator display shows 6.4×10^3

6.4×10^3 means $6.4 \times 1000 = 6400$

What number does each of the following calculator displays show?

   a 2.4×10^2 **b** 3.6×10^2 **c** 7.8×10^3 **d** 8.2×10^3

Estimations

You should have an idea if the answer to a calculation is about the right size or not. Here are some ways of checking answers.

- First, when it is a multiplication, you can check that the final digit is correct.
- Second, you can round off numbers and do a mental calculation to see if an answer is about the right size.
- Third, you can check by doing the inverse operation.

Example 8.6 ▷   Explain why these calculations must be wrong.

   a $23 \times 45 = 1053$ **b** $19 \times 59 = 121$

   a The last digit should be 5, because the product of the last digits is 15. That is, $23 \times 45 = \ldots 5$

   b The answer is roughly $20 \times 60 = 1200$.

Example 8.7 ▶ Estimate the answers to each of these calculations.

a $\dfrac{21.3 + 48.7}{6.4}$ **b** 31.2×48.5 **c** $359 \div 42$

a Round the numbers on the top to $20 + 50 = 70$. Round off 6.4 to 7. Then $70 \div 7 = 10$

b Round to 30×50, which is $3 \times 5 \times 100 = 1500$

c Round to $360 \div 40$, which is $36 \div 4 = 9$

Example 8.8 ▶ By using the inverse operation, check if each calculation is correct.

a $450 \div 6 = 75$ **b** $310 - 59 = 249$

a By the inverse operation, $450 = 6 \times 75$. This is true and can be checked mentally: $6 \times 70 = 420$, $6 \times 5 = 30$, $420 + 30 = 450$

b By the inverse operation, $310 = 249 + 59$. This addition must end in 8 as $9 + 9 = 18$, so the calculation cannot be correct.

Exercise 8C

1 Explain why these calculations must be wrong.

a $24 \times 42 = 1080$ **b** $51 \times 73 = 723$ **c** $\dfrac{34.5 + 63.2}{9.7} = 20.07$

d $360 \div 8 = 35$ **e** $354 - 37 = 323$

2 Estimate the answer to each of these calculations.

a $2768 - 392$ **b** 231×18 **c** $792 \div 38$ **d** $\dfrac{36.7 + 23.2}{14.1}$

e 423×423 **f** $157.2 \div 38.2$ **g** $\dfrac{135.7 - 68.2}{15.8 - 8.9}$ **h** $\dfrac{38.9 \times 61.2}{39.6 - 18.4}$

FM **3** Delroy had £10. In his shopping basket he had a magazine costing £2.65, some batteries costing £1.92, and a tape costing £4.99. Without adding up the numbers, how could Delroy be sure he had enough to buy the goods in the basket? Explain a quick way for Delroy to find out if he could afford a 45p bar of chocolate as well.

FM **4** Amy bought 6 bottles of pop at 46p per bottle. The shopkeeper asked her for £3.16. Without working out the correct answer, explain why this is wrong.

FM **5** A pencil costs 27p. I need eight. Will £2 be enough to pay for them? Explain your answer clearly.

FM **6** In a shop I bought a 53p comic and a £1.47 model car. The till said £54.47. Why?

7 Estimate the value the arrow is pointing at in each of these.

 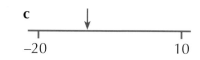

a   0.7   3.7   b   0   6.3   c   −20   10

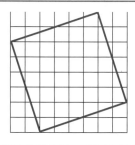

1 Without working out areas or counting squares, explain why the area of the square shown must be between 36 and 64 grid squares.

2 Now calculate the area of the square.

3 Using an 8 × 8 grid, draw a square with an area of exactly 50 grid squares.

Adding and subtracting decimals

Example 8.9

Work out:

a 64.06 + 178.9 + 98.27   **b** 20 − 8.72 − 6.5

The numbers need to be lined up in columns with their decimal points in line. Blank places are filled with zeros. Part **b** needs to be done in two stages.

a
$$
\begin{array}{r}
64.06 \\
178.90 \\
+\ 98.27 \\
\hline
341.23 \\
{\scriptstyle 2\ 2\ 1\ \ 1}
\end{array}
$$

b
$$
\begin{array}{r}
{\scriptstyle 1\ 9\ 9\ 1} \\
2\cancel{0}.\cancel{0}0 \\
-\ 8.72 \\
\hline
11.28
\end{array}
\qquad
\begin{array}{r}
{\scriptstyle 0\ 1} \\
1\cancel{1}.28 \\
-\ 6.50 \\
\hline
4.78
\end{array}
$$

Example 8.10

In a science lesson, a pupil adds 0.45 kg of water and 0.72 kg of salt to a beaker that weighs 0.09 kg. He then pours out 0.6 kg of the mixture. What is the total mass of the beaker and mixture remaining?

This has to be set up as an addition and subtraction problem. That is:

0.09 + 0.45 + 0.72 − 0.6

The problem has to be done in two stages:

$$
\begin{array}{r}
0.09 \\
0.45 \\
+\ 0.72 \\
\hline
1.26 \\
{\scriptstyle 1\ \ 1}
\end{array}
\qquad
\begin{array}{r}
{\scriptstyle 0\ 1} \\
\cancel{1}.26 \\
-\ 0.60 \\
\hline
0.66
\end{array}
$$

So the final mass is 0.66 kg or 660 grams.

MNU 3-07a

Exercise 8D

1 Work out each of the following.

a 8.3 + 4.6	**b** 8.3 − 4.9	**c** 5.1 + 2.6 + 1.4
d 9.6 + 6.5 − 2.2	**e** 8.3 + 6.9 − 2.1	**f** 6.7 + 3 − 5.7
g 4.5 − 1.2 − 2.3	**h** 8.2 − 2.9 − 2.7	
i 4.5 cm + 2.1 cm + 8.6 cm	**j** 7.3 m − 3.7 m − 2.5 m	

2 Work out each of the following.

a 4.32 + 65.09 + 172.3   b 8.7 + 9 + 14.02 + 1.03
c 11.42 + 15.72 − 12.98   d 42.7 + 67.3 − 35.27
e 19.87 + 2.8 − 13.46   f 12 − 5.09 + 3.21
g 23.9 + 8 − 9.25   h 7.05 + 2.9 + 7 + 0.64
i 7.25 + 19.3 − 12.06   j 21.35 + 6.72 − 12.36 − 5.71

3 There are 1000 metres in a kilometre. Calculate each of the following. (Work in kilometres.)

a 7.45 km + 843 m + 68 m   b 3.896 km + 723 m + 92 m
c 8.76 km + 463 m − 892 m   d 16 km − 435 m − 689 m
e 7.8 km + 5.043 km − 989 m

4 There are 1000 grams in a kilogram. Calculate the mass of the following shopping baskets. (Work in kilograms.)

a 3.2 kg of apples, 454 g of jam, 750 g of lentils, 1.2 kg of flour
b 1.3 kg of sugar, 320 g of strawberries, 0.65 kg of rice

5 In an experiment a beaker of water has a mass of 1.104 kg. The beaker alone weighs 0.125 kg. What is the mass of water in the beaker (in kilograms)?

6 A rectangle is 2.35 m by 43 cm. What is its perimeter (in metres)?

7 A piece of string is 5 m long. Pieces of length 84 cm, 1.23 m and 49 cm are cut from it. How much string is left (in metres)?

Extension   Work

Centimetres and millimetres both show lengths. The first length shown on the rule below, AB, can be given as 1.6 cm, 16 mm or $1\frac{3}{5}$ cm.

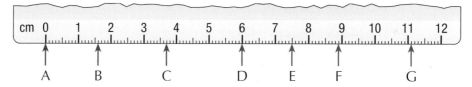

Write each length shown below:

i in centimetres as a decimal.   ii in millimetres.   iii in centimetres as a fraction.

a AC   b BD   c CE   d DE   e EF   f EG

Efficient calculations

You should have your own calculator, so that you can get used to it. Make sure that you understand how to use the basic functions (×, ÷, +, −) and the square, square root and brackets keys. They are different even on scientific calculators.

Example 8.11 Use a calculator to work out: **a** $\dfrac{242 + 118}{88 - 72}$ **b** $\dfrac{63 \times 224}{32 \times 36}$

The line that separates the top numbers from the bottom numbers acts both as a divide sign (÷) and as brackets.

a Key the calculation as: $(242 + 118) \div (88 - 72) = 22.5$

b Key the calculation as: $(63 \times 224) \div (32 \times 36) = 12.25$

Example 8.12 Use a calculator to work out: **a** $\sqrt{1764}$ **b** 23.4^2 **c** $52.3 - (30.4 - 17.3)$

a Some calculators need the square root after the number has been keyed, some need it before: $\sqrt{1764} = 42$

b Most calculators have a special key for squaring: $23.4^2 = 547.56$

c This can be keyed in exactly as it reads: $52.3 - (30.4 - 17.3) = 39.2$

MTH
4-06a

Exercise 8E

1 Without using a calculator, work out the value of each of these.

a $\dfrac{17 + 8}{7 - 2}$ **b** $\dfrac{53 - 8}{3.5 - 2}$ **c** $\dfrac{19.2 - 1.7}{5.6 - 3.1}$

2 Use a calculator to do the calculations in Question 1. Do you get the same answers? For each part, write down the sequence of keys that you pressed to get the answer.

3 Work out the value of each of these. Round your answers to 1 dp if necessary.

a   **b**   **c** $\dfrac{132 + 88}{78 - 28}$ **d** $\dfrac{792 + 88}{54 - 21}$

e   **f**   **g** $\dfrac{107 + 853}{24 \times 16}$ **h** $\dfrac{57 - 23}{18 - 7.8}$

Ex 8.11, 8.12, 8E
— difficult to categorise
— probably level 5 or a difficult level 4 but not sure which category to put them in

4 Est...

No... 1 dp. Is it about the same?

5 Wo...

a   **b**   **c** 2.6^2 **d** 3.9^2

e   **f**   **g** $(5.2 - 1.8)^2$ **h** $(2.5 + 6.1)^2$

MTH
4-06a

6 W...

a $8.3 - (4.2 - 1.9)$ **b** $12.3 + (3.2 - 1.7)^2$ **c** $(3.2 + 1.9)^2 - (5.2 - 2.1)^2$

7 A calculator shows an answer of

$$2.33333333333$$

Write this as a mixed number or a top-heavy fraction.

Previously Cons division would be required only with a calculator & long multiplication would be general/credit. But MNU 3-03a seems open ended so I have used this category.

Extension Work

On your calculator you may have a key or a function above a key marked x^{-1} ($x!$). Find out what this key does. For example, on some calculators you can key: [key] [x!] and the display shows 6, and you can key [key] [key] [x!] and the display shows 5040. Similarly, investigate what the key marked x^{-1} does.

Long multiplication and long division

Example 8.13

Work out 36 × 43.

Below are four examples of the ways this calculation can be done. The answer is 1548.

Box method (partitioning)

×	30	6	
40	1200	240	1440
3	90	18	108
			1548

Column method (expanded working)

$$\begin{array}{rl} & 36 \\ \times & 43 \\ \hline & 18 \quad (3 \times 6) \\ & 90 \quad (3 \times 30) \\ & 240 \quad (40 \times 6) \\ & 1200 \quad (40 \times 30) \\ \hline & 1548 \end{array}$$

Column method (compacted working)

$$\begin{array}{rl} & 36 \\ \times & 43 \\ \hline & 108 \quad (3 \times 36) \\ & 1440 \quad (40 \times 36) \\ \hline & 1548 \end{array}$$

Chinese method

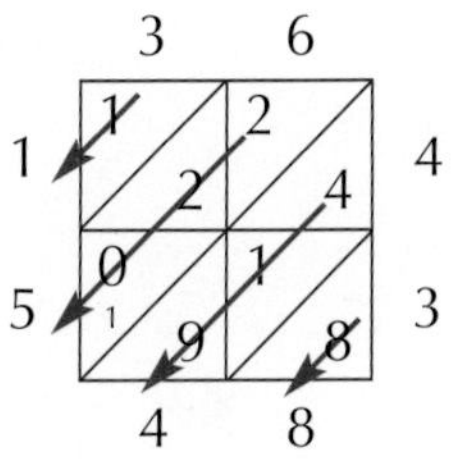

Example 8.14

Work out 543 ÷ 31.

Below are two examples of the ways this can be done. The answer is 17, remainder 16.

Subtracting multiples

$$\begin{array}{rl} & 543 \\ - & 310 \quad (10 \times 31) \\ \hline & 233 \\ - & 155 \quad (5 \times 31) \\ \hline & 78 \\ - & 62 \quad (2 \times 31) \\ \hline & 16 \end{array}$$

Traditional method

$$\begin{array}{r} 17 \\ 31\overline{)543} \\ \underline{31} \\ 233 \\ \underline{217} \\ 16 \end{array}$$

MNU 3-03a

Exercise 8F

MNU 3-03a

1 Work out each of the following multiplication and division problems. Use any method you are happy with.

a 35 × 6	**b** 42 × 5	**c** 27 × 3	**d** 58 × 7
e 92 ÷ 4	**f** 144 ÷ 9	**g** 135 ÷ 5	**h** 152 ÷ 8

2 Work out each of the following long multiplication problems. Use any method you are happy with.

    a 17×23 **b** 32×42 **c** 19×45 **d** 56×46

    e 12×346 **f** 32×541 **g** 27×147 **h** 39×213

3 Work out each of the following long division problems. Use any method you are happy with. Some of the problems will have a remainder.

    a $684 \div 19$ **b** $966 \div 23$ **c** $972 \div 36$ **d** $625 \div 25$

    e $930 \div 38$ **f** $642 \div 24$ **g** $950 \div 33$ **h** $800 \div 42$

Decide whether each of the following 10 problems involves long multiplication or long division. Then do the appropriate calculation, showing your method clearly.

4 Each day 17 Jumbo jets fly from London to San Francisco. Each jet can carry up to 348 passengers. How many people can travel from London to San Francisco each day?

5 A company has 897 boxes to move by van. The van can carry 23 boxes at a time. How many trips must the van make to move all the boxes?

6 The same van does 34 miles to a gallon of petrol. How many miles can it do if the petrol tank holds 18 gallons?

7 The school photocopier can print 82 sheets a minute. If it runs without stopping for 45 minutes, how many sheets will it print?

8 The RE department has printed 525 sheets on Buddhism. These are put into folders in sets of 35. How many folders are there?

9 a To raise money, Wath Running Club are going to do a relay race from Wath to Edinburgh, running a 384 kilometre route. Each runner will run 24 kilometres. How many runners will be needed to cover the distance?

    b Sponsorship will bring in £32 per kilometre. How much money will the club raise?

10 Blank CDs are 45p each. How much will a box of 35 CDs cost. Give your answer in pounds.

11 The daily newspaper sells advertising by the square inch. On Monday, it sells 232 square inches at £15 per square inch. How much money does it get from this advertising?

12 The local library has 13 000 books. Each shelf holds 52 books. How many shelves are there?

13 How many bubble packs of 48 nails can be filled from a carton of 400 nails?

Extension Work

The box method can be used to do decimal multiplications. For example, 2.5 × 4.8 can be worked out as follows.

×	4	0.8	Sum of row
2	8	1.6	9.6
0.5	2	0.4	2.4
		Total	12.0

Use the box method to calculate 1.4 × 2.4.

Check your answer with a calculator.

LEVEL BOOSTER

4
I can write large numbers in words or using figures.
I can round numbers to the nearest 10 or 100.
I can add and subtract simple decimals up to two decimal places.
I can recall multiplication facts up to 10 × 10.

5
I can round numbers to one decimal place.
I can use bracket, square and square root keys on a calculator.
I can add and subtract decimals up to two decimal places.
I can multiply and divide decimals up to two decimal places.

6
I can round numbers to two decimal places.
I can multiply and divide by powers of 10.
I can approximate decimals when solving numerical problems.

National Test questions

4

1 *2001 4–6 Paper 1*

The table shows the approximate populations of five different places:

a Which of these places has a population of about **seventy thousand**?

b Use the table to complete these sentences:

The population of **Harrogate** is about **10 times** as big as the population of ......

The population of ...... is about **100 times** as big as the population of **Harrogate**.

The population of **Sheffield** is about ...... times as big as the population of **Ash Vale**.

Place	Approximate population
London	7 000 000
Sheffield	700 000
Harrogate	70 000
Ash Vale	7000
Binbrook	700

2 *2006 4–6 Paper 1*

Work out the missing numbers.

In each part, you can use the first line to help you.

a $16 \times 15 = 240$

$16 \times .... = 480$

b $46 \times 44 = 2024$

$46 \times 22 = ...$

c $600 \div 24 = 25$

$600 \div .... = 50$

MNU
3-01a

3 *2003 5–7 Paper 1*

a I pay **£16.20** to travel to work each week.
I work for **45 weeks** each year.

How much do I pay to travel to work each year?

Show your working.

b I could buy one season ticket that would let me travel for **45 weeks**.
It would cost **£630**.

How much is that per week?

MNU
3-03a

 4 *2007 5–7 Paper 2*

Kate buys **24 cans** of lemonade.
She buys the cans in **packs of 4**.
Each pack costs **£1.20**.

Steve buys **24 cans** of lemonade.
He buys the cans in **packs of 6**.
Each pack costs **£1.60**.

Kate pays more for her 24 cans than Steve pays for his 24 cans.

How much more?

Pack of 4
Cost £1.20

Pack of 6
Cost £1.60

MNU
3-03a

 5 *2001 Paper 1*

a A football club is planning a trip. The club hires 234 coaches. Each coach holds 52 passengers. How many passengers is that altogether?

b The club wants to put one first aid kit into each of the 234 coaches. The first aid kits are sold in boxes of 18. How many boxes does the club need?

6 *2002 Paper 1*

a Peter's height is 0.9 m. Lucy is 0.3 m taller than Peter. What is Lucy's height?

b Lee's height is 1.45 m. Misha is 0.3 m shorter than Lee. What is Misha's height?

c Zita's height is 1.7 m. What is Zita's height in centimetres?

MNU
3-03a

There are two types of taxes – direct tax and indirect tax.

Direct tax is tax taken directly from what you earn, for example income tax.

Indirect tax is tax taken from what you spend, for example VAT.

Direct tax

Income tax
Each person has a tax allowance. This is the amount they are allowed to earn without paying income tax.

Tax rates
Basic rate: First £36 000 of taxable pay is taxed at the rate of 20%.

> **Example 1**
> Mr Gallagher's tax allowance is £5435.
> He earns £25 000.
> His taxable pay is £25 000 – £5435 = £19 565
>
> So his income tax is:
> Basic rate: 20% of £19 565 = £3913

Indirect tax

VAT
Value added tax is charged at three different rates on goods and services.

Standard rate (17.5%)
You pay VAT on most goods and services in the UK at the standard rate.

Reduced rate (5%)
In some cases, a reduced rate of VAT is charged, for example children's car seats and domestic fuel or power.

Zero rate (0%)
There are some goods on which you do not pay any VAT, for example:
- Food
- Books, newspapers and magazines
- Children's clothes
- Special exempt items, such as equipment for disabled people

> **Example 2**
> Work out the 17.5% VAT charged on a bicycle costing £180 excluding VAT.
>
> 10% of £180 = £18
> 5% of £180 = £9
> 2.5% of £180 = £4.50
> So 17.5% of £180 = £31.50

Use the information on taxes to answer these questions.

1. Sam earnt £20 000 last year. He spent £5000 of his earnings on a new car. What percentage of his earnings is this?

2. Hollie earnt £16 000 last year. This year she had a pay increase of 5%. How much does she earn now?

3. Miss Howe receives her gas bill. What is the rate of VAT that she will have to pay?

4. Mr Legg buys a wheelchair. What is the rate of VAT that he pays?

5. Bradley bought a new child seat. The cost was £90 excluding VAT.
   a What rate of VAT is charged?
   b Work out the total cost of the child seat including VAT.

6. Kerry bought a mobile phone. The cost was £260 excluding 17.5% VAT.
   Work out the cost including VAT.

7. Mrs Pritchard earns £24 000. Her tax allowance is £6000. She pays tax on the rest at 20%.
   a How much does she pay tax on?
   b How much tax does she pay?

8. Miss France earns £14 000. Her tax allowance is £5600. She pays tax on the rest at 20%.
   a How much does she pay tax on?
   b How much does she earn after the tax is deducted?

9. Mr Ladds earns £5500. His tax allowance is £6200.
   a Explain why he does not pay any tax.
   b How much more can he earn before he has to pay tax?

	2002	2003	2004	20
7.4	13.556.1	13,269.7	13,025.9	12.84
2.9	9.742.6	9.6		
6.9	719.2	6		
0.9	1.287.9	1		
3.6	1,022.7			
3.5	2,966.0			
0.6	1,168			
4.2	2,33			
2.9	2			
0.2	1			
5.1				
1.1				
9				

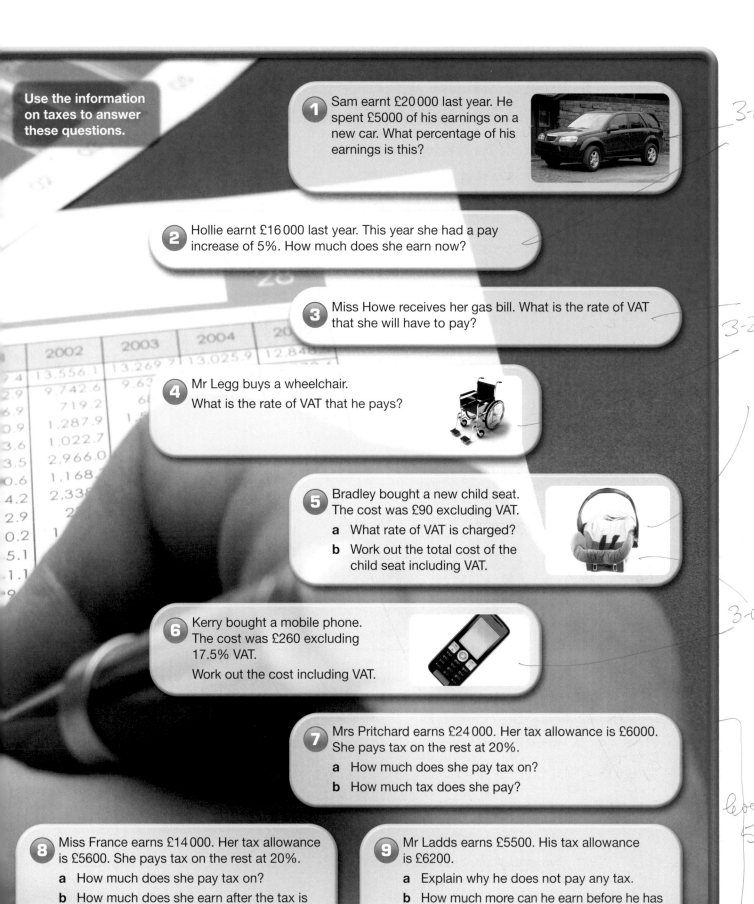

109

This chapter is going to show you

- How to recognise congruent shapes
- How to transform 2-D shapes by combinations of reflections, rotations and translations
- How to solve problems using ratio

What you should already know

- How to reflect a 2-D shape in a mirror line
- How to rotate a 2-D shape about a point
- How to translate a 2-D shape
- How to use ratio

Congruent shapes

All the triangles on the grid below are reflections, rotations or translations of Triangle A. What do you notice about them?

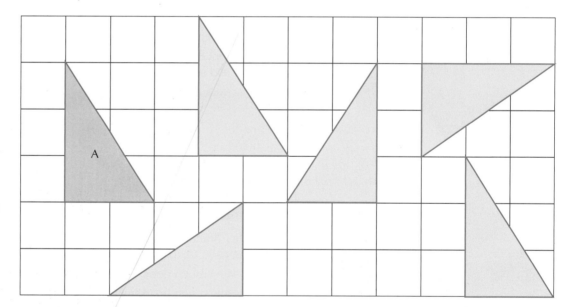

You should remember that the image triangles are exactly the same shape and size as the object Triangle A.

Two shapes are said to be **congruent** if they are exactly the same shape and size. Reflections, rotations and translations all produce images that are congruent to the original object. For shapes that are congruent, all the corresponding sides and angles are equal.

Example 9.1  Which two shapes below are congruent?

a   b   c   d

Shapes **b** and **d** are exactly the same shape and size, so **b** and **d** are congruent.
Tracing paper can be used to check that two shapes are congruent.

Exercise 9A

1) For each pair of shapes below, state whether or not they are congruent. (Use tracing paper to help if you are not sure.)

a    b    c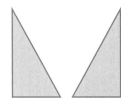

d 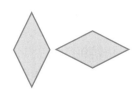   e 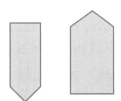   f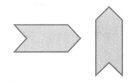

2) Which pairs of shapes on the grid below are congruent?

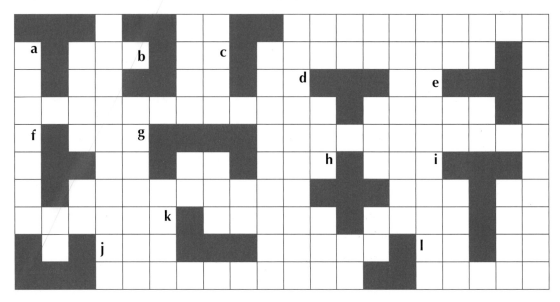

3 Which of the shapes below are congruent?

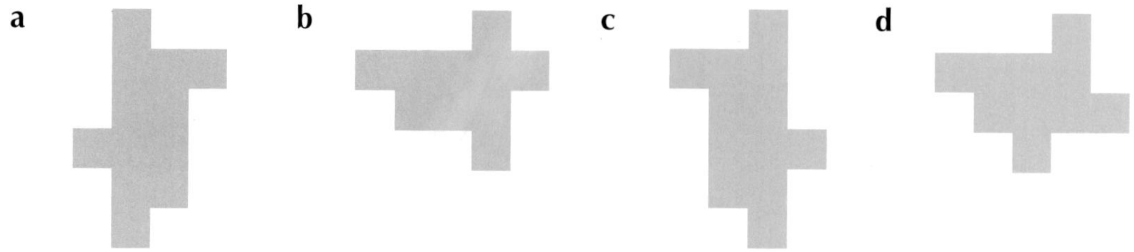

a  b  c  d

4 Two congruent right-angled triangles are placed together with two of their equal sides touching to make another shape, as shown in the diagram below.

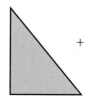 + make an isosceles triangle:

a How many different shapes can you make? To help, you can cut out the triangles from a piece of card.

b Repeat the activity using two congruent isosceles triangles.

c Repeat the activity using two congruent equilateral triangles.

Extension **Work**

The 4-by-4 pinboard is divided into two congruent shapes.

Use square-dotted paper to show the number of different ways this can be done.

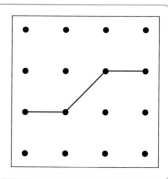

Combinations of transformations

The three single transformations you have met so far and the notation that we use to explain these transformations are shown below.

Reflections Mirror line

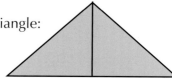

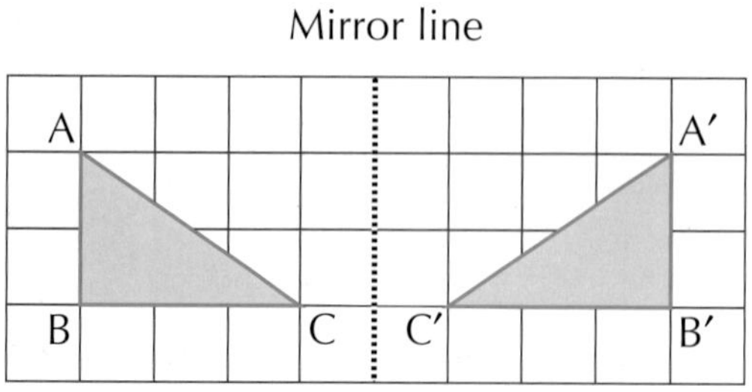

Triangle ABC is mapped onto triangle A'B'C' by a reflection in the mirror line. The object and the image are congruent.

Rotations

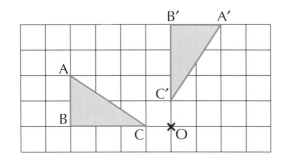

Triangle ABC is mapped onto triangle A'B'C' by a rotation of 90° clockwise about the centre of rotation O. The object and the image are congruent.

MTH 4-19a (handwritten)

Translations

See note Book 2 Pg 123 (handwritten)

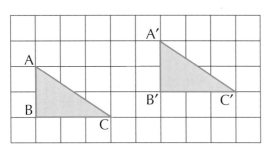

MTH 4-18 b. (handwritten)

Triangle ABC is mapped onto triangle A'B'C' by a translation of five units to the right, followed by one unit up. The object and the image are congruent.

Example 9.2 shows how a shape can be transformed by a combination of two of the above transformations.

Example 9.2

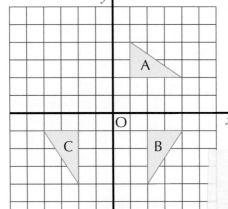

MTH 4-19a (handwritten)

Which two transformations map triangle A onto triangle C?.

Firstly, a rotation of 90° clockwise about the origin O maps A onto B. Secondly a reflection in the y-axis maps B onto C.

So, triangle A is mapped onto triangle C by a rotation of 90° clockwise about the origin O, followed by a reflection in the y-axis.

Exercise 9B

Tracing paper and a mirror will be use

Qns will need modificn if translation is to be avoided (handwritten)

1 Copy the diagram opposite onto squared paper.

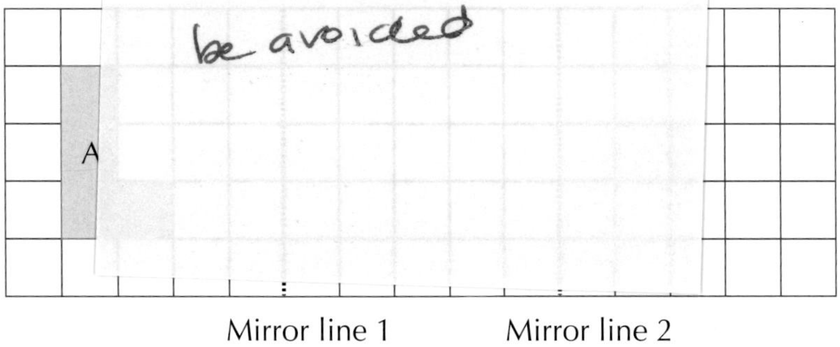

   a Reflect shape A in mirror line 1 to give shape B.

   b Reflect shape B in mirror line 2 to give shape C.

MTH 3-19 a (handwritten)

Mirror line 1   Mirror line 2

   c Describe the single transformation that maps shape A onto shape C.

5

2 Copy the diagram opposite onto squared paper.

   a Reflect shape A in the *x*-axis to give shape B.

   b Reflect shape B in the *y*-axis to give shape C.

   c Describe the single transformation that maps shape A onto shape C.

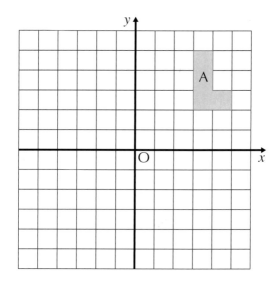

3 Copy the diagram opposite onto squared paper.

   a Rotate shape A 90° clockwise about the origin O to give shape B.

   b Rotate shape B 90° clockwise about the origin O to give shape C.

   c Describe the single transformation that maps shape A onto shape C.

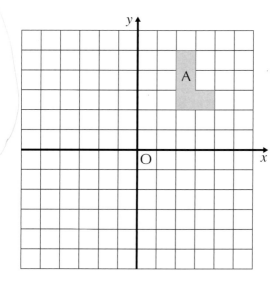

4 Copy the diagram below onto squared paper.

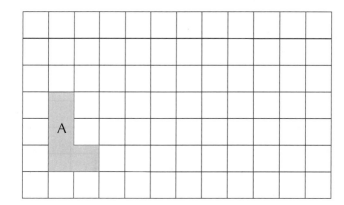

   a Translate shape A three units to the right, followed by two units up, to give shape B.

   b Translate shape B four units to the right, followed by 1 unit down, to give shape C.

   c Describe the single transformation that maps shape A onto shape C.

Extension **Work**

Copy the triangles A, B, C, D, E and F onto a square grid, as shown.

1 Find a single transformation that will map:

   a A onto B

   b E onto F

   c B onto E

   d C onto B

2 Find a combination of two transformations that will map:

   a A onto C

   b B onto F

   c F onto D

   d B onto E

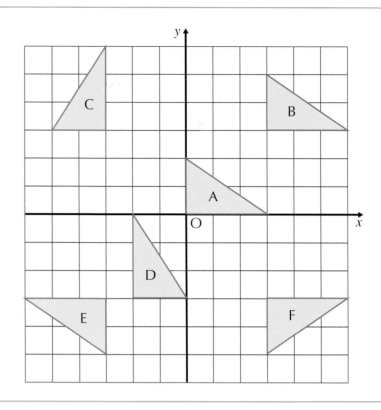

Reflections in two mirror lines

A shape can be reflected in two perpendicular mirror lines as Example 9.3 shows.

Example 9.3 ▷   Reflect the 'L' Shape in mirror line 1, then in mirror line 2.

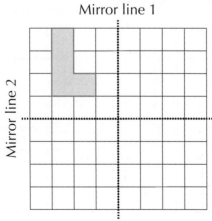

Reflecting in mirror line 1 gives:

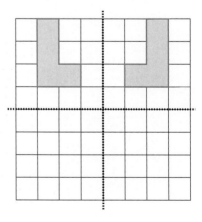

Example 9.3
continued

Reflecting both shapes in mirror line 2 gives:

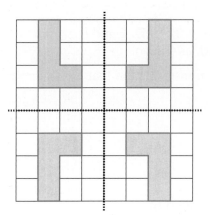

MTH 3-19a

Exercise 9C

1 Copy each of the following shapes onto centimetre-squared paper and reflect it in both mirror lines shown.

a
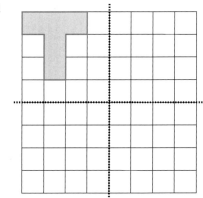

b
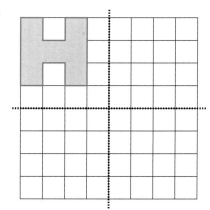

c
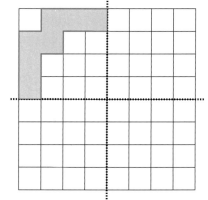

MTH 3-19a

d

2 Copy each of the following diagrams onto centimetre-squared paper and reflect the shape in both mirror lines.

a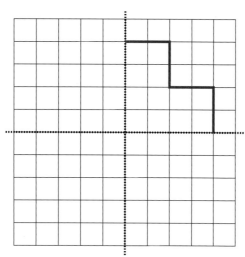

b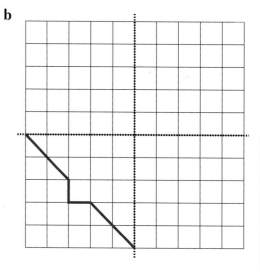

Extension Work

1 Copy the diagram onto centimetre-squared paper and reflect the shape in the two diagonal mirror lines.

2 Make up some of your own examples to show how a shape can be reflected in two diagonal lines.

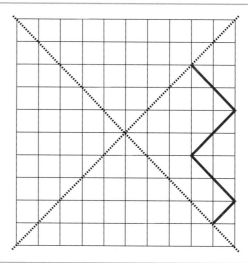

Shape and ratio

Ratio can be used to compare lengths and areas of 2-D shapes, as Examples 9.4 and 9.5 show.

Example 9.4

A ———— B
12 mm

C ═══════════════ D
4.8 cm

To find the ratio of the length of the line segment AB to the length of the line segment CD, change the measurements to the smallest unit and then simplify the ratio. So the ratio is 12 mm : 4.8 cm = 12 mm : 48 mm = 1 : 4. Remember that ratios have no units in the final answer.

Example 9.5 ▶ Find the ratio of the area of rectangle A to the area of rectangle B, giving the answer in its simplest form.

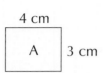

8 cm

4 cm

A | 3 cm

B | 5 cm

The ratio is 12 cm² : 40 cm² = 3 : 10

5

Exercise 9D

1 In each of the following, find the ratio of the length AB to the length CD. Remember to simplify the ratio where possible.

a A ——2 cm—— B   C ——4 cm—— D

b A ——2 cm—— B   C ——5 cm—— D

c A ——3 cm—— B   C ——6 cm—— D

d A ——3 cm—— B   C ——5 cm—— D

e A ——4 cm—— B   C ——6 cm—— D

2 Express each of the following ratios in its simplest form.

a 10 mm : 25 mm   **b** 2 mm : 2 cm   **c** 36 cm : 45 cm

d 40 cm : 2 m   **e** 500 m : 2 km

3 In each of the following, find the ratio of the area of rectangle A to the area of rectangle B. Remember to simplify the ratio where possible.

a 3 cm

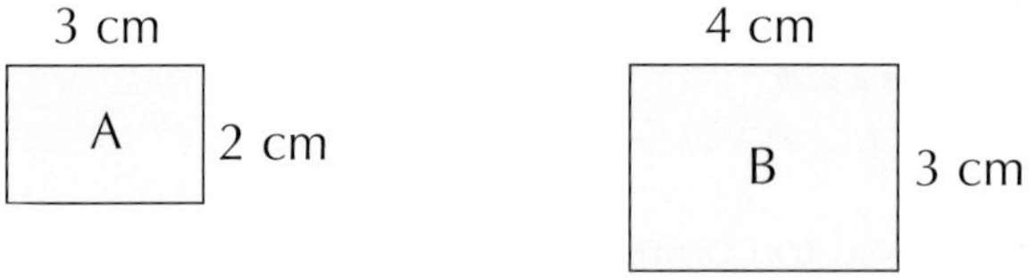

A | 2 cm

4 cm

B | 3 cm

b 4 cm

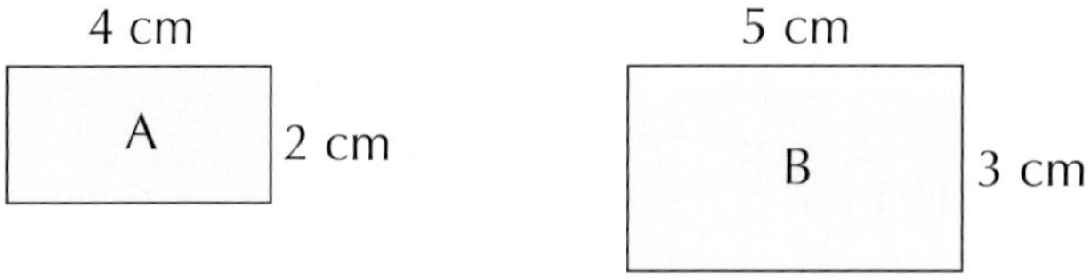

A | 2 cm

5 cm

B | 3 cm

c 5 cm

A | 2 cm

10 cm

B | 3 cm

d

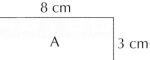

8 cm

A

3 cm

9 cm

B

4 cm

e

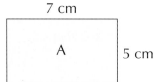

7 cm

A

5 cm

10 cm

B

6 cm

④ For the two squares shown, find each of the following ratios, giving your answers in their simplest form.

2 cm

A 2 cm

6 cm

B

6 cm

a The length of a side of square A to the length of a side of square B

b The perimeter of square A to the perimeter of square B

c The area of square A to the area of square B

MTH
4-17b

Extension Work

1 Three rectangles A, B and C are arranged as in the diagram. The ratio of the length of A to the length of B to the length of C is 3 cm : 6 cm : 9 cm = 1 : 2 : 3. Find each of the following ratios in the same way, giving your answers in their simplest form.

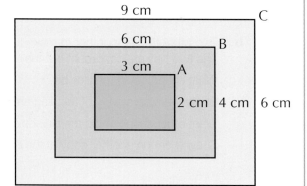

9 cm — C

6 cm — B

3 cm — A

2 cm | 4 cm | 6 cm

a The width of A to the width of B to the width of C

b The perimeter of A to the perimeter of B to the perimeter of C

b The area of A to the area of B to the area of C

2 a Find the ratio of the area of the pink square to the area of the yellow surround, giving your answer in its simplest form.

b Express the area of the pink square as a fraction of the area of the yellow surround.

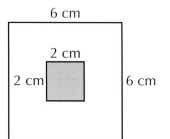

6 cm

2 cm

2 cm

6 cm

MTH
4-17b

6

4 I can reflect a shape in a mirror line.

5 I can recognise congruent shapes.

I can recognise and visualise simple transformations in 2-D shapes.

I can solve problems using ratio.

National Test questions

1 *2007 3–5 Paper 2*

a The diagram shows how two congruent 'F-tiles' fit together to make a rectangle.

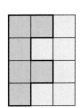

On a copy of the diagram, show how the two congruent 'F-tiles' can fit together to make this shape:

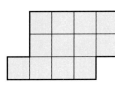

OMIT

b Two other tiles fit together to make a different shape. The two tiles are congruent but they are **not 'F-tiles'**.

What shape could the tiles be?

Show them on a copy of the diagram.

What other shape could the tiles be?

Show them on another copy of the diagram.

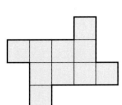

2 *2006 3–5 Paper 2*

The square grid shows a rectangle reflected in **two mirror lines**.

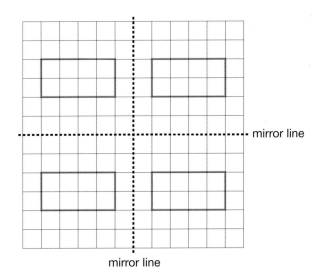

mirror line

mirror line

Copy the square grid and show **the triangle** reflected in the two mirror lines.

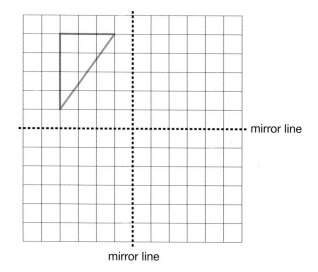

- - - mirror line

mirror line

MTH 3 -19 a

3 *2002 Paper 1*

Four squares join together to make a bigger square.

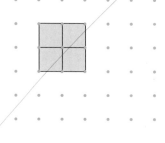

OMIT

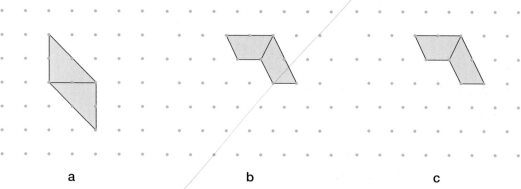

a   b   c

a   **Four** congruent triangles join together to make a bigger triangle. On a copy of the diagram, draw **two more** triangles to complete the drawing of the bigger triangle.

b   Four congruent trapezia join to make a bigger trapezium. On a copy of the diagram, draw **two more** trapezia to complete the drawing of the bigger trapezium.

c   Four congruent trapezia join together to make a **parallelogram**.
On a copy of the diagram, draw **two more** trapeziums to complete the drawing of the parallelogram.

4 *1999 Paper 2*

a Nigel pours 1 carton of apple juice and 3 cartons of orange juice into a big jug.
What is the ratio of apple juice to orange juice in Nigel's jug?

b Lesley pours 1 carton of apple juice and 1½ cartons of orange juice into another big jug.
What is the ratio of apple juice to orange juice in Lesley's jug?

c Tandi pours 1 carton of apple juice and 1 carton of orange juice into another big jug. She wants only half as much apple juice as orange juice in her jug. What should Tandi pour into her jug now?

5 *1996 Paper 1*

Julie has written a computer program to transform pictures of tiles.
There are **only two instructions** in her program:

Reflect vertical or **Rotate 90° clockwise**.

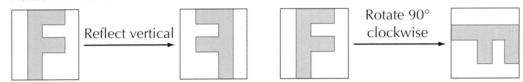

a Julie wants to transform the first pattern to the second pattern:

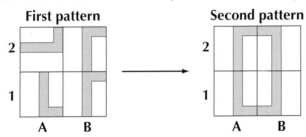

Copy and complete the instructions to transform the tiles B1 and B2. You must use only **Reflect vertical** or **Rotate 90° clockwise**.

A1 Tile is in the correct position.

A2 Reflect vertical, and then Rotate 90° clockwise.

B1 Rotate 90° clockwise, and then ......

B2 ......

b Paul starts with the first pattern that was on the screen:

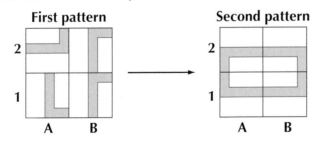

Copy and complete the instructions for the transformations of A2, B1 and B2 to make Paul's pattern. You must use only **Reflect vertical** or **Rotate 90° clockwise**.

A1 Reflect vertical, and then Rotate 90° clockwise.

A2 Rotate 90° clockwise, and then......

B1 ......

B2 ......

This chapter is going to show you

- How to solve more difficult equations
- How to substitute into a formula
- How to create your own expressions and formulae

What you should already know

- How to add, subtract and multiply negative numbers

Puzzle mappings

The mappings you are going to meet will contain an unknown value, often written as x. This is called the **unknown** of the mapping. The puzzle is to find the value of x, which you will do by **inverse mapping**.

Example 10.1 Find the value of x in the mapping:

$$x \longrightarrow \boxed{\times 3} \longrightarrow 12$$

The inverse of $\times 3$ is $\div 3$. So, use the inverse mapping:

$$4 \longleftarrow \boxed{\div 3} \longleftarrow 12$$

which gives $x = 4$

Example 10.2 Find the value of A in the mapping:

$$A \longrightarrow \boxed{+ 5} \longrightarrow 16$$

The inverse of $+ 5$ is $- 5$. So, use the inverse mapping:

$$11 \longleftarrow \boxed{- 5} \longleftarrow 16$$

which gives $A = 11$

Exercise 10A

1 Find the unknown in each of these mappings.

a $x \longrightarrow \boxed{+ 3} \longrightarrow 17$ **b** $y \longrightarrow \boxed{\times 4} \longrightarrow 20$ **c** $p \longrightarrow \boxed{- 2} \longrightarrow 8$

d $q \longrightarrow \boxed{\times 2} \longrightarrow 16$ **e** $t \longrightarrow \boxed{+ 5} \longrightarrow 19$ **f** $m \longrightarrow \boxed{- 3} \longrightarrow 12$

g $A \longrightarrow \boxed{+ 7} \longrightarrow 20$ **h** $B \longrightarrow \boxed{- 4} \longrightarrow 5$ **i** $p \longrightarrow \boxed{\times 5} \longrightarrow 15$

2 A teacher put some puzzle mappings on the board. Someone rubbed out parts of each problem. Copy and complete each mapping.

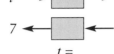

a $x \longrightarrow \boxed{} \longrightarrow 9$

$\longleftarrow \boxed{-4}$

$x =$

b $A \longrightarrow \boxed{} \longrightarrow$

$\longleftarrow \boxed{\div 2} \longleftarrow 12$

$A =$

c $y \longrightarrow \boxed{\times 3} \longrightarrow$

$\longleftarrow \boxed{} \longleftarrow 15$

$y =$

d $t \longrightarrow \boxed{} \longrightarrow 9$

$7 \longleftarrow \boxed{} \longleftarrow$

$t =$

e $m \longrightarrow \boxed{} \longrightarrow 2$

$5 \longleftarrow \boxed{} \longleftarrow$

$m =$

f $B \longrightarrow \boxed{-3} \longrightarrow 14$

$\longleftarrow \boxed{+3} \longleftarrow$

$B =$

3 Find the missing number in each of these.

a $3 + \boxed{} = 11$

b $4 \times \boxed{} = 12$

c $10 - \boxed{} = 3$

d $5 \times \boxed{} = 30$

e $8 + \boxed{} = 12$

f $9 - \boxed{} = 7$

g $4 + \boxed{} = 15$

h $3 \times \boxed{} = 18$

i $12 - \boxed{} = 9$

j $6 \times \boxed{} = 18$

k $15 - \boxed{} = 9$

l $7 + \boxed{} = 15$

4 Solve each of the following equations.

a $x + 5 = 12$

b $2s = 10$

c $t + 3 = 12$

d $g - 5 = 12$

e $4x = 20$

f $4x = 12$

g $v + 9 = 39$

h $x - 3 = 11$

i $6x = 24$

j $q + 5 = 26$

k $5x = 35$

l $p - 8 = 17$

Extension Work

Using only whole positive numbers, in how many different ways can you complete each of the following? Show all your answers.

a $\boxed{} + \boxed{} = 9$

b $\boxed{} \times \boxed{} = 24$

c $\boxed{} - \boxed{} = 7$

More puzzle mappings

All the puzzle mappings that you met in the last section had only one operation. This section deals with puzzle mappings that have more than one operation.

Example 10.3

Find the value of x in the mapping:

$x \longrightarrow \boxed{\times 5} \longrightarrow \boxed{+3} \longrightarrow 18$

Put in the inverse of each operation and work backwards:

$? \longleftarrow \boxed{\div 5} \longleftarrow \boxed{-3} \longleftarrow 18$

$3 \longleftarrow 15 \longleftarrow 18$

which gives $x = 3$

Example 10.4

Find the value of *y* in the mapping:

$$y \longrightarrow \boxed{+2} \longrightarrow \boxed{\times 3} \longrightarrow 18$$

Put in the inverse of each operation and work backwards:

$$? \longleftarrow \boxed{-2} \longleftarrow \boxed{\div 3} \longleftarrow 18$$
$$4 \longleftarrow 6 \longleftarrow 18$$

which gives *y* = 4

1 Use inverse mapping to find the value of *x* in each of the following.

a $x \longrightarrow \boxed{\times 2} \longrightarrow \boxed{+3} \longrightarrow 13$ **b** $x \longrightarrow \boxed{\times 3} \longrightarrow \boxed{+5} \longrightarrow 11$

c $x \longrightarrow \boxed{\times 2} \longrightarrow \boxed{+9} \longrightarrow 17$ **d** $x \longrightarrow \boxed{+1} \longrightarrow \boxed{\times 5} \longrightarrow 35$

e $x \longrightarrow \boxed{+3} \longrightarrow \boxed{\times 4} \longrightarrow 16$ **f** $x \longrightarrow \boxed{+2} \longrightarrow \boxed{\times 7} \longrightarrow 21$

g $x \longrightarrow \boxed{\times 4} \longrightarrow \boxed{+5} \longrightarrow 29$ **h** $x \longrightarrow \boxed{\times 5} \longrightarrow \boxed{+3} \longrightarrow 28$

i $x \longrightarrow \boxed{\times 3} \longrightarrow \boxed{+4} \longrightarrow 25$ **j** $x \longrightarrow \boxed{+2} \longrightarrow \boxed{\times 5} \longrightarrow 30$

2 Copy and complete the missing parts of each of these puzzle mappings.

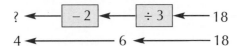

a $x \longrightarrow \boxed{+5} \longrightarrow \boxed{} \longrightarrow 16$
$\longleftarrow \boxed{} \longleftarrow \boxed{\div 2} \longleftarrow$
$x =$

b $y \longrightarrow \boxed{} \longrightarrow \boxed{\times 3} \longrightarrow 15$
$\longleftarrow \boxed{-2} \longleftarrow \boxed{} \longleftarrow$
$y =$

c $t \longrightarrow \boxed{\times 4} \longrightarrow \boxed{} \longrightarrow 31$
$\longleftarrow \boxed{} \longleftarrow \boxed{-3} \longleftarrow$
$t =$

d $w \longrightarrow \boxed{} \longrightarrow \boxed{+5} \longrightarrow 17$
$\longleftarrow \boxed{\div 4} \longleftarrow \boxed{} \longleftarrow$
$w =$

e $m \longrightarrow \boxed{\times 2} \longrightarrow \boxed{} \longrightarrow 19$
$\longleftarrow \boxed{} \longleftarrow \boxed{+1} \longleftarrow$
$m =$

f $g \longrightarrow \boxed{} \longrightarrow \boxed{-3} \longrightarrow 27$
$\longleftarrow \boxed{\div 5} \longleftarrow \boxed{} \longleftarrow$
$g =$

3 Pete had a number rule in his head. He used the rule on any number given to him.

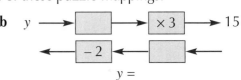
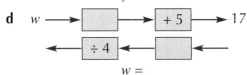
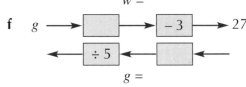

> Multiply by 2. Then subtract 5.

a What number did Pete give in reply to each of the following?
  i 7
  ii 3
  iii 10

b What number was given to Peter when he replied as follows?
  i 19
  ii 9
  iii 21

MTH 2-15a

In how many different ways can you fill in the operation boxes in each of these mapping diagrams? Show all your answers.

MTH 2-15a

a   2 ⟶ ☐ ⟶ ☐ ⟶ 20

b   16 ⟶ ☐ ⟶ ☐ ⟶ 1

Solving equations

An **equation** is formed when an expression is put equal to a number or another expression.

The equations you will meet contain only one unknown value, which is often represented by x. This is called the **unknown** of the equation. To find the value of the unknown, the equation has to be **solved**.

One way to solve equations is to use inverse mapping.

Example 10.5   Solve the equation $5x - 4 = 11$.

The mapping which gives this equation is:

$x \longrightarrow \boxed{\times 5} \longrightarrow \boxed{-4} \longrightarrow 11$

The inverse is:

$? \longleftarrow \boxed{\div 5} \longleftarrow \boxed{+4} \longleftarrow 11$

$3 \longleftarrow \qquad 15$

which gives $x = 3$

See note on Bk 2 p 91 → if CfE doesn't include mappings, should we include 'inverse mappings'?

Example 10.6   Solve the equation $4x + 2 = 22$.

The mapping which gives this equation is:

$x \longrightarrow \boxed{\times 4} \longrightarrow \boxed{+2} \longrightarrow 22$

Working the mapping backwards:

Subtract 2: $22 - 2 = 20$

Divide by 4: $20 \div 4 = 5$

So, the solution is $x = 5$

MTH 3-15a

Exercise 10C

1 i   Write the equation which is given by each of the following mappings.

ii   Use inverse mapping to solve each equation.

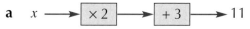

a $x \longrightarrow \boxed{\times 2} \longrightarrow \boxed{+ 3} \longrightarrow 11$

b $x \longrightarrow \boxed{\times 3} \longrightarrow \boxed{+ 1} \longrightarrow 16$

c $t \longrightarrow \boxed{\times 5} \longrightarrow \boxed{+ 4} \longrightarrow 34$

d $t \longrightarrow \boxed{\times 4} \longrightarrow \boxed{- 3} \longrightarrow 13$

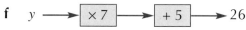

e $y \longrightarrow \boxed{\times 2} \longrightarrow \boxed{- 1} \longrightarrow 13$

f $y \longrightarrow \boxed{\times 7} \longrightarrow \boxed{+ 5} \longrightarrow 26$

2 i Write the mapping which is given by each of the following equations.

   ii Use inverse mapping to solve each equation.

    a $3x + 4 = 19$ **b** $2x + 5 = 11$ **c** $4x - 1 = 23$

    d $5x - 3 = 17$ **e** $3x + 1 = 22$ **f** $6x - 5 = 7$

3 Solve each of the following equations by first writing the inverse of the mapping given by the equation.

    a $2x + 3 = 15$ **b** $4x + 1 = 29$ **c** $3x + 4 = 25$

    d $5x - 1 = 34$ **e** $2x - 3 = 13$ **f** $4x - 3 = 37$

4 Solve each of the following equations.

    a $2x + 3 = 17$ **b** $4x - 1 = 19$ **c** $5x + 3 = 18$

    d $2y - 3 = 13$ **e** $4z + 5 = 17$ **f** $6x - 5 = 13$

    g $10b + 9 = 29$ **h** $2r - 3 = 9$ **i** $3x - 11 = 1$

    j $7p + 5 = 82$ **k** $5x + 7 = 52$ **l** $9x - 8 = 55$

Extension Work

$$x \longrightarrow \boxed{\times 2} \longrightarrow \boxed{+1} \longrightarrow \boxed{\times 3} \longrightarrow y$$

a Find the value of y when:

   i $x = 5$ **ii** $x = 4$ **iii** $x = 3$

b Find the value of x when:

   i $y = 39$ **ii** $y = 51$ **iii** $y = 57$

c Find the negative decimal value of x when $x \longrightarrow x$.

Substituting into expressions

Replacing the letters in an expression by numbers is called **substitution**.

Substituting different numbers will give an expression different values. You need to be able to substitute negative numbers as well as positive numbers into expressions.

Example 10.7 What is the value of $5x + 7$ when: **i** $x = 3$ **ii** $x = -1$

i When $x = 3$, $5x + 7 = 5 \times 3 + 7 = 22$

ii When $x = -1$, $5x + 7 = 5 \times (-1) + 7 = -5 + 7 = 2$

Exercise 10D

1 Write down the value of each expression for each value of x.

    a $x + 3$ **i** $x = 4$ **ii** $x = 5$ **iii** $x = -1$

    b $7 + x$ **i** $x = 6$ **ii** $x = 2$ **iii** $x = -5$

    c $3x$ **i** $x = 7$ **ii** $x = 3$ **iii** $x = -5$

    d $4x$ **i** $x = 3$ **ii** $x = 5$ **iii** $x = -1$

    e $3x + 4$ **i** $x = 5$ **ii** $x = 4$ **iii** $x = -2$

MTH 3-15a

MTH 3-14a

f	$5x - 1$	i	$x = 3$	ii	$x = 2$	iii	$x = -6$
g	$3x + 5$	i	$x = 3$	ii	$x = 7$	iii	$x = -1$
h	$4x + 20$	i	$x = 4$	ii	$x = 5$	iii	$x = -3$
i	$8 + 7x$	i	$x = 2$	ii	$x = 6$	iii	$x = -2$
j	$93 + 4x$	i	$x = 10$	ii	$x = 21$	iii	$x = -3$

2 If $a = 2$ and $b = 3$, find the value of each of the following.

   a $3a + b$ **b** $a + 3b$ **c** $3a + 5b$ **d** $4b - 3a)$

3 If $c = 5$ and $d = 2$, find the value of each of the following.

   a $2c + d$ **b** $6c - 2d$ **c** $3d + 7c$ **d** $3c - 5d$

4 If $e = 4$, $f = 3$ and $g = 2$, find the value of each of the following.

   a $ef + g$ **b** $eg - f$ **c** efg **d** $3e + 2f + 5g$

5 If $h = -4$, $j = 7$ and $k = 5$, find the value of each of the following.

   a hjk **b** $4k + fj$ **c** $5h + 4j + 3k$ **d** $3hj - 2hk$

Extension Work

1 What values of n can be substituted into n^2 that give n^2 a value less than 1?

2 What values of n can be substituted into $(n - 4)^2$ that give $(n - 4)^2$ a value less than 1?

3 What values of n can be substituted into $\frac{1}{n}$ that give $\frac{1}{n}$ a value less than 1?

4 Find at least five different expressions in x that give the value 10 when $x = 2$ is substituted into them.

Substituting into formulae

Formulae occur in all sorts of situations. A common example is the conversion between metric and imperial units.

Example 10.8   The formula for converting kilograms (K) to pounds (P) is given by:

$$P = 2.2K$$

Convert 10 kilograms to pounds.

Substituting $K = 10$ into the formula gives: $P = 2.2 \times 10 = 22$

So, 10 kg is 22 pounds.

Example 10.9   The formula for the volume, V, of a box with length b, width w and height h, is given by:

$$V = bwh$$

Calculate the volume of a box whose length is 8 cm, width is 3 cm and height is 2 cm.

Substitute the values given into the formula: $V = 8 \times 3 \times 2 = 48$

So, the volume of the box is 48 cm³.

1 The area, A, of a rectangle is found using the formula $A = LB$, where L is its length and B its width. Find A when:

   a $L = 8$ and $B = 7$ **b** $L = 6$ and $B = 1.5$

2 The surface area, A, of a coil is given by the formula $A = 6rh$. Find A when:

   a $r = 6$ and $h = 17$ **b** $r = 2.5$ and $h = 12$

3 The sum, S, of the angles in a polygon with n sides is given by the formula $S = 180(n - 2)°$. Find S when:

   a $n = 7$ **b** $n = 12$

4 If $V = u + ft$, find V when:

   a $u = 40$, $f = 32$ and $t = 5$ **b** $u = 12$, $f = 13$ and $t = 10$

5 If $D = \dfrac{M}{V}$, find D when:

   a $M = 28$ and $V = 4$ **b** $M = 8$ and $V = 5$

FM **6** A magician charges £25 for every show he performs, plus an extra £10 per hour spent on stage. The formula for calculating his charge is $C = 10t + 25$, where C is the charge in pounds and t is the length of the show in hours.

How much does he charge for a show lasting the following durations?
   i   1 hour   **ii**   3 hours   **iii**   2 hours

7 The area (A) of the triangle shown is given by the formula $A = \frac{1}{2}bh$.

Find the area when:
   i $h = 12$ cm and $b = 5$ cm
   ii $h = 9$ cm and $b = 8$ cm

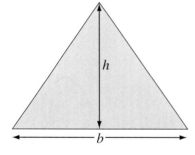

FM **8** $F = 2C + 30$ approximately converts temperatures in degrees Celsius (C) to degrees Fahrenheit (F).

Convert approximately each of these temperatures to degrees Fahrenheit.
   a   45 °C   **b**   40 °C   **c**   65 °C   **d**   100 °C

9 The surface area (S) of this cuboid is given by the formula:

$$S = 2ab + 2bc + 2ac$$

   a   Find the surface area, when
         $a = 3$ m, $b = 4$ m and $c = 5$ m.
   b   **i**   Find the surface area when $a = 3$ cm,
            and a, b and c are all the same length.
         ii   What name is given to this cuboid?

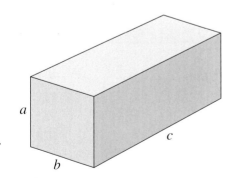

The triangle numbers are given by the following formula:

$$T = \frac{n(n + 1)}{2}$$

The first triangle number is found by substituting in $n = 1$, which gives:

$$T = 1 \times \frac{(1 + 1)}{2} = 1$$

a Find the next four triangle numbers.

b Find the 99th triangle number.

Creating your own expressions and formulae

The last section showed you some formulae which could be used to solve problems. In this section, you need to write your own formulae to help solve given problems.

You will need to choose a letter to represent each variable in a problem, and use it when you write the formula. Usually this will be the first letter of the word which describes the variable. For example, V often represents volume and A is often used for area.

Example 10.10 ▷ Find an expression for the sum, S, of any three consecutive whole numbers.

Let the smallest number be n.
The next number is $(n + 1)$ and the third number is $(n + 2)$. So,

$$S = n + (n + 1) + (n + 2)$$
$$S = n + n + 1 + n + 2$$
$$S = 3n + 3$$

Example 10.11 ▷ How many months are there in: **i** 5 years

ii t years?

There are 12 months in a year, so **i** in 5 years there will be $12 \times 5 = 60$ months

ii in t years there will be $12 \times t = 12t$ months

Exercise 10F

1 Using the letters suggested, construct a simple formula in each case.

a The sum, S, of three numbers a, b and c.

b The product, P, of two numbers x and y.

c The difference, D, between the ages of two people. The older person is a years old and the other person is b years old.

d The sum, S, of four consecutive integers. Let the first integer be n.

e The number of days, D, in W weeks.

f The average age, A, of three boys whose ages are m, n and p years.

2 How many days are there in:

    a   1 week?   **b**   3 weeks?   **c**   *w* weeks?

3 A girl is now 13 years old.

    a   How old will she be in:

        i   1 year?   **ii**   5 years?   **iii**   *t* years?

    b   How old was she:

        i   1 year ago?   **ii**   3 years ago?   **ii**   *m* years ago?

4 A car travels at a speed of 30 mph. How many miles will it travel in the following durations?

    a   1 hour   **b**   2 hours   **c**   *t* hours

5 How many grams are there in the following?

    a   1 kg   **b**   5 kg   **c**   *x* kg

6 How many minutes are there in *m* hours?

7 Write down the number that is half as big as:

    a   20   **b**   6   **c**   *b*

8 Write down the number that is twice as big as:

    a   4   **b**   7   **c**   *T*

9 If a boy runs at *b* miles per hour, how many miles does he run in *k* hours?

10 **a**   What is the cost, in pence, of 6 papers at 35 pence each?

    b   What is the cost, in pence, of *k* papers at 35 pence each?

    c   What is the cost, in pence, of *k* papers at *q* pence each?

11 A boy is *b* years old and his mother is 6 times as old.

    a   Find the mother's age in terms of *b*.

    b   Find the sum of their ages in *y* years time.

12 Mr Speed's age is equal to the sum of the ages of his three sons. The youngest son is aged *x* years, the eldest is 10 years older than the youngest and the middle son is 4 years younger than the eldest. How old is Mr Speed?

Extension Work

The formula for the volume of a cylinder is $V = \pi r^2 h$, where r is the radius and h is the height.

MTH 3-15b

Take π as 3.14 and work out the volume of these cylinders:

Give your answers to the nearest whole number.

a $r = 5$ cm, $h = 10$ cm

b $r = 12$ cm, $h = 20$ cm

c $r = 7$ cm, $h = 12$ cm

d diameter $= 18$ cm, $h = 7$ cm

LEVEL BOOSTER

4 I can substitute positive numbers into simple expressions, for example work out the value of $3x + 2y$ when $x = 3$ and $y = 4$.

I can find the input value for a simple mapping such as:

$$x \longrightarrow \boxed{+\ 14} \longrightarrow 7$$

I can use inverse functions to find input values such as:

$$x \longrightarrow \boxed{} \longrightarrow 7$$
$$x \longleftarrow \boxed{\div\ 3} \longleftarrow$$

5 I can use inverse functions with two operations to find input values, for example:

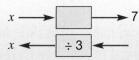

I can solve equations of the type $3x + 7 = 10$, by using inverse flow diagrams.

I can substitute positive and negative numbers into algebraic expressions, for example work out the value of $4a - 3b$ when $a = 3$ and $b = -2$.

I can substitute positive and negative numbers into formulae, for example working out the value of $A = 2b + 2w$, when $b = 5$ and $w = 3$.

I can devise algebraic formula to represent simple facts such as the distance travelled by a car doing 40 mph in t hours.

1 *2002 3–5 Paper 2*

Here is some information about a school:

There are **3 classes** in **year 8**. Each class has **27 pupils**.

There are **4 classes** in **year 9**. Each class has **25 pupils**.

a Use the information to match each question with the correct calculation. The first one is done for you.

Question

Calculation

How many **classes** are there altogether in years 8 and 9?

3 + 4

3 − 4

4 − 3

There are more **classes** in year 9 than in year 8. How many more?

$(3 \times 27) + (4 \times 25)$

$(3 + 27) + (4 + 25)$

How many **pupils** are there altogether in years 8 and 9?

$(3 \times 27) - (4 \times 25)$

$(4 + 25) - (3 + 27)$

There are more **pupils** in year 9 than in year 8. How many more?

$(4 \times 25) - (3 \times 27)$

2 *2002 3–5 Paper 1*

a I can think of three different rules to change **6** to **18**:

6 → 18

Complete these sentences to show what these rules could be:

First rule: **add** ......

Second rule: **multiply by** ......

Third rule: **multiply by 2, then** ......

b Now I think of a new rule.

The new rule changes 10 to 5 **and** it changes 8 to 4:

10 → 5   8 → 4

Write what this new rule could be.

3 *2003 3–5 Paper 1*

a The number chain below is part of a **doubling** number chain.

Write down the two missing numbers.

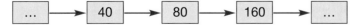

b The number chain below is part of a **halving** number chain.

Write down the two missing numbers.

40 → 20 → 10 → ... → ...

4 *2007 3–5 Paper 2*

Look at this equation:

$$4 + a = b$$

Write a pair of numbers for a and b to make the equation true.

Now write a **different** pair of numbers for a and b to make the equation true.

5 *2002 Paper 1*

Look at this table:

	Age in years
Ann	a
Ben	b
Cindy	c

Copy the table below and write in words the meaning of each equation.
The first one is done for you.

a	$b = 30$	Ben is 30 years old
b	$a + b = 69$	
c	$b = 2c$	
d	$\dfrac{a + b + c}{3} = 28$	

CHAPTER 11

Statistics 2

This chapter is going to show you

- How to read information from a range of charts and diagrams
- How to create simple pie charts

What you should already know

- How to find mode, median, mean and range for small data sets

Information from charts

We often see charts in magazines and papers, giving us a lot of different types of information.

Example 11.1

Here are the results of a girls' long-jump competition.

The table shows how high they jumped in centimetres.

	1st jump	2nd jump	3rd jump	4th jump
Amy	218	105	233	297
Donna	154	108	287	176
Gaynor	202	276	95	152
Joy	165	197	240	295

a   How far did Gaynor jump on her 3rd jump?

b   Who improved with every jump?

c   Who won the competition?

All the information is found by reading the table.

a   Gaynor jumped 95cm on her 3rd jump.

b   Joy improved with every jump, the only girl to do that.

c   Amy had the longest jump of 297cm, so she won the competition.

Exercise 11A

FM 1 The chart below shows the distances, in miles, between certain towns in the UK.

Birmingham				
159	Exeter			
144	302	Holyhead		
206	365	247	Newcastle	
76	235	149	129	Sheffield

4

a How far apart are Exeter and Newcastle?

b How far apart are Birmingham and Holyhead?

c Which town is 235 miles from Exeter?

d Which two towns are 206 miles from each other?

e How much further away from Newcastle is Exeter than Sheffield?

2 The table shows who is able to babysit on which nights:

	Mon	Tue	Wed	Thu	Fri	Sat	Sun
Alice		✓		✓			✓
Davinder		✓	✓	✓	✓		
Kylie	✓					✓	
Suzie				✓			✓
Teresa	✓	✓	✓				

a On which days can Alice babysit?

b Who is available to babysit on Wednesday?

c Mr and Mrs Carter used one of the babysitters last Thursday. What is the probability that this was: **i** Davinder? **ii** Kylie?

3 This table shows some information about the subjects taken by five Y11 pupils:

	Maths	Geology	History	Literature
Eli	✓		✓	✓
Dan	✓	✓	✓	
Gill	✓	✓		✓
Eve	✓		✓	✓
Fynn	✓	✓		

This table shows some information about their families:

	Dad	Mum	Brothers	Sisters
Eli		✓	1	0
Dan	✓		0	2
Gill	✓	✓	2	1
Eve		✓	1	1
Fynn	✓	✓	0	0

a How many of the pupils took geology?

b Which subjects did Eli take?

c One pupil said, 'Last night my brother helped me with my geology homework'. Who was this pupil?

d In the literature lesson, one pupil was talking about their brother and sister fighting the previous night. Which pupils could this have been?

4 The table shows some information about pupils in a Y8 class.

Eye colour	Number of boys	Number of girls
Blue	7	8
Brown	5	6
Green	2	4

a How many pupils are in the class?

b How many of the pupils have brown eyes?

c One pupil in the class is chosen at random. What is the probability that this pupil:

   i has blue eyes?

   ii is a girl with green eyes?

   iii is a boy?

5 In a group of five friends, Amos, Billy, Celine, Dot and Elvin:

Amos, Celine and Elvin could play the piano.
Billy, Dot and Celine could play the guitar.
Amos, Billy and Elvin could play the clarinet.
Amos and Dot could read music.

a Create a table showing all this information.

b Which of the friends could:

   i read music and play the guitar?

   ii play the piano and the guitar?

   iii play the piano and the clarinet?

c One of the friends who could play the guitar won a raffle. What is the probability that this was:

   i Billy?

   ii Elvin?

d One of the friends who could read music was late for rehearsals. What is the probability that this was:

   i Dot?

   ii Elvin?

Extension Work

Max and Joanne were planning a day out in Derbyshire using the trains. They wanted to set off from Dore, stopping at Hathersage for morning coffee. They then wanted to go out to Hope for lunch and then onto Edale for a cream tea in the afternoon, returning back to Dore before six o'clock.

Dore	07.21	09.21	10.21	12.21
Grindleford	07.29	09.29	10.29	12.29
Hathersage	07.32	09.32	10.32	12.32
Bamford	07.36	09.36	10.36	12.36
Hope	07.39	09.39	10.39	12.39
Edale	07.47	09.47	10.47	12.47

Edale	15.28	16.30	18.02
Hope	15.34	16.36	18.08
Bamford	15.37	16.39	18.11
Hathersage	15.40	16.42	18.14
Grindleford	15.44	16.46	18.18
Dore	15.53	16.53	18.25

Use the timetables above to plan this day for them with suitable train times.

Circular bar charts

Charts can come in all shapes and sizes. Circles are a popular way of displaying information.

Example 11.2

Toads and Frogs hibernate in the winter.

The shaded parts of the chart show when they hibernate.

Use the chart to answer these questions.

a For how many months do frogs hibernate in winter?

b It has been said that 'toads hibernate for $\frac{1}{4}$ of their life'.
Is this correct? Explain your answer.

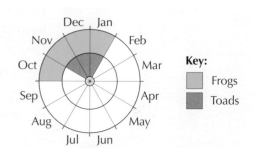

Key:
Frogs
Toads

By looking at the chart:

a Frogs hibernate from October to January – 4 months.

b Toads hibernate from November to January – this is 3 months, which is $\frac{1}{4}$ of 12 months (a year). So yes, the statement is true.

Exercise 11B

1 The diagram shows the hours four security guards spent on duty at a secure factory site.

a Who works the longest hours?
b Who works the shortest hours?
c Saquib says, 'I work for $\frac{1}{3}$ of the day at this place'.
Is Saquib correct? Explain your answer.

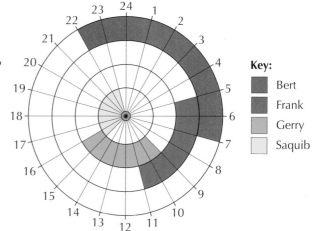

Key:
Bert
Frank
Gerry
Saquib

2 The diagram shows the time that Gerrard spends each day on certain activities.

a How many hours does Gerrard spend doing the following activities?
  i Sleeping
  ii Eating
  iii Working
b How many hours of the day does he have left for other activities?

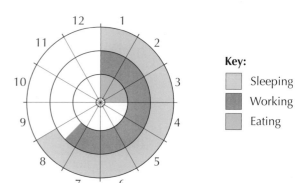

Key:
Sleeping
Working
Eating

3 The diagram shows the months
of various sporting seasons in England.

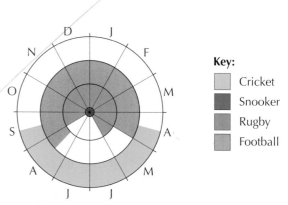

Key:
- Cricket
- Snooker
- Rugby
- Football

a For how many months in the year:
  i   does the cricket season last?
  ii does the rugby season last?
  iii is snooker played?

b Amy says, 'The football season
lasts for half of the year'.

Is she right? Explain your answer.

Omit

Extension **Work**

Imagine the Simpson family: Dad, Mum, Grandpa, Son, Daughter and Baby.

Create a series of circular bar charts to illustrate what you estimate would be
an average day for each of them, including time spent:

  sleeping   eating   working   watching TV

Reading pie charts

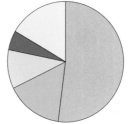

In the picture, which colour represents 'Unfit adults'? How do you know?

The pie chart is used because it shows the proportion of the whole amount and is quite
easy to interpret.

Sometimes you will have to read information from pie charts, and sometimes you will be
asked to draw them.

In a pie chart, the information is represented by a whole circle (a pie) and each category
is represented by a sector of the circle (a slice of the pie).

Example 11.3 This pie chart shows the proportion of British and foreign cars
sold one weekend at a car salesroom. 40 cars were sold.

British cars

Foreign cars

a How many British cars were sold?

b How many foreign cars were sold?

You can see from the pie chart that $\frac{1}{4}$ of the cars sold
were British and $\frac{3}{4}$ were foreign. So:

a $\frac{1}{4}$ of 40 = 10: 10 British cars were sold.

b $\frac{3}{4}$ of 40 = 30: 30 foreign cars were sold.

*MNU
4-20a*

Example 11.4 ▶

The pie chart shows how one country disposed of 3000 kg of waste in 2006.

How much waste was disposed of by:

a landfill? **b** burning?

c dumping at sea? **d** chemical treatment?

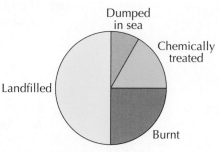

From the pie chart you can see that:

a $\frac{1}{2}$ of the waste was landfilled = $\frac{1}{2}$ of 3000 kg = 1500 kg landfilled

b $\frac{1}{4}$ of the waste was burnt = $\frac{1}{4}$ of 3000 kg = 750 kg burnt

c $\frac{30}{360} = \frac{1}{12}$ of the waste was dumped at sea, i.e. 3000 ÷ 12 = 250 kg dumped at sea

d $\frac{60}{360} = \frac{1}{6}$ of the waste was treated by chemicals, i.e. 3000 ÷ 6 = 500 kg chemically treated

Exercise 11C

① 900 pupils in a school were asked to vote for their favourite subject.
The pie chart illustrates their responses.

How many voted for:

a PE? **b** science? **c** maths?

② One weekend in Edale, a café sold 300 drinks. The pie chart illustrates the different drinks that were sold.

How many of the following drinks were sold that weekend?

a Soft drinks **b** Tea

c Hot chocolate **d** Coffee

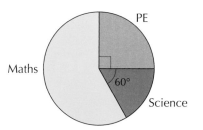

③ The pie chart illustrates how, in one week, 450 kg of kilograms of butter were sold at a supermarket.

How many kilograms of butter were sold on the following days?

a Monday **b** Tuesday **c** Wednesday

d Thursday **e** Friday **f** Saturday

g Sunday

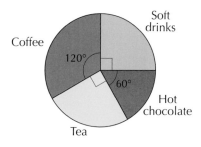

④ Pat conducated a survey about fruit and nut nut chocolate. She asked 30 of her friends how often they ate it. The pie chart illustrates her results.

How many of these friends:

a never ate fruit and nut chocolate?

b sometimes ate fruit and nut chocolate?

c called fruit and nut their favourite chocolate?

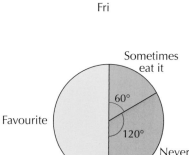

5 The pie chart shows Joe's activities one Wednesday.
It covers a 24-hour time period.

How long did Joe spend:

a at school? **b** at leisure?

c travelling? **d** sleeping?

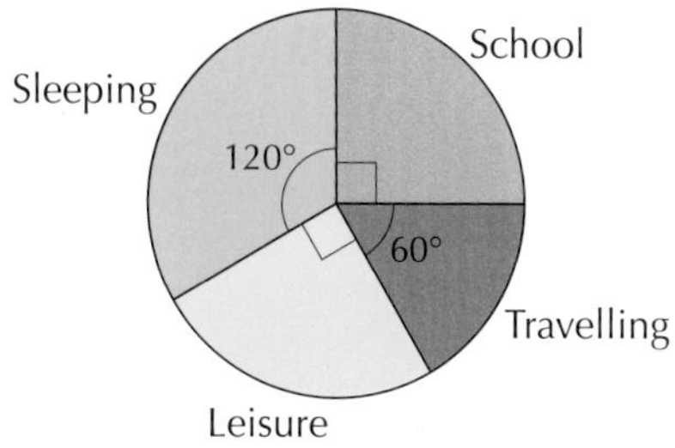

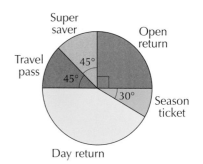

6 On a train one morning, the guard inspected all the tickets in order to report how many of each type there were.
The pie chart illustrates his results for the 240 tickets he saw that morning.

How many of the following tickets did he see that morning?

a Open return **b** Season ticket

c Day return **d** Travel pass

e Super saver

Extension Work

Design a poster to show information about 20 pupils in your class. Either include pie charts that you have drawn yourself or use a spreadsheet to produce the pie charts. Make sure that any pie chart you produce has labels and is easy to understand.

Pie charts and percentages

We are often presented with pie charts showing percentages. The simplest of these are split into ten sections where each section represents 10%, like the ones shown below.

Example 11.5 ▸

The pie chart shows the favourite snack of some Year 8 pupils:

It shows that:

'Fruit' occupies 1 sector, hence 10% gave fruit as their favourite.

'Chocolate' occupies 3 sectors, hence 30% gave chocolate as their favourite.

'Crisps' occupies 4 sectors, hence 40% gave crisps as their favourite.

'Biscuits' occupies 2 sectors, hence 20% gave biscuits as their favourite.

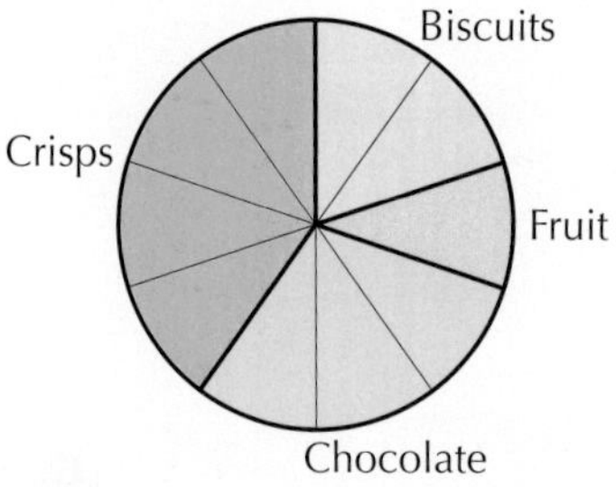

Example 11.6

The two pie charts show how late the plumbers of the UK and France are. Use them to compare the punctuality of plumbers in both countries.

Creating tables can help to interpret the data. (Remember each division represents 10% so half a sector represents 5%.)

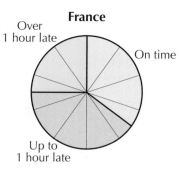

This table can be created from the data in the pie charts.

We can see that:

- a higher percentage of plumbers in the UK are on time.

- the same percentage of plumbers are up to 1 hour late in both countries.

	UK	France
On time	40%	35%
Up to 1 hour late	40%	40%
Over 1 hour late	20%	25%

- a higher percentage of plumbers in France are over 1 hour late.

Exercise 11D

1 The pie chart shows the percentage of people of different ages travelling on buses.

What percentage of people that travel on buses are aged:

a   under 10?   b   10 to 20?

c   21 to 30?   d   31 to 50?

e   over 50?

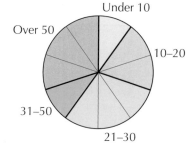

2 The pie chart shows the percentage of wild animals seen in one region of the Peak District one weekend.

What percentage of the wild animals were:

a   hedgehogs?   b   foxes?

c   rabbits?   d   squirrels?

e   badgers?

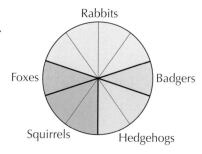

3 The pie chart shows the percentage of various school subjects that pupils chose as their favourite.

What percentage of the pupils said their favourite subject was the following?

a   Maths   b   English

c   Science   d   History

e   PE

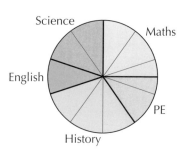

4 The pie chart shows the percentage of various sci-fi shows on TV that pupils chose as their favourite.

What percentage of the pupils said their favourite sci-fi show was:

a Doctor Who? **b** Battlestar Galactica?

c Star Trek? **d** Heroes?

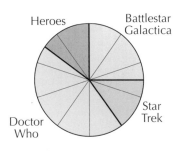

5 The pie chart shows the percentage of various age groups living in Chesterfield.

What percentage of the people in Chesterfield were aged:

a under 12? **b** 12–20?

c 21–50? **d** 51–70?

e over 70?

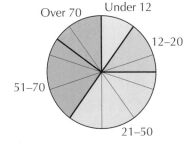

6 The pie chart shows the percentage of various age groups living in Bournemouth.

What percentage of the people living in Bournemouth were aged:

a under 12? **b** 12–20?

c 21–50? **d** 51–70?

e over 70?

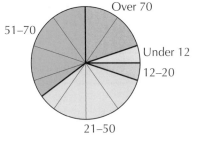

7 The pie chart shows the percentage of various age groups living in a village in Africa.

What percentage of the people living in this African village were aged:

a under 12? **b** 12–20?

c 21–50? **d** 51–70?

e over 70?

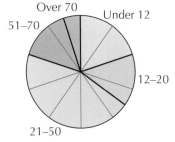

FM **8** Use the information in questions 5, 6 and 7 to decide which of the following statements are TRUE and which are FALSE.

a There is a greater percentage of under-12s in Chesterfield than Bournemouth.

b There is a greater percentage of over-70s in Chesterfield than Bournemouth.

c There is a greater percentage of people aged 12–20 in Chesterfield than Bournemouth.

d There is an equal percentage of people aged 51–70 in Chesterfield and Bournemouth.

e There is a smaller percentage of under-12s in Chesterfield than the village in Africa.

f There is a smaller percentage of over-70s in the village in Africa than Bournemouth.

g There is a smaller percentage of people aged 51–70 in the village in Africa than Bournemouth.

1 Use the following facts about spectator sport in Australia to draw three pie charts, illustrating these facts.

- A higher percentage of under-20s go to football than cricket or hockey
- A higher percentage of 21–30s go to hockey than cricket or football
- A lower percentage of 31–50s go to hockey than cricket or football
- A higher percentage of over-50s go to cricket than football or hockey

2 Investigate similar statistics for the UK. Create three pie charts reflecting what you have found.

Information from other diagrams

You will come across many different types of diagram or chart giving information. The following exercise shows you a variety of these.

Exercise 11E

1 Abby wanted to find out why people in some countries lived longer than people in other countries.

She picked 15 countries and found out:
- the population.
- the number of doctors per million people.
- the average length of life.

She plotted these graphs to help her look for links:

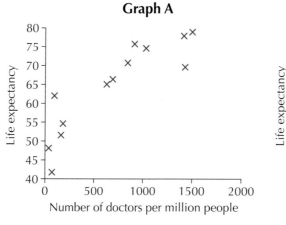

Graph A

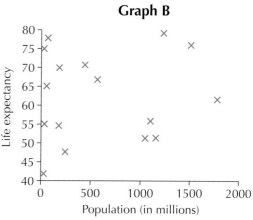

Graph B

a What does graph A show about possible links between length of life and the number of doctors per million people in a country?

b What does graph B show about possible links between length of life and a country's population?

c Abby is told that another country has:
- a population of about 100 million.
- about 800 doctors per million people.

Use the graphs above to estimate the average length of life for this country.

2 There are 24 pupils in Mr Lockwood's class.
He did a survey of how the pupils in his class travelled to school.
He started to draw a pie chart to show his results.

a Four of his pupils travel by car.

   i Sketch a copy of the pie chart, showing these four pupils.

   ii The only pupils now not shown are those who travel by taxi. How many pupils travel by taxi?

b There are 36 pupils in Mrs Casey's class.
She did the same survey and drew a pie chart to show her results.

How many of Mrs Casey's pupils travelled by:

   i taxi?   **ii** bicycle?   **iii** car?

c Mr Lockwood said, 'Mrs Casey's chart shows fewer pupils travelling by bus than mine does'.

He is wrong. Explain why.

3 Paul and Sean both have five attempts at long jump.
The diagram below represents the lengths of these jumps.

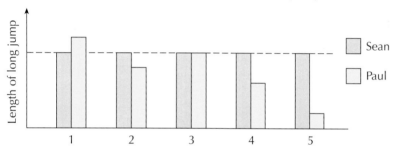

Use the diagram to decide which of the following statements is true, which is false, or whether you cannot tell.

i Sean jumped the same length every time.

ii One of Paul's jumps was 2m long.

iii The mean length of Paul's jumps is less than the mean for Sean's jumps.

iv The range of jumps is the same for both boys.

v The median length of jumps is the same for both.

4 A vending machine in a youth club sells snacks at the following prices.

Crisps	30p
Chocolate bars	45p
Drinks	60p
Baguettes	£1.00
Sandwiches	£1.50

MNU 4-20a

Aaran writes down the amounts of money which different people spend one evening during each hour the club is open.

Amounts of money spent during each hour		
6pm to 7pm	7pm to 8pm	8pm to 9pm
60p	£1.05	£2.50
90p	75p	£2.10
75p	90p	£2.40
30p	60p	£1.05
60p	£1.60	£2.10
90p	60p	£1.45
75p	£1.05	90p
60p	60p	£2.00

a What is the mode amount spent?

b

	6pm to 7pm	7pm to 8pm	8pm to 9pm
Under 70p			
70p to £1.49			
£1.50 to £1.99			
£2 or more			

i Copy and complete the table above.

ii Which is the modal group?

iii What do you notice about the amounts of money people spent at different times in the evening?

Extension Work

Helen and Leila are planning to go on a walking holiday in September. They are trying to choose where to go and have the information on the right:

Choose which place you would like to go to for a walking holiday and use the diagrams to explain your choice.

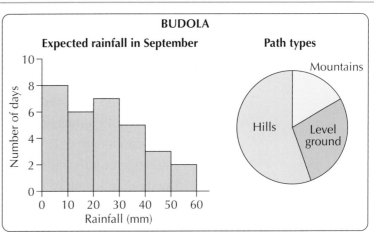

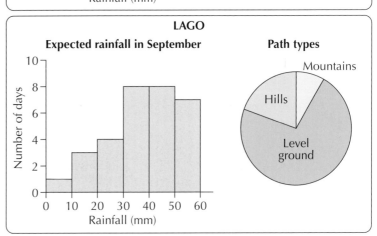

LEVEL BOOSTER

4
I can read information from simple tables.
I can read information from a range of different sorts of bar charts.

5
I can read pie charts.
I can create simple pie charts.
I can read information from real life graphs.

National Test questions

1 *2007 3–5 Paper 1*

The lengths of babies are measured at different ages. The graph shows the longest and shortest a baby boy is likely to be.

a Write down the numbers missing from the sentences below:

A baby boy is **8 weeks old**.

The **longest** he is likely to be is about ...... cm.

The **shortest** he is likely to be is about ...... cm.

b A **34 week old** baby is **72 cm** long.

Copy the graph and mark a cross on it to show this information.

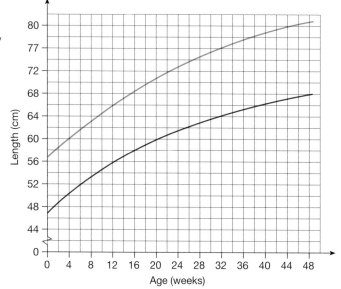

2 *2006 3–5 Paper 2*

The chart shows the average length of pregnancy for different mammals:

Use the information in the table to answer these questions:

a Which mammal has an average length of pregnancy of **1 year**?

b Which mammal has an average length of pregnancy of **50 weeks**?

c A human has an average length of pregnancy of **about 9 months**. Which other mammal also has an average length of pregnancy of about 9 months?

Mammal	Average length of pregnancy
Dolphin	276 days
Horse	337 days
Seal	350 days
Whale	365 days
Camel	406 days
Elephant	640 days

3 *2005 3–5 Paper 1*

a Jane asked **27 people**: "Do you like school dinners?"
The bar chart shows her results for 'Yes' and 'No'.

Copy the bar chart and complete it to show her results for 'Don't know'.

b This pictogram also shows her results for 'Yes' and 'No'.

Yes	◯ ◯ ◯ ◯
No	◯ ◯
Don't know	

Copy the pictogram and complete it to show her results for 'Don't know'.

4 *2006 3–5 paper 1*

Red kites are large birds that were very rare in England.

Scientists set free some red kites in 1989 and hoped that they would build nests.

The diagrams show how many nests the birds built from 1991 to 1996.

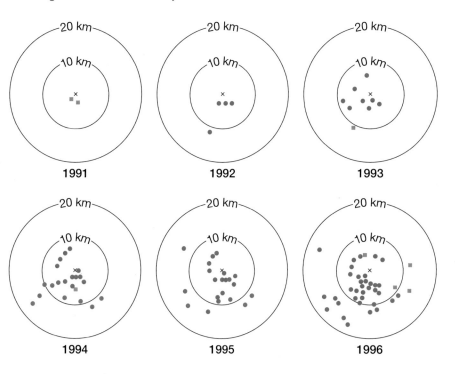

Key:

× shows where the birds were set free

■ represents a nest without eggs

● represents a nest with eggs

Use the diagrams to answer these questions:

a Which was the first year there were nests **with eggs**?

b In **1993**, how many nests were **without eggs**?

c In **1995**, how many nests were **more than 10 km** from where the birds were set free?

d Explain what happened to the **number** of nests over the years.

e Now explain what happened to the **distances** of the nests from where the birds were set free, over the years.

Wear glasses

Do not wear glasses

5 *2001 Paper 1*

There are 60 pupils in a school. 6 of these pupils wear glasses.

a The pie chart is not drawn accurately.

What should the angles be? Show your working.

b Exactly half of the 60 pupils in the school are boys.

From this information, is the percentage of boys in this school that wear glasses 5%, 6%, 10%, 20%, 50% or not possible to tell?

6 *2001 Paper 2*

A teacher asked two different classes: 'What type of book is your favourite?'

a Results from Class A (total 20 pupils) are shown on the right.

Draw a pie chart to show this information. Show your working and draw your angles accurately.

Type of book	Frequency
Crime	3
Non-fiction	13
Fantasy	4

b The pie chart on the right shows the results from all of Class B.

Each pupil had only one vote.

The sector for non-fiction represents 11 pupils.

How many pupils are in Class B? Show your working.

Class B

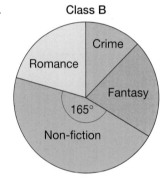

Crime

Romance

Fantasy

165°

Non-fiction

7 *2005 3–5 Paper 2*

Look at this information:

In 1976, a man earned £16.00 each week.

The pie chart shows how this man spent his money:

a How much did the man spend on **food** each week?

b Now look at this information:

In 2002, a man earned £400.00 each week.

This table shows how he spent his money:

Rent	£200
Food	£100
Entertainment	£50
Other	£50

Draw a pie chart like the one below and complete it to show how the man spent his money.

Remember to **label** each sector of the pie chart.

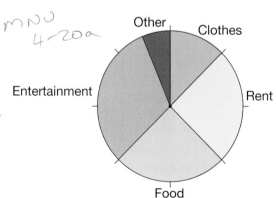

Other

Clothes

Entertainment

Rent

Food

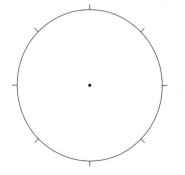

FM Football attendances

The Sheffield football teams have had various support over the years as they have moved in and out of the divisions. Below is a table comparing their attendances over the years 1989 to 2007.

Year	Sheffield Wednesday			Sheffield United		
	Level	Place	Attendance	Level	Place	Attendance
1989	1	15	20 035	3	2	12 279
1990	1	18	20 928	2	2	17 008
1991	2	3	26 196	1	13	21 609
1992	1	3	29 578	1	9	21 805
1993	1	7	27 264	1	14	18 985
1994	1	7	27 187	1	20	19 562
1995	1	13	26 596	2	8	14 408
1996	1	15	24 877	2	9	12 904
1997	1	7	25 714	2	5	16 675
1998	1	13	28 706	2	6	17 936
1999	1	12	26 745	2	8	16 258
2000	1	19	24 855	2	16	13 700
2001	2	17	19 268	2	10	17 211
2002	2	20	20 882	2	13	18 031
2003	2	21	20 327	2	3	18 073
2004	3	16	22 336	2	8	21 646
2005	3	5	23 100	2	8	19 594
2006	2	19	24 853	2	2	23 650
2007	2	9	23 638	1	18	30 512

Use the information to answer the questions.

1 Which team had:

  a the lowest average attendance and when?

  b the highest average attendance and when?

2 How many years were both Sheffield clubs playing at the same level?

3 **a** What was the highest position that each team achieved at each level?

b What was the lowest position that each team achieved at each level?

4 What is the modal level for each team?

5 What is the range of levels played at for each team?

6 What is the range of the average attendances for each club?

7 What is the median average attendance of each team?

8 For how many of the years did Sheffield United have a higher average attendance than Sheffield Wednesday?

9 Find the total of the average attendances for both Sheffield teams, for every year and make a suitable comment.

MNU
L4-20a

MTH
4-20b

<table>
<tr><td>**This chapter is going to show you**

● How to add and subtract fractions with any denominators
● How to use BODMAS with more complex problems
● How to solve problems using decimals, fractions, percentages and units of measurement</td><td>**What you should already know**

● How to add and subtract fractions with the same denominator
● How to find equivalent fractions
● How to use the four operations with decimals</td></tr>
</table>

Fractions

This section recalls some of the rules you have already met about fractions.

Example 12.1 ▷

    a   How many sevenths are in 4 whole ones?

    b   How many fifths are in $3\frac{3}{5}$?

    a   There are 7 sevenths in one whole, so there are $4 \times 7 = 28$ sevenths in 4 whole ones.

    b   There are $3 \times 5 = 15$ fifths in 3 whole ones, so there are $15 + 3 = 18$ fifths in $3\frac{3}{5}$.

Example 12.2 ▷

Write the following as mixed numbers.

    a $\frac{48}{15}$ **b** $\frac{24}{18}$

    a $48 \div 15 = 3$ remainder 3, so $\frac{48}{15} = 3\frac{3}{15}$, which cancels to $3\frac{1}{5}$.

    Note: It is usually easier to cancel after the fraction has been written as a mixed number rather than before.

    b $24 \div 18 = 1$ remainder 6, so $\frac{24}{18} = 1\frac{6}{18}$, which is $1\frac{1}{3}$ in its simplest form.

Exercise 12A

1 Find the missing number in each of these fractions.

    a $\frac{5}{3} = \frac{\square}{9}$ **b** $\frac{9}{8} = \frac{\square}{16}$ **c** $\frac{25}{9} = \frac{\square}{27}$

    d $\frac{8}{5} = \frac{\square}{15}$ **e** $\frac{12}{7} = \frac{48}{\square}$ **f** $\frac{20}{9} = \frac{80}{\square}$

    g $\frac{8}{5} = \frac{\square}{15}$ **h** $\frac{7}{2} = \frac{\square}{6}$ **i** $\frac{13}{3} = \frac{52}{\square}$

2 **a** How many sixths are in 1?   **b** How many sixths are in 3?

    c How many eighths are in 1?   **d** How many eighths are in 4?

3 **a** How many sixths are in $3\frac{5}{6}$?   **b** How many eighths are in $4\frac{1}{2}$?

    c How many tenths are in $2\frac{2}{5}$?   **d** How many ninths are in $5\frac{7}{9}$?

4 Convert each of these top-heavy fractions to a mixed number.

    a $\frac{3}{2}$ **b** $\frac{7}{5}$ **c** $\frac{9}{7}$ **d** $\frac{17}{8}$ **e** $\frac{15}{2}$ **f** $\frac{22}{7}$

    g $\frac{32}{15}$ **h** $\frac{17}{5}$ **i** $\frac{12}{5}$ **j** $\frac{13}{6}$ **k** $\frac{9}{4}$ **l** $\frac{41}{10}$

5 Convert each of these mixed numbers to a top-heavy fraction.

    a $1\frac{1}{4}$ **b** $2\frac{1}{2}$ **c** $3\frac{1}{6}$ **d** $4\frac{2}{7}$ **e** $5\frac{1}{8}$ **f** $2\frac{3}{5}$

    g $1\frac{7}{8}$ **h** $3\frac{3}{4}$ **i** $3\frac{2}{5}$ **j** $2\frac{3}{11}$ **k** $4\frac{5}{8}$ **l** $3\frac{2}{9}$

6 Write each of the following as a mixed number in its simplest form.

    a $\frac{14}{12}$ **b** $\frac{15}{9}$ **c** $\frac{24}{21}$ **d** $\frac{35}{20}$ **e** $\frac{28}{20}$ **f** $\frac{70}{50}$

    g $\frac{28}{24}$ **h** $\frac{26}{12}$ **i** $\frac{44}{24}$ **j** $\frac{32}{10}$ **k** $\frac{36}{24}$ **l** $\frac{75}{35}$

7 Write these fractions as mixed numbers. (Cancel if necessary.)

    a Seven-thirds   **b** Sixteen-sevenths   **c** Twelve-fifths   **d** Nine-halves

    e $\frac{20}{7}$ **f** $\frac{24}{5}$ **g** $\frac{13}{3}$ **h** $\frac{19}{8}$ **i** $\frac{146}{12}$ **j** $\frac{78}{10}$ **k** $\frac{52}{12}$ **l** $\frac{102}{9}$

Extension **Work**

Use this example to work through the questions below: $830 \text{ cm} = 8\frac{3}{10} \text{ m}$. $6200 \text{ g} = 6\frac{1}{5} \text{ kg}$.

1 Write the fraction of a metre given by:

    i 715 cm   **ii** 2300 mm   **iii** 405 cm   **iv** 580 cm   **v** 1550 mm   **vi** 225 cm

2 Write the fraction of a kilogram given by:

    i 2300 g   **ii** 4050 g   **iii** 7500 g   **iv** 5600 g   **v** 1225 g   **vi** 6580 g

Adding and subtracting fractions

When the denominators of two fractions are not the same, they must be made the same before the numerators are added or subtracted. To do this, we need to find the Lowest Common Multiple (LCM) of the denominators.

Example 12.3   Add:

    a $\frac{2}{5} + \frac{1}{4}$ **b** $\frac{2}{3} + \frac{2}{7}$ **c** $\frac{1}{3} + \frac{5}{6} + \frac{3}{4}$

    a The common denominator is 20, as this is the lowest common multiple of 4 and 5, hence $\frac{2}{5} + \frac{1}{4} = \frac{8}{20} + \frac{5}{20} = \frac{13}{20}$

    b The common denominator is 21, so $\frac{2}{3} + \frac{2}{7} = \frac{14}{21} + \frac{6}{21} = \frac{20}{21}$

    c The common denominator is 12, so $\frac{1}{3} + \frac{5}{6} + \frac{3}{4} = \frac{4}{12} + \frac{10}{12} + \frac{9}{12} = \frac{23}{12} = 1\frac{11}{12}$

    Note: The last answer is a top-heavy fraction, so should be written as a mixed number.

Example 12.4

Subtract:

a $\frac{2}{3} - \frac{1}{4}$ **b** $\frac{5}{6} - \frac{4}{9}$

a The common denominator is 12, so $\frac{2}{3} - \frac{1}{4} = \frac{8}{12} - \frac{3}{12} = \frac{5}{12}$

b The common denominator is 18, so $\frac{5}{6} - \frac{4}{9} = \frac{15}{18} - \frac{8}{18} = \frac{7}{18}$

Exercise 12B

1 Find the lowest common multiple of the following pairs of numbers.

a (3, 4)   **b** (5, 6)   **c** (3, 5)   **d** (2, 3)

e (4, 5)   **f** (2, 4)   **g** (6, 9)   **h** (4, 6)

2 Add the following fractions.

a $\frac{2}{3} + \frac{1}{4}$ **b** $\frac{2}{5} + \frac{1}{6}$ **c** $\frac{1}{3} + \frac{2}{5}$ **d** $\frac{1}{3} + \frac{1}{2}$

e $\frac{1}{5} + \frac{1}{4}$ **f** $\frac{1}{2} + \frac{1}{4}$ **g** $\frac{5}{6} + \frac{1}{9}$ **h** $\frac{1}{6} + \frac{1}{4}$

3 Subtract the following fractions.

a $\frac{1}{3} - \frac{1}{4}$ **b** $\frac{2}{5} - \frac{1}{6}$ **c** $\frac{2}{5} - \frac{1}{3}$ **d** $\frac{1}{2} - \frac{1}{3}$

e $\frac{2}{5} - \frac{1}{4}$ **f** $\frac{1}{2} - \frac{1}{4}$ **g** $\frac{5}{6} - \frac{1}{9}$ **h** $\frac{5}{6} - \frac{3}{4}$

4 Convert the following fractions to equivalent fractions with a common denominator, and then work out the answer, cancelling down or writing as a mixed number if appropriate:

a $\frac{1}{3} + \frac{1}{4}$ **b** $\frac{1}{6} + \frac{1}{3}$ **c** $\frac{3}{10} + \frac{1}{4}$ **d** $\frac{1}{8} + \frac{5}{6}$

e $\frac{4}{15} + \frac{3}{10}$ **f** $\frac{7}{8} + \frac{5}{6}$ **g** $\frac{7}{12} + \frac{1}{4}$ **h** $\frac{3}{4} + \frac{1}{3} + \frac{1}{2}$

i $\frac{2}{3} - \frac{1}{8}$ **j** $\frac{5}{6} - \frac{1}{3}$ **k** $\frac{3}{10} - \frac{1}{4}$ **l** $\frac{8}{9} - \frac{1}{6}$

m $\frac{4}{15} - \frac{1}{10}$ **n** $\frac{7}{8} - \frac{5}{6}$ **o** $\frac{7}{12} - \frac{1}{4}$ **p** $\frac{3}{4} + \frac{1}{3} - \frac{1}{2}$

Extension Work

The ancient Egyptians only used unit fractions, that is fractions with a numerator of 1. So they would write $\frac{5}{8}$ as $\frac{1}{2} + \frac{1}{8}$.

1 Write the following as the sum of two unit fractions.

a $\frac{3}{8}$ **b** $\frac{3}{4}$

c $\frac{7}{12}$ **d** $\frac{2}{3}$

2 Write the following as the sum of three unit fractions.

a $\frac{7}{8}$ **b** $\frac{5}{6}$

c $\frac{5}{8}$ **d** $\frac{23}{24}$

5

6

Order of operations

MTH
4-03b

B	– Brackets
O	– pOwers
DM	– Division and Multiplication
AS	– Addition and Subtraction

B	– Brackets
I	– Indices
DM	– Division and Multiplication
AS	– Addition and Subtraction

BODMAS and BIDMAS are ways of remembering the order in which mathematical operations are carried out.

Example 12.5

Work out each of the following, using the order of operations given by BODMAS. Show each step of the calculation.

a $10 - 3 \times 2$ **b** $5 \times (7 + 3) - 5$ **c** $18 \div 3 \times 2$

a Firstly, work out the multiplication, which gives: $10 - 6$

Then work out the subtraction to give: 4

b Firstly, work out the bracket, which gives: $5 \times 10 - 5$

Secondly, the multiplication, which gives: $50 - 5$

Finally, the subtraction to give: 45

c There is a choice between division and multiplication, so decide on the order by working from left to right.

Work out the left-hand operation first, which gives: 6×2

Then work out the remaining operation to give: 12

Example 12.6

Work out:

a $2 \times 3^2 + 6 \div 2$ **b** $(2 + 3)^2 \times 8 - 6$

Show each step of the calculation.

a Firstly, work out the power, which gives: $2 \times 9 + 6 \div 2$

Secondly, the division and multiplication, which gives: $18 + 3$

Finally, the addition to give: 21

b Firstly, work out the bracket, which gives: $5^2 \times 8 - 6$

Secondly, the power, which gives: $25 \times 8 - 6$

Thirdly, the multiplication, which gives: $200 - 6$

Finally, the subtraction to give: 194

Exercise 12C

1 Write the operation that you do first in each of these calculations, and then work out each calculation.

a $5 + 4 \times 7$ **b** $18 - 6 \div 3$ **c** $7 \times 7 + 2$ **d** $16 \div 4 - 2$

e $(5 + 4) \times 7$ **f** $(18 - 6) \div 3$ **g** $7 \times (7 + 2)$ **h** $16 \div (4 - 2)$

i $5 + 9 - 7 - 2$ **j** $2 \times 6 \div 3 \times 4$ **k** $12 - 15 + 7$ **l** $12 \div 3 \times 6 \div 2$

5

MTH
4-03b

2 Work out the following, showing each step of the calculation.

a $3 + 4 + 4^2$ **b** $3 + (4 + 4)^2$ **c** $3 \times 4 + 4^2$ **d** $3 \times (4 + 4)^2$

e $5 + 3^2 - 7$ **f** $(5 + 3)^2 - 7$ **g** $2 \times 6^2 + 2$ **h** $2 \times (6^2 + 2)$

i $\dfrac{200}{4 \times 5}$ **j** $\dfrac{80 + 20}{4 \times 5}$ **k** $\sqrt{(4^2 + 3^2)}$ **l** $\dfrac{(2 + 3)^2}{6 - 1}$

m $3.2 - (5.4 + 6.1) + (5.7 - 2.1)$ **n** $8 \times (12 \div 4) \div (2 \times 2)$

3 Write out each of the following and insert brackets to make the calculation true.

a $3 \times 7 + 1 = 24$ **b** $3 + 7 \times 2 = 20$ **c** $2 \times 3 + 1 \times 4 = 32$

d $2 + 3^2 = 25$ **e** $5 \times 5 + 5 \div 5 = 26$ **f** $5 \times 5 + 5 \div 5 = 10$

g $5 \times 5 + 5 \div 5 = 6$ **h** $15 - 3^2 = 144$

Extension **Work**

By putting brackets in different places, one calculation can be made to give many different answers. For example:

$$4 \times 6 + 4 - 3 \times 8 + 1 = 24 + 4 - 24 + 1 = 5$$

without brackets, but with brackets, it could be:

$$4 \times (6 + 4) - 3 \times (8 + 1) = 4 \times 10 - 3 \times 9 = 40 - 27 = 13$$

Put brackets into the appropriate places in the calculation above, to obtain answers of:

a 33 **b** 17 **c** 252 **d** 1

Multiplying decimals

This section will give you more practice on multiplying integers and decimals.

Example 12.7 Find:

a 0.2×3 **b** 0.2×0.3 **c** 40×0.8

 levels

a $2 \times 3 = 6$. There is one decimal place in the multiplication, so $0.1 \times 6 = 0.6$.

b $2 \times 3 = 6$. There are two decimal places in the multiplication, so there are two in the answer. So, $0.2 \times 0.3 = 0.06$.

c Rewrite the problem as an equivalent product, that is $40 \times 0.8 = 4 \times 8 = 32$.

Example 12.8 A sheet of card is 0.5 mm thick. How thick is a pack of card containing 80 sheets?

This is a multiplication problem:

$$0.5 \times 80 = 5 \times 8 = 40 \text{ mm}$$

See note
page 166 Book 2.

1 Without using a calculator, write down the answers to the following.

a	0.2×3	**b**	0.4×2
c	0.6×6	**d**	0.7×2
e	0.2×4	**f**	0.8×4
g	0.6×1	**h**	0.3×3
i	0.7×8	**j**	0.5×8
k	0.9×3	**l**	0.6×9

MNU 3-07a

2 Without using a calculator, write down the answers to the following.

a	0.2×0.3	**b**	0.4×0.2
c	0.6×0.6	**d**	0.7×0.2
e	0.2×0.4	**f**	0.8×0.4
g	0.6×0.1	**h**	0.3×0.3
i	0.7×0.8	**j**	0.5×0.8
k	0.9×0.3	**l**	0.6×0.9

3 Without using a calculator, work out the following.

a	30×0.8	**b**	0.6×20
c	0.6×50	**d**	0.2×60
e	0.3×40	**f**	0.4×50
g	0.7×20	**h**	0.2×90
i	0.5×80	**j**	70×0.6
k	30×0.1	**l**	80×0.6

level5

4 Without using a calculator, work out the following.

a	0.02×0.4	**b**	0.8×0.04
c	0.07×0.08	**d**	0.006×0.9
e	0.8×0.005	**f**	0.06×0.03
g	0.01×0.02	**h**	0.07×0.07

5 Without using a calculator, work out the following.

a	300×0.8	**b**	0.06×400
c	0.6×500	**d**	0.02×600
e	0.005×8000	**f**	300×0.01
g	600×0.006	**h**	0.04×8000

MNU 3-07a

FM **6** Screws cost 0.6p. A company orders 2000 screws.
How much will this cost?

7 A grain of sand weighs 0.6 milligrams.
How much would 500 grains weigh?

This extension work is about using powers with decimals.

$$0.1 \times 0.1 = 0.1^2 = 0.01$$
$$0.1 \times 0.1 \times 0.1 = 0.1^3 = 0.001$$
$$0.1 \times 0.1 \times 0.1 \times 0.1 = 0.1^4 = 0.0001$$

level 5

1 Using the calculations above, write down the answers to the following.

   a 0.1^5 **b** 0.1^6 **c** 0.1^7 **d** 0.1^{10}

2 Write down the answers to each of these.

   a 0.2^2 **b** 0.3^2 **c** 0.4^2 **d** 0.5^2

   e 0.2^3 **f** 0.3^3 **g** 0.4^3 **h** 0.5^3

Dividing decimals

This section gives more practice on dividing integers and decimals.

Example 12.9

Work out:

   a $0.8 \div 2$ **b** $0.8 \div 0.2$ **c** $20 \div 0.5$ **d** $0.16 \div 0.4$ **e** $400 \div 0.8$

level 5

   a $0.8 \div 2 = 0.4$ because $0.4 + 0.4 = 0.8$

   b Rewrite the sum as equivalent divisions, $0.8 \div 0.2 = 8 \div 2 = 4$. You must multiply both numbers by 10 at a time, to keep the calculation equivalent.

   c Rewriting this as equivalent divisions gives:
$$20 \div 0.5 = 200 \div 5 = 40$$

   d Rewriting this as equivalent divisions gives:
$$0.16 \div 0.4 = 1.6 \div 4 = 0.4$$

   e Rewriting this as equivalent divisions gives:
$$400 \div 0.8 = 4000 \div 8 = 500$$

Example 12.10

Work out the calculations below. These contain more decimal places than those you have been doing.

   a $0.8 \div 0.04$ **b** $0.04 \div 0.2$ **c** $50 \div 0.02$

In each case, rewrite as an equivalent calculation, so that the division is by a whole-number.

   a $0.8 \div 0.04 = 8 \div 0.4 = 80 \div 4 = 20$

   b $0.04 \div 0.2 = 0.4 \div 2 = 0.2$

   c $50 \div 0.02 = 500 \div 0.2 = 5000 \div 2 = 2500$

Exercise 12E

1 Without using a calculator, work out the following.

a	$0.4 \div 2$	**b**	$0.6 \div 2$
c	$0.6 \div 1$	**d**	$0.9 \div 3$
e	$0.2 \div 1$	**f**	$0.8 \div 2$
g	$0.18 \div 3$	**h**	$0.12 \div 3$

2 Without using a calculator, work out the following.

a	$0.4 \div 0.2$	**b**	$0.6 \div 0.2$
c	$0.6 \div 0.1$	**d**	$0.9 \div 0.3$
e	$0.2 \div 0.1$	**f**	$0.8 \div 0.2$
g	$0.18 \div 0.3$	**h**	$0.12 \div 0.3$
i	$0.16 \div 0.2$	**j**	$0.8 \div 0.2$
k	$0.8 \div 0.1$	**l**	$0.24 \div 0.8$
m	$0.2 \div 0.2$	**n**	$0.8 \div 0.8$
o	$0.9 \div 0.9$	**p**	$0.4 \div 0.1$

3 Without using a calculator, work out out the following.

a	$200 \div 0.4$	**b**	$300 \div 0.2$
c	$40 \div 0.8$	**d**	$200 \div 0.2$
e	$90 \div 0.3$	**f**	$40 \div 0.4$
g	$50 \div 0.1$	**h**	$400 \div 0.2$
i	$300 \div 0.5$	**j**	$400 \div 0.5$
k	$400 \div 0.1$	**l**	$200 \div 0.1$
m	$30 \div 0.5$	**n**	$50 \div 0.5$
o	$60 \div 0.5$	**p**	$400 \div 0.4$

4 Without using a calculator, work out the following.

a	$0.4 \div 0.02$	**b**	$0.06 \div 0.1$
c	$0.9 \div 0.03$	**d**	$0.2 \div 0.01$
e	$0.06 \div 0.02$	**f**	$0.09 \div 0.3$

5 Without using a calculator, work out the following.

a	$40 \div 0.08$	**b**	$200 \div 0.02$
c	$400 \div 0.05$	**d**	$200 \div 0.01$
e	$24 \div 0.02$	**f**	$4000 \div 0.02$

FM **6** Bolts cost 0.3p. How many can I buy with £60 (= 6000p)?

7 Grains of salt weigh 0.2 mg. How many grains are in a kilogram (= 1 000 000 mg) of salt?

1 Given that $46 \times 34 = 1564$, write down the answers to each of these.

    a 4.6×34 **b** 4.6×3.4

    c $1564 \div 3.4$ **d** $15.64 \div 0.034$

level 5

2 Given that $57 \times 32 = 1824$, write down the answers to each of these.

    a 5.7×0.032 **b** $0.57 \times 32\,000$

    c 5700×0.32 **d** 0.0057×32

3 Given that $2.8 \times 0.55 = 1.540$, write down the answers to each of these.

    a 28×55 **b** $154 \div 55$

    c $15.4 \div 0.028$ **d** 0.028×5500

LEVEL BOOSTER

4
I can multiply simple decimals by a whole number by using addition.
I can divide simple decimals by a whole number.

5
I can simplify fractions by cancelling common factors.
I can add and subtract simple fractions.
I know the correct order of operations, including using brackets.
I can multiply simple decimals without using a calculator.

6
I can add and subtract fractions by writing them with a common denominator.
I can multiply and divide decimals.

1 *2007 4–6 Paper 1*

Here are six number cards:

$$2 \quad 4 \quad 6 \quad 8 \quad 10 \quad 12$$

a Choose two of these six cards to make a fraction that is equivalent to $\frac{1}{3}$.

b Choose two of these six cards to make a fraction that is **greater than** $\frac{1}{2}$ but **less than** 1.

MTH 3-07b

2 *2006 4–6 Paper 1*

Write down the numbers missing from the boxes:

$$4 \times \boxed{} + 20 = 180 \qquad 4 \times 20 + \boxed{} = 180 \qquad 4 \times \boxed{} - 20 = 180$$

MTH 4-03b

3 *2004 5–7 Paper 1*

Look at this diagram:

The diagram can help you work out some fraction calculations.

Calculate:

$$\frac{1}{12} + \frac{1}{4} =$$

$$\frac{1}{3} + \frac{1}{4} =$$

$$\frac{1}{3} - \frac{1}{6} =$$

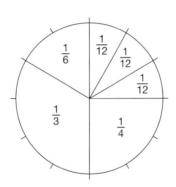

MTH 3-07b

4 *2005 5–7 Paper 2*

Use your calculator to work out the answers to:

$$(48 + 57) \times (61 - 19) =$$

$$\frac{48 + 57}{61 - 19} =$$

MTH 4-03b.

5 *2005 5–7 Paper 1*

How many eighths are there in one quarter?

Now work out $\frac{3}{4} + \frac{1}{8}$.

MTH 3-07b

6 *2007 5–7 Paper 1*

Write down the numbers missing from these fraction sums:

$$\frac{1}{4} + \frac{\boxed{}}{8} = 1 \qquad \frac{1}{3} + \frac{8}{\boxed{}} = 1$$

Shopping for bargains

The more you buy, the more you save

Collect 15 points for every litre
When you have 5000 points you receive a £5 voucher to spend in store

**Petrol £1.20 per litre
Diesel £1.30 per litre**

1

a How many litres would you need to buy to collect a voucher?

b Petrol is £1.20 a litre.

How much would you spend on petrol before you receive a voucher?

c Estimate the number of weeks it would take to receive a voucher if you use an average of 30 litres of petrol each week.

2 Nina uses an average of 40 litres of diesel each week. Diesel is £1.30 per litre.

a How much does she spend on diesel each week?

b Her car uses 1 litre of diesel for every 14 miles travelled. If Nina drives 140 fewer miles each week, how much will she save each week?

c If the price of diesel goes up by 10p a litre, how much more would she spend on diesel in a year (52 weeks)?

3 Here is some information about three business people and their company cars.

	Car fuel	Annual distance travelled (km)	CO_2 emissions (grams per km)
Managing director	Diesel	14 000	140
Secretary	Petrol	8 000	200
Delivery driver	Diesel	22 000	110

The company wants to encourage each person to reduce the CO_2 emissions.

a Work out the annual amount of CO_2 emissions for each car.
Give your answer in kilograms.

b The company wants each person to reduce the CO_2 emissions by reducing each person's travelling by 10%.
Work out the reduction in CO_2 emissions for each car.
Give your answer in kilograms.

Chocolate
Only £1 Was £1.19

Mint sauce
3 for £2 Normally 85p each

Almost Butter
Buy one get one free £1.38

Milk
2 for £2 or £1.25 each

Cheese
Save £1 was £3.25

Scotch eggs
Were £1.15 Save 20% Now 92p

Grillsteaks
520g Half price
Was £2.99 Now £1.49

Baby shampoo
Save $\frac{1}{3}$ Was £2.47 Now £1.64

Luxury Crisps
2 for £2.50 £1.49 each

Yoghurts
48p each Buy 3 get 3 free

Bread 95p

Coffee £3.90

Baked beans 45p

Orange juice £1.30

5 Matt decides to take up all the offers shown.

  a How much will he save on each offer compared with the full price?

  b How much will he save altogether?

4 You have £20 to spend but you have to buy, bread, coffee, baked beans and orange juice.

  a How much do these four items cost altogether?

  b How much does this leave you to spend on other items?

  c Using the offers, make two different shopping lists of items you could now afford to buy. Try to spend as close to £20 altogether as possible. (*Hint:* You can buy single items but then you would not get the offer price.)

6 The shopping can be ordered on the Internet and delivered to your home.

The delivery charge is £4.50.

The journey to the supermarket and back is 8 miles altogether.

It costs 60p per mile to run your car.

Explain the advantages and disadvantages of having the shopping delivered.

CHAPTER 13 Algebra 5

This chapter is going to show you

- How to expand and then simplify expressions
- How to solve a range of linear equations
- How to construct equations and solve them
- How to change the subject of a formula

What you should already know

- The arithmetic of negative numbers

Expansion of brackets

In algebra, brackets occur often. They may form part of all kinds of expressions and equations – from the simplest to the most complicated.

Expansion means removing the brackets from an expression or equation by multiplying each term inside the brackets by the term outside the brackets. Look at Example 13.1 to see how this works with numbers.

Example 13.1

Expand and simplify $3(5 + 2)$.

Multiply each term in the brackets by 3: $3 \times 5 + 3 \times 2$

$= 15 + 6 = 21$

Check by working out the bracket first: $3(5 + 2) = 3 \times 7 = 21$

The same rule can be applied to algebraic terms, as Example 13.2 shows.

Example 13.2

Expand each of these.

a $2(4 + 3y)$ **b** $3(5p - 2)$

a Multiply each term in the brackets by 2: $2(4 + 3y)$

$= 2 \times 4 + 2 \times 3y$

$= 8 + 6y$

b Multiply each term in the brackets by 3: $3(5p - 2)$

$= 3 \times 5p + 3 \times (-2)$

$= 15p + -6$

$= 15p - 6$

Note: Neither $8 + 6y$ nor $15p - 6$ can be simplified because 8 and $6y$ are not like terms and neither are $15p$ and 6.

H-14a

1. Copy and complete each of the following.

   a $2(4 + 5)$ $= 2 \times 9 =$ ☐

   $2 \times 4 + 2 \times 5 = 8 +$ ☐ $=$ ☐

   $2(4 + 5)$ $= 2 \times 4 + 2 \times 5$

   b $3(2 + 7)$ $= 3 \times$ ☐ $=$ ☐

   $3 \times 2 + 3 \times 7 =$ ☐ $+$ ☐ $=$ ☐

   $3(2 + 7)$ $=$ ☐ $\times$ ☐ $+$ ☐ $\times$ ☐

   c $5(4 + 3)$ $=$ ☐ $\times$ ☐ $=$ ☐

   $5 \times$ ☐ $+ 5 \times$ ☐ $=$ ☐ $+$ ☐ $=$ ☐

   $5(4 + 3)$ $=$ ☐ $\times$ ☐ $+$ ☐ $\times$ ☐

   d $4(5 + 2)$ $=$ ☐ $\times$ ☐ $=$ ☐

   ☐ $\times$ ☐ $+$ ☐ $\times$ ☐ $=$ ☐ $+$ ☐ $=$ ☐

   $4(5 + 2)$ $=$ ☐ $\times$ ☐ $+$ ☐ $\times$ ☐

2. Copy and complete each of the following.

   a $3(2 + t)$ $= 3 \times 2 + 3 \times t =$ ☐ $+$ ☐

   b $5(m + 4) = 5 \times m + 5 \times 4 =$ ☐ $+$ ☐

   c $4(3 - k)$ $= 4 \times 3 + 4 \times (-k) =$ ☐ $-$ ☐

   d $2(w - 4) = 2 \times w + 2 \times (-4) =$ ☐ $-$ ☐

   e $3(4 + k)$ $= 3 \times$ ☐ $+$ ☐ $\times$ ☐ $=$ ☐ $+$ ☐

   f $5(q + 2)$ $=$ ☐ $\times$ ☐ $+ 5 \times$ ☐ $=$ ☐ $+$ ☐

   g $4(5 - t)$ $=$ ☐ $\times$ ☐ $+$ ☐ $\times$ ☐ $=$ ☐ $-$ ☐

   h $2(n - 3)$ $=$ ☐ $\times$ ☐ $+$ ☐ $\times$ ☐ $=$ ☐ $-$ ☐

3. Expand each of the following.

   a $3(4 + k)$ b $5(m + 7)$ c $4(3 + t)$ d $2(5 - n)$ e $3(w - 2)$

   f $6(h - 2)$ g $5(3 + g)$ h $2(f - 7)$ i $3(1 - q)$

4. Copy and complete each of the following.

   a $3(2m + 4) = 3 \times 2m + 3 \times 4 = 6m +$ ☐

   b $5(3 + 2t)$ $= 5 \times 3 + 5 \times 2t =$ ☐ $+$ ☐

   c $4(3w - 2)$ $= 4 \times$ ☐ $+ 4 \times$ ☐ $=$ ☐ $-$ ☐

   d $2(5 + 4k)$ $= 2 \times$ ☐ $+ 2 \times$ ☐ $=$ ☐ $+$ ☐

   e $3(5d + 2)$ $=$ ☐ $\times$ ☐ $+$ ☐ $\times$ ☐ $=$ ☐ $+$ ☐

   f $5(4 - 3q)$ $=$ ☐ $\times$ ☐ $+$ ☐ $\times$ ☐ $=$ ☐ $-$ ☐

   g $4(2n + 7)$ $=$ ☐ $\times$ ☐ $+$ ☐ $\times$ ☐ $=$ ☐ $+$ ☐

5 Expand each of the following.

a $3(2a + 3)$ **b** $2(4 - 3k)$ **c** $5(1 + 3p)$

d $4(2q - 3)$ **e** $3(4 + 2t)$ **f** $7(4 + 3m)$

g $2(5y - 3)$ **h** $4(3 - 2n)$ **i** $5(2m + 4)$

j $3(3p - 2)$ **k** $6(5 + 3y)$ **l** $2(3k - 4)$

Extension **Work**

In a magic square, each row, each column and each diagonal add up to the same amount.

1 Show that the square below is a magic square.

2 Using different values for x, y and m, see how many magic squares you can create.

$x + m$	$x + y - m$	$x - y$
$x - y - m$	x	$x + y + m$
$x + y$	$x - y + m$	$x - m$

Solving equations

You have met several different types of linear equations so far. They were solved by finding the inverse mapping of each equation.

Example 13.3 ▷ Solve each of these equations.

a $3x = 15$ **b** $n + 7 = 15$ **c** $4t - 3 = 17$

a $3x = 15$ gives:

$$x \longrightarrow \boxed{\times 3} \longrightarrow 15$$
$$5 \longleftarrow \boxed{\div 3} \longleftarrow 15$$

So, $x = 5$

b $n + 7 = 15$ gives:

$$n \longrightarrow \boxed{+ 7} \longrightarrow 15$$
$$8 \longleftarrow \boxed{- 7} \longleftarrow 15$$

So, $n = 8$

c $4t - 3 = 17$ gives:

$$t \longrightarrow \boxed{\times 4} \longrightarrow \boxed{- 3} \longrightarrow 17$$
$$5 \longleftarrow \boxed{\div 4} \longleftarrow \boxed{+ 3} \longleftarrow 17$$

So, $t = 5$

When an equation has brackets in it, three operations are needed to solve the equation. Look at example 13.4 to see how this works.

Example 13.4 ▶ Solve $3(2x + 4) = 30$.

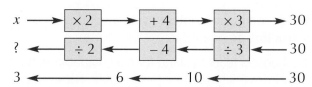

So, $x = 3$

Exercise 13B

1 Solve each of the following equations.

a	$4x = 12$	**b**	$5x = 30$	**c**	$2m = 14$
d	$3n = 15$	**e**	$2x = 7$	**f**	$2x = 11$
g	$x + 7 = 8$	**h**	$x + 3 = 18$	**i**	$x + 5 = 23$
j	$x - 3 = 11$	**k**	$x - 4 = 17$	**l**	$x + 3 = 19$

2 Solve each of the following equations.

a	$4n + 1 = 21$	**b**	$5n + 3 = 18$	**c**	$3m + 4 = 19$
d	$7x + 2 = 23$	**e**	$2x - 1 = 11$	**f**	$4m - 3 = 17$
g	$5x + 3 = 33$	**h**	$2n - 7 = 15$	**i**	$2k - 5 = 3$
j	$10x + 7 = 47$	**k**	$5x - 3 = 22$	**l**	$4n + 17 = 25$

3 Solve each of the following equations.

a	$3(2t + 5) = 33$	**b**	$2(5m + 3) = 36$	**c**	$5(2m + 1) = 45$
d	$4(3k + 2) = 56$	**e**	$2(2t - 3) = 18$	**f**	$4(3x - 2) = 28$

4 Ewan's dad helped him with his homework, but he got most of it wrong. In each case, explain what is wrong and then correct it.

> **a** $5x + 3 = 13$
> $x = 13 - 5$
> $x = 8$
>
> **b** $3m - 4 = 11$
> $m = 11 + 4 - 3$
> $m = 12$
>
> **c** $2(3x + 4) = 38$
> $x = 38 \div 2 - 4 - 3$
> $x = 12$
>
> **d** $4(5m + 3) = 28$
> $m = 28 \div 4 - 3 + 5$
> $m = 9$

Extension Work

Solve each of the following equations.

a	$1.5x + 3.6 = 5.4$	**b**	$2.4x + 7.1 = 13.1$	**c**	$3.4m - 4.3 = 7.6$
d	$5.6k - 2.9 = 5.5$	**e**	$4.5n - 3.7 = 12.5$	**f**	$1.8t + 7.1 = 18.8$
g	$28 - 3.6x = 11.8$	**h**	$31.3 - 2.8x = 27.1$	**i**	$2.4 - 1.8m = 8.7$

Constructing equations to solve problems

The first step in solving a problem using algebra is to write down an equation. This is called **constructing** an equation.

You need to choose a letter to stand for each variable in the problem. This might be x or the first letter of words which describe the variable. For example, t is often used to stand for time.

Example 13.5

I think of a number, multiply it by 5 and add 7 to the result. I get the answer 22. What is the number I first thought of?

Let my number be x.

Multiplying it by 5 gives: $5x$

Adding 7 to $5x$ gives: $5x + 7$

The answer has to be 22, so form the equation: $5x + 7 = 22$

Now solve the equation using inverse mapping:

$$5x + 7 = 22$$

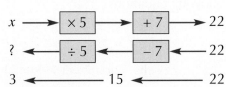

So my number is 3.

Exercise 13C

1. Write down an algebraic expression for each of the following.
    a   The number which is 5 more than x.
    b   The number which is 4 less than x.
    c   The number which is 17 more than m.
    d   The number which is 11 less than n.
    e   The number which is 3 times as large as q.
    f   The number which is twice the size of m.

2. a   Two numbers add up to 100. If one of the numbers is x, write an expression for the other.
    b   The difference between two numbers is 8. If the smaller of the two numbers is y, write an expression for the larger number.
    c   Jim and Ann have 18 marbles between them. If Jim has p marbles, how many marbles does Ann have? Write an expression for this.

③ James thinks of a number rule:

Double the number and add 3.

   a   Using *n* for the number, write James's rule as an algebraic expression.

   b   James replies '17' when Helen gives him a number. Write down the equation this gives and solve it.

   c   James replies '25' when Kirstie gives him a number. Write down the equation this gives and solve it.

④ Billy pays £5 for four cups of tea, which includes a tip of £1. Using *c* for the price of a cup of tea, write down the equation this gives and solve it.

⑤ A rectangle has a perimeter of 24. The length is twice as long as the width, *w*.

   a   Write an expression for the length *x* in terms of *w*.

   b   Write an equation from the information given about the perimeter of this rectangle.

   c   Solve this equation to find the length and width of the rectangle.

Extension **Work**

1   The sum of two consecutive even numbers is 54. The smallest number is *n*.

   a   What is the larger number?

   b   Write down and simplify an equation to represent the above information.

   c   Solve your equation to find the value of *n*.

2   The sum of two consecutive odd numbers is 208. The smallest number is *n*.

   a   What is the larger number?

   b   Write down and simplify an equation to represent the above information.

   c   Solve your equation to find the value of *n*.

3   John and his brother together weigh 185 kg. John weighs *x* kg. His brother weighs 3 kg less than John.

   a   Write down John's brothers weight in terms of *x*.

   b   Write down and simplify an equation to represent the above information.

   c   Solve your equation to find the value of *x*.

4   The sum of Joy and Mary's ages is 70. Joy is *y* years old. Mary is four times as old as Joy.

   a   Write down Mary's age in terms of *y*.

   b   Write down and simplify an equation to represent the above information.

   c   Solve your equation to find the value of *y*.

Lines and equations

Look at the diagram on the right.

The coordinates on the dashed line are:

(0, 4) (1, 4) (2, 4) (3, 4) (4, 4) (5, 4) (6, 4)

Notice that the second number, the y-coordinate, is 4 every time.

Therefore, the dashed line is said to have the equation:

$y = 4$

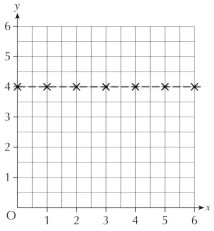

Now look at the next diagram on the right.

The coordinates shown in this dashed line are:

(2, 0) (2, 1) (2, 2) (2, 3) (2, 4) (2, 5) (2, 6)

Notice that the first number, the x-coordinate, is 2 every time.

Therefore, the dashed line is said to have the equation:

$x = 2$

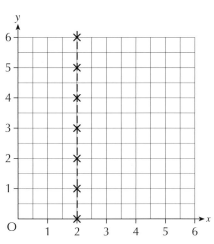

Exercise 13D

① Look at each diagram. Write out the coordinates shown on each dashed line and state its equation.

a

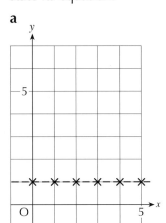

b

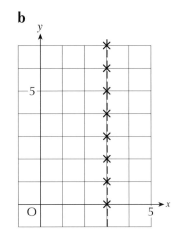

c

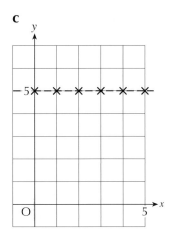

② Draw simple diagrams to show the straight lines with the following equations.

    a $y = 2$ **b** $x = 3$ **c** $y = 3$

    d $x = 1$ **e** $x = 6$ **f** $y + 5$

3 Draw a grid with each axis from 0 to 5.

   i Draw each pair of lines given below on the grid.

   ii Write down the coordinates of the point where each pair of lines cross.

     a $x = 1$ and $y = 3$ **b** $x = 2$ and $y = 4$ **c** $x = 5$ and $y = 1$

     d What do you notice about the crossing coordinates for each pair of lines?

     e Work out the coordinates of the point where the following lines cross:
       $x = 17$ and $y = 28$

4 Look at each diagram.

a 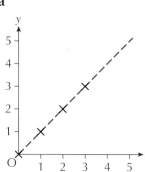   **b** 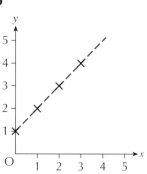   **c**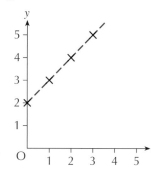

d 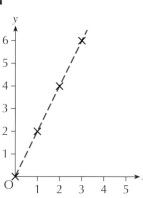   **e** 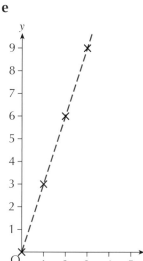   **f**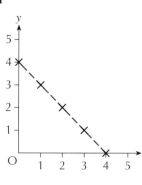

   i Write down the coordinates of each of the points marked on the dashed lines.

   ii Do you notice anything special about the numbers?

   iii In each case, try to write the rule that converts y to x.

Extension Work

1 Write down at least four coordinates (x, y) that fit the rule $y = 2x + 1$.

2 Draw a suitable grid, plot these points and draw the straight line that joins the points.

3 Repeat the above to draw lines with the following equations.

    a $y = 2x + 3$ **b** $y = 2x + 5$ **c** $y = 2x + 4$

6

Real-life graphs

Graphs are used to show a relationship that exists between two variables.

Example 13.6 ▷ Draw a sketch graph to illustrate that a hot cup of tea will take about 20 minutes to get cold.

The graph is shown below. The two axes are labelled Temperature and Time, with time on the horizontal axis and graduated in minutes.

The temperature starts at *hot* at 0 minutes, and is at *cold* after 20 minutes.

Note: The graph has a negative gradient. That is, it slopes downwards from left to right.

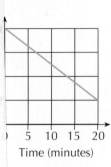

Time (minutes)

Handwritten annotations: MTH 4-21a; see ex 13.7 in Bk 2-7 same content is coded; L3 ex 13.8 in (and Bk 3)

Exercise 13E

① Match the four graphs shown here to the following situations.

a The amount of petrol in a car tank on a long journey which is filled up at the end of the journey.

b The cost of electricity against the amount of electricity used.

c The temperature on a sunny day as the Sun comes up, stays out all day then goes down at night.

d The amount of water in a bucket with a small leak.

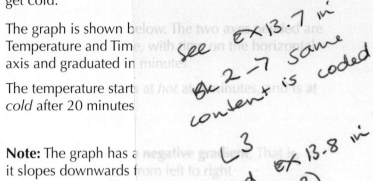

Graph 1   Graph 2

Graph 3   Graph 4

Handwritten annotation: MNU 4-20a

② The graph shows a car park's charges.

a How much are the charges for each of these stays?
  i 30 minutes
  ii Less than 1 hour
  iii 2 hours
  iv 2 hours 59 minutes
  v 3 hours 30 minutes
  vi 6 hours

b For how long can a person park for each of these amounts?
  i £1   **ii** £2   **iii** £5

c This type graph is called a step graph. Explain why it is given this name.

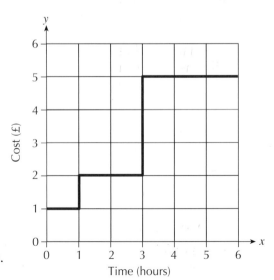

FM ③ A country's parcel post costs are given in the table shown.

MTH
4-21a

Draw a step graph to show charges against weight.

Weight	Cost
0 grams to 500 grams	£1.00
Above 500 grams and up to 1 kg	£2.50
Above 1 kg and up to 2 kg	£3.00
Above 2 kg and up to 3 kg	£4.50
Above 3 kg and up to 5 kg	£7.00

④ Match the four graphs shown here to the following situations.

MNU
4-20a

a The amount John gets paid against the number of hours he works.

b The temperature of an oven against the time it is switched on.

c The amount of tea in a cup as it is drunk.

d The cost of posting a letter compared to the weight.

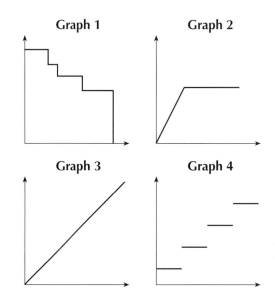

Graph 1   Graph 2

Graph 3   Graph 4

Extension Work

1 Harry decides to take a bath.
The graph shows the depth of water in the bath.

MNU 4-20a

Match each section of the graph to the events below.
i The bath gets topped up with hot water.
ii Harry lays back for a soak.
iii Harry gets in the bath.
iv The hot and cold taps are turned on.
v The cold tap is turned off and only the hot tap is left on.
vi Harry washes himself.
vii The plug is pulled and the bath empties.
viii Harry gets out of the bath.
ix The hot tap is turned off and Harry gets ready to dip in.

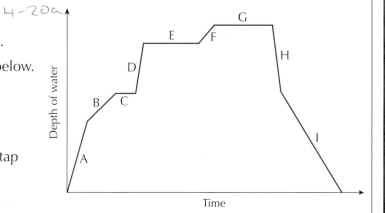

2 Draw graphs to show these other bath stories.

a Jade turns the taps on, then starts talking to her friend on the phone. The bath overflows. Jade rushes back in and pulls the plug.

MTH
4-21a

b Jane decides to wash her dog. She fills the bath with a few inches of water then puts the dog in. The dog jumps around and whilst being washed splashes most of the water out of the bath. Jane pulls the plug and the small amount of water left empties out.

c Jake fills the bath then gets in. Then the phone rings and Jake gets out dripping a lot of water on the floor. He gets back in the bath, finishes his bath, gets out and pulls the plug.

4 I can simplify algebraic expressions by collecting like terms, for example $3a + 5m + 2a - 3m = 5a + 2m$.

I can solve simple equations of the form $4x = 32$.

5 I can solve equations of the form $6 = \frac{21}{x}$.

I can solve equations of the type $3x + 7 = 10$, for example, where the solution may be fractional or negative.

I can expand brackets such as $4(2a - 1) = 8a - 4$.

I can use algebra to represent a practical situation.

I can recognise and draw lines of the form $y = 2$ and $x = 3$.

6 I can solve equations of the type $2(3x - 8) = 14$, for example, where the solution may be fractional or negative.

I can solve equations of the type $4x + 9 = 3 + x$, for example, where the solution may be fractional or negative.

I can use algebra to set up an equation to represent a practical situation.

I can draw and interpret graphs that describe real-life situations.

National Test questions

1 *2000 Paper 2*

Joanne is cooking dinner. Her rule for working out how much rice to cook is:

Number of spoonfuls of rice = Double the number of people and then add one

MTH 3-13a

For example: For three people she cooks seven spoonfuls of rice

Write Joanne's rule as a formula. Use S for the number of spoonfuls of rice and P for the number of people.

2 *1999 Paper 1*

The diagram shows a rectangle $(n + 3)$ cm long and $(n + 2)$ cm wide. It has been split into four smaller rectangles.

Copy the diagram and write a number or an expression for the area of each small rectangle.

One has been done for you:

MTH 3-14a

	n cm	3 cm
n cm	.... cm²	$3n$ cm²
2 cm	.... cm²	.... cm²

3 *2005 4–6 Paper 1*

Solve these equations:

$$3y + 1 = 16$$

$$18 = 4k + 6$$

MTH 3-15a.

FM Train timetable

Use the timetable to answer the questions.

Sheffield - Barnsley - Huddersfield/Leeds

Mondays to Fridays

									G													
Sheffield	0516	0536	0550	0614	0636	0649	0704	0725	0736	0751	0808	0836	0851	0908	0936	0951	1008	1036	1051	1108	1136	1151
Meadowhall	0522	0542	0556	0620	0642	0655	0710	0731	0742	0757	0814	0842	0857	0914	0942	0957	1014	1042	1057	1114	1142	1157
Chapeltown	0528	0548	—	0626	0648	—	0716	—	0748	—	0820	0848	—	0920	0948	—	1020	1048	—	1120	1148	—
Elsecar	0533	—	—	0631	—	—	0721	—	—	—	0825	—	—	0925	—	—	1025	—	—	1125	—	—
Wombwell	0537	0555	—	0635	0655	—	0725	—	0755	—	0829	0855	—	0929	0955	—	1029	1055	—	1129	1155	—
Barnsley	0542	0601	0611	0641	0701	0710	0731	0748	0801	0812	0835	0901	0912k	0935	1001	1012	1035	1101	1112	1135	1201	1212
Dodworth	—	0607	—	—	0707	—	—	—	0807	—	—	0907	—	—	1007	—	—	1107	—	—	1207	—
Silkstone Common	—	0611	—	—	0711	—	—	—	0811	—	—	0911	—	—	1011	—	—	1111	—	—	1211	—
Penistone	—	0618	—	—	0718	—	—	—	0825n	—	—	0918	—	—	1018	—	—	1118	—	—	1218	—
Denby Dale	—	0625	—	—	0724	—	—	—	0831	—	—	0924	—	—	1024	—	—	1124	—	—	1224	—
Shepley	—	0630	—	—	0729	—	—	—	0836	—	—	0929	—	—	1029	—	—	1129	—	—	1229	—
Stocksmoor	—	0632	—	—	0732	—	—	—	0839	—	—	0932	—	—	1032	—	—	1132	—	—	1232	—
Brockholes	—	06360	—	—	0736	—	—	—	0843	—	—	0936	—	—	1036	—	—	1136	—	—	1236	—
Honley	—	639	—	—	0738	—	—	—	0845	—	—	0938	—	—	1038	—	—	1138	—	—	1238	—
Berry Brow	—	0642	—	—	0741	—	—	—	0848	—	—	0941	—	—	1041	—	—	1141	—	—	1241	—
Lockwood	—	0644	—	—	0744	—	—	—	0851	—	—	0944	—	—	1044	—	—	1144	—	—	1244	—
Huddersfield	—	0650	—	—	0749	—	—	—	0856	—	—	0949	—	—	1049	—	—	1149	—	—	1249	—
Darton	—	—	—	0646	—	—	0736	—	—	—	0840	—	—	0940	—	—	1040	—	—	1140	—	—
Wakefield Kirkgate	—	—	0629	0658	—	0729	0747	—	—	0829	0852	—	0929	0952	—	1029	1052	—	1129	1152	—	1229
Normanton	—	—	0633	0702	—	0733	0752	—	—	—	0856	—	—	0956	—	—	1056	—	—	1156	—	—
Castleford	—	—	—	0710	—	—	0800	—	—	—	0904	—	—	1004	—	—	1104	—	—	1204	—	—
Woodlesford	—	—	—	0719	—	—	0809	—	—	—	0913	—	—	1013	—	—	1113	—	—	1213	—	—
Leeds	—	—	0650	0733	—	0750	0823	—	—	0851	0927	—	0950	1027	—	1050	1127	—	1150	1227	—	1250

Notes: **G** Through train from Retford   **k** Arrives 7 minutes earlier   **n** Arrives 1818

1 How long does the 0536 from Sheffield take to get to Huddersfield?

2 How long does the 1008 from Sheffield take to get to Leeds?

3 How long does the 0635 from Wombwell take to get to Normanton?

4 What is the last station before Huddersfield?

5 If you arrive at Sheffield station at 0730, how long will you have to wait for the next train to Leeds?

MNU – 4-20a

6 Only two trains a day from Sheffield in the morning do not go any further than Barnsley. What times do these trains leave Sheffield?

7
  a The first 'fast' train to Leeds leaves Sheffield at 0550. How many stations, except Sheffield and Leeds, does it stop at?

  b How long does the train take to get from Sheffield to Wakefield Kirkgate?

  c How many stations does a 'slow' train from Sheffield to Leeds stop at, except at Sheffield and Leeds?

8 Ken lives in Penistone. He wants to catch the 0718 to Huddersfield. It takes him 15 minutes to walk to the station. On the way he buys a paper which can take up to 2 minutes. He likes to be at the station at least 5 minutes early. What time should he leave home?

9 What is special about the 0751 fast train to Leeds from Sheffield?

10 If you arrive at Sheffield station at half past eight in the morning, how long do you have to wait before you can catch a train to Elsecar?

11 Frank, who lives in Barnsley, has an interview in Leeds at 11 am. The hotel where the interview is being held is 5 minutes' walk from the station. What is the time of the latest train that Frank can catch from Barnsley?

12 Mary, who lives in Wombwell, is meeting her friend for coffee in Huddersfield at 10 am. The café is 10 minutes from the station. What time train should Mary catch to get to Huddersfield in time?

13 Ahmed lives in Elsecar and has to get to Huddersfield to catch a train that leaves Huddersfield at 0757. Which train should he catch from Elsecar?

14 What time does the 0851 from Sheffield arrive at Barnsley station?

15 How long does the 0736 from Sheffield take to get to Penistone?

CHAPTER 14 Solving problems

This chapter is going to show you

- How to investigate problems involving numbers and measures
- How to identify important information in a question
- How to interpret information from tables
- How to use examples to prove a statement is true or false
- How to use proportion or ratio

What you should already know

- When to use symbols or words to describe a problem
- When to use tables, diagrams and graphs
- How to break down a calculation into simpler steps
- How to find examples to match a statement

Number and measures

A leaflet has 12 pages. The pages have stories, adverts or both on them. Half of the pages have both. The number of pages which have adverts only is twice the number of pages which have stories only. How many pages have stories only?

Example 14.1 ▶ Use the digits 1, 2 and 3 and the multiplication sign × once only to make the largest possible answer.

Write down different examples:

$1 \times 32 = 32$	$1 \times 23 = 23$
$2 \times 31 = 62$	$2 \times 13 = 13$
$3 \times 21 = 63$	$3 \times 12 = 12$

The largest possible answer is $3 \times 21 = 63$.

1 Two consecutive numbers add up to 13. What are the numbers?

2 Two consecutive numbers add up to 29. What are the numbers?

3 Two consecutive numbers add up to 37. What are the numbers?

4 Two consecutive numbers multiply together to give 30. What are the numbers?

5 Two consecutive numbers multiply together to give 90. What are the numbers?

6 Two consecutive numbers multiply together to give 56. What are the numbers?

7 **a** Copy and complete the table.

Powers of 3	Working out	Answer	Units digit
3^1	3	3	3
3^2	3×3	9	9
3^3	$3 \times 3 \times 3$	27	7
3^4	$3 \times 3 \times 3 \times 3$	81	1
3^5	$3 \times 3 \times 3 \times 3 \times 3$	243	
3^6			
3^7			
3^8			

b What is the units digit of 3^{12}?

8 **a** Use your calculator to find two consecutive odd numbers which multiplied together give an answer of 143.

b Use the digits 1, 3 and 4 and the multiplication sign $\times$ once only to make the largest possible answer.

9 Here is a magic square. Each row, column and diagonal adds up to 15.

8	1	6
3	5	7
4	9	2

Complete these magic squares so that each row, column and diagonal adds up to 15.

4		8
	7	

2		4
	7	

6		7
	6	

10 A map has a scale of 1 cm to 3 km. The road between two towns is 5 cm on the map. Calculate the actual distance between the two towns.

11 Which is the greater mass, 3 kg or 7 pounds (lb)? Use the conversion 1 kg $\approx$ 2.2 lb.

12 Which is the greater length, 10 miles or 15 kilometres? Use conversion 5 miles $\approx$ 8 kilometres.

OMIT

Extension Work

Make up a recipe in imperial units. For example: 6 ounces of flour, 2 pints of water, etc. Use metric conversions and rewrite the recipe in metric units. If you need to find out the conversions, use a textbook or the Internet.

Using words and diagrams to solve problems

There are three chickens A, B and C. A and B have a total mass of 5 kg. A and C have a total mass of 6 kg. B and C have a total mass of 7 kg. What is the mass of each chicken?

Example 14.2 ▷ A gardener charges £8 per hour. Write down a formula, in words, for the total charge when the gardener is hired for several hours. Work out the cost of hiring the gardener for 6 hours.

The formula is:

The charge is equal to the number of hours worked multiplied by eight pounds

If the gardener is hired for 6 hours, the charge $= 6 \times £8$
$$= £48$$

So, the charge is £48.

Example 14.3 ▷ I think of a number, add 3 and then double it. The answer is 16. What is the number?

Working this flowchart backwards gives:

The answer is 5.

Exercise 14B

1 I think of a number, double it and add 1. The answer is 19.

Work the flow diagram backwards to find the number.

2 I think of a number, multiply it by 3 and subtract 5. The answer is 25.

a Copy and complete the flow diagram.
b Work backwards to find the number.

3 I think of a number, divide it by 2 and add 5. The answer is 11.

a Copy and complete the flow diagram.
b Work backwards to find the number.

4 I think of a number, multiply by 2 and add 7. The answer is 15.

Work backwards to find the number.

5 I think of a number, divide it by 3 and subtract 2. The answer is 5.

Work backwards to find the number.

6 A man and his suitcase weigh 84 kg. The suitcase weighs 12 kg. What is the weight of the man?

7 Two numbers add up to 43. One of the numbers is 19. What is the other number?

FM **8** **a** A tool hire company charges £8 per day to hire a tool. Write down a formula, in words, for the total charge when a tool is hired for a number of days.

b Work out the cost for 10 days.

c A different company uses a table to work out their charges.

1 day	2 to 3 days	4 to 5 days	More than 5 days
£12	£10 per day	£8 per day	£7.50 per day

Use the table to work out the total cost of hiring a tool from this company for:
i 3 days. **ii** 5 days. **iii** 8 days.

9

a Draw the next pattern in the sequence.
b How many squares will the fifth pattern have?
c Write down a rule to work out the number of squares in the next pattern.

Extension **Work**

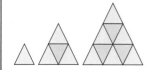

Equilateral triangles are pieced together to make a pattern of triangles as shown. The first diagram has only one small triangle. How many small triangles are in the next two diagrams? Extend the pattern and work out a rule for the number of small triangles in the next pattern.

Logical solutions and best value

Look at the recipe. This is for four people. How much of each ingredient is needed to make a chocolate cake for eight people?

Chocolate cake
500g flour
100g sugar
35g cocoa powder
60g butter

Example 14.4 ▷ Give an example to show that any even number multiplied by any other even number always gives an even number.

Two examples are:
$$2 \times 4 = 8 \qquad 10 \times 6 = 60$$

Both 8 and 60 are even numbers.

Example 14.5 ▷ Take any three consecutive numbers. Add the first number to the third number and divide the answer by 2. What do you notice?

Take, for example, 1, 2, 3 and 7, 8, 9. These give:
$$1 + 3 = 4 \qquad 7 + 9 = 16$$
$$4 \div 2 = 2 \qquad 16 \div 2 = 8$$

Whichever three consecutive numbers you choose, you should always get the middle number.

Exercise 14C

1. Copy and complete each of the following number problems, filling in the missing digits.

   a
   ```
      3 □
   +  □ 7
   ───────
      4 9
   ```

   b
   ```
      4 □
   +  □ 3
   ───────
      7 6
   ```

   c
   ```
      1 3 □
   +    □ 7
   ─────────
      □ 4 9
   ```

   d
   ```
      8 □
   −  □ 2
   ───────
      4 5
   ```

   e
   ```
      2 3 8
   − □ □ □
   ─────────
      1 1 7
   ```

   f
   ```
      □ 3 5
   ×      4
   ─────────
      5 □ □
   ```

2. Write down an example to show that when you add two odd numbers, the answer is always an even number.

3. Write down an example to show that when you add two even numbers, the answer is always an even number.

4. Write down an example to show that when you add an odd number to an even number, the answer is always an odd number.

5. Write down an example to show that when you multiply together two odd numbers, the answer is always an odd number.

6 Write down an example to show that when you multiply an odd number by an even number, the answer is always an even number.

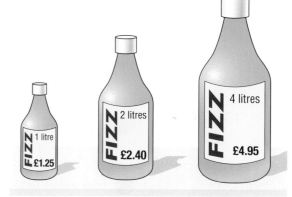

7 Which bottle is the best value for money?

8 Which is the better value for money?

  a 6 litres for £12 or 3 litres for £9.

  b 4 kg for £10 or 8 kg for £18.

  c 200 g for £4 or 300 g for £5.

  d Six chocolate bars for £1.50 or four chocolate bars for 90p.

9 A recipe uses 250 g of meat and makes a meal for five people. How many grams of meat would be needed to make a meal for 15 people?

Extension **Work**

Invent your own recipes for two people. Rewrite them for four people and then for five people. Remember that you cannot have half an egg!

Proportion

Look at the picture.
Can you work out how many pints are in 3 litres?

A litre of water is a pint and three-quarters

Example 14.6 A café sells four cakes for £6. How much will ten cakes cost?

Two cakes cost £3

So ten cakes cost $5 \times 3 = £15$

Exercise 14D

1 An orange drink is made using one part orange juice to four parts water. How many litres of orange juice and water are needed to make:

  a 5 litres of orange drink?   **b** 20 litres of orange drink?

2 A supermarket uses $\frac{3}{4}$ of its space for food and the rest for non-food items. It had 100 square metres for non-food items. How many square metres did it have for food?

3 A green paint is made by mixing three parts of blue paint with seven parts of yellow paint. How many litres of blue and yellow paint are needed to make:

    a   20 litres of green paint?   **b**   5 litres of green paint?

4 5 miles is approximately 8 km.

    a   How many miles are equal to 24 km?

    b   How many kilometres are equal to 25 miles?

5 30 cm is approximately 1 foot. Approximately how many feet are there in:

    a   120 cm?   **b**   15 cm?   **c**   45 cm?

6 Four cakes cost £10. What will twelve cakes cost?

7 Six towels cost £18. What will three towels cost?

8 Ten candles cost £12. What will 15 candles cost?

9 A lorry travels at 60 miles per hour on the motorway.

    a   How far will it travel in 3 hours?

    b   How far will it travel in 15 minutes?

    c   How far will it travel in 3 hours and 15 minutes?

10 In 15 minutes a car travelled 12 km. If it continued at the same speed, how far did it travel in:

    a   30 minutes?   **b**   45 minutes?   **c** 1 hour?

11 In 30 minutes, 40 litres of water runs through a pipe. How much water will run through the pipe in:

    a   60 minutes?   **b**   15 minutes?   **c** 45 minutes?

12 Roast ham costs 80p for 100 grams. How much will 250 grams cost?

Extension Work

Design a spreadsheet that a shopkeeper could use to double her prices.

Ratio

John and Mary are sharing the sweets. John wants twice as many sweets as Mary, and there are 21 sweets altogether. Can you work out how many sweets each gets?

Example 14.7

Michael has 32 CDs. Alice has three times as many as Michael. How many CDs do they have altogether?

Alice has three times as many CDs as Michael, so Alice has $3 \times 32 = 96$ CDs.

This means that altogether they have $32 + 96 = 128$ CDs.

Example 14.8

James and Briony are two goalkeepers. James has let in twice as many goals as Briony. Altogether they have let in 27 goals. How many goals has James let in?

You need to find two numbers that add up to 27. One number is double the other.

By trying different pairs of numbers, you will find that the answers are 18 and 9.

So, James has let in 18 goals.

Example 14.9

Alex has 21 pencils. The ratio of coloured pencils to black pencils is 2 : 1. How many coloured pencils does Alex have?

The ratio of 2 : 1 means that there are twice as many coloured pencils as there are black pencils.

By trying different pairs of numbers, you will find that the answers are 14 and 7.

So, Alex has 14 coloured pencils.

Example 14.10

Simplify each of these ratios.

a   18 : 12   **b**   20 : 100   **c**   35 minutes : 15 minutes   **d**   2 cm : 25 mm

a   18 and 12 will both divide by 6. So, $18 : 12 = (18 \div 6) : (12 \div 6)$
$$= 3 : 2$$

b   20 and 100 can be done in two stages. First divide by 10 and then by 2.
$$20 : 100 = 2 : 10 \ (\div 10)$$
$$= 1 : 5 \ \ (\div 2)$$

c   When units are in a ratio, they can be ignored when both units are the same. So, in this case:
$$35 \text{ minutes} : 15 \text{ minutes} = 35 : 15$$
$$= (35 \div 5) : (15 \div 5)$$
$$= 7 : 3$$

d   When the units are different, one unit must be changed to make it the same as the other unit. So, in this case:
$$2 \text{ cm} : 25 \text{ mm} = 20 \text{ mm} : 25 \text{ mm}$$
$$= 20 : 25$$
$$= 4 : 5$$

Exercise 14E

1 Simplify each of these ratios.

a 6 : 4	**b** 10 : 25	**c** 21 : 7	**d** 6 : 9
e 5 : 20	**f** 8 : 2	**g** 12 : 3	**h** 20 : 15
i 4 : 12	**j** 32 : 8	**k** 15 : 3	**l** 100 : 25
m 400 : 1000	**n** 500 : 1000	**o** 100 : 70	**p** 100 : 750
q 120 : 30	**r** 24 : 6	**s** 20 : 300	**t** 50 : 250

2 Simplify each of these ratios.
   a 6 hours : 4 hours   **b** 10 minutes : 25 minutes   **c** 21 days : 7 days
   d 6 kg : 9 kg   **e** 5 cm : 20 cm   **f** 8 litres : 2 litres

3 Simplify each of these ratios.
   a 1 hour : 30 minutes   **b** 15 minutes : 1 hour   **c** 1 week : 7 days
   d 1 kg : 200 g   **e** 20 mm : 1 cm   **f** 1 litre : 2000 ml

4 Harriet and Richard go shopping. Altogether they buy 66 items. Harriet buys twice as many items as Richard. How many items does Harriet buy?

5 At a concert there are half as many males as females. There are 240 people altogether. How many females are at the concert?

6 180 people see a film at the cinema. The number of children to the number of adults are in the ratio 2 : 1. How many children see the film?

7 In a fishing contest the number of trout caught to the number of carp caught is in the ratio 1 : 2. The total number of trout and carp is 24. How many carp were caught?

8 A bakery makes 1200 loaves. The ratio of white to brown is 3 : 1. How many brown loaves did the bakery make?

9 A do-it-yourself shop sells paints. The ratio of gloss paint to emulsion paint sold on one day is 1 : 3. If they sell 80 litres of paint, how much gloss paint do they sell?

Extension Work

Draw a cube of side 1 cm. Now draw a cube of side 2 cm.

1 Investigate what happens to the total length of all the edges of a cube as you double its dimensions.

2 The surface area of the small cube is 6 cm² as there are six faces. Work out the surface area of the bigger cube. Then investigate what happens to the surface area of a cube when you double its dimensions.

3 Extend the problem to a cube of side 3 cm. Then consider cuboids.

4
I can develop a strategy for solving problems.
I can use mathematics to solve practical problems.
I can use simple proportions in problems.
I can write a simple formula in words.

5
I can identify the information needed to solve a problem.
I can check a result to see if it is sensible.
I can describe situations mathematically using symbols, words or diagrams.

National Test questions

1 *2007 3–5 Paper 1*

Here are the rules for a number grid:

12 — This number is the **sum** of the numbers in the middle row.

10 | 2

20 — This number is the **product** of the numbers in the middle row.

Copy the number grids below and use the rules to write in the missing numbers.

a

... / 4 | 7 / ...

b

12 / 9 | ... / ...

c

10 / ... | ... / 24

MTH 3-13a

2 *2006 3–5 Paper 2*

A bottle contains 250ml of cough mixture.

One adult and **one child** need to take cough mixture **four times a day** every day for **five days**.

Will there be enough cough mixture in the bottle?

Explain your answer.

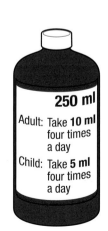

250 ml
Adult: Take **10 ml** four times a day
Child: Take **5 ml** four times a day

MNU 3-03a

3 *2006 3–5 Paper 1*

a I am thinking of a number.
My number is a **multiple of 4**.

Which of the statements below is true?

My number must be even
My number must be odd
My number could be odd or even

Explain how you know.

b I am thinking of a **different** number.
My number is a **factor of 20**.

Which of the statements below is true?

My number must be even
My number must be odd
My number could be odd or even

Explain how you know.

MTH
3-05a

4 *2005 3–5 Paper 2*

The screens of widescreen and standard televisions look different. They have different proportions.

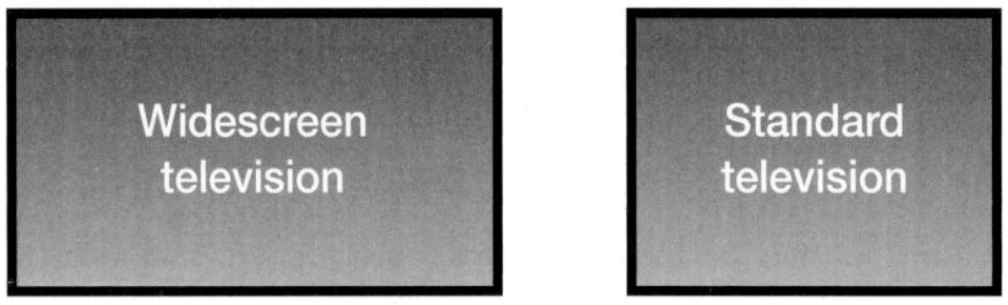

Widescreen television	Standard television
Ratio of height to width is **9 : 16**	Ratio of height to width is **3 : 4**

Keri starts to draw scale drawings of the televisions. For each, the height is 4.5 cm.

What should the **width** in centimetres of **each scale** drawing be?

4.5 cm **Widescreen** television

4.5 cm **Standard** television

MTH
3-17b

This chapter is going to show you

- How to draw plans, elevations and scale drawings
- How to solve problems using coordinates
- How to construct a triangle given three sides
- How to use bearings
- How to solve problems involving cuboids

What you should already know

- How to draw nets of 3-D shapes
- How to plot coordinates
- How to construct triangles from given data
- How to measure and draw angles
- How to calculate the surface area of cuboids

Plans and elevations

A **plan** is the view of a 3-D shape when it is looked at from above. An **elevation** is the view of a 3-D shape when it is looked at from the front or from the side.

Example 15.1

The 3-D shape shown is drawn on an isometric grid. Notice that the paper must be used the correct way round, so always check that the dots form vertical columns.

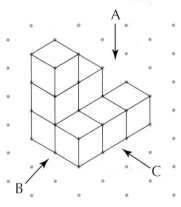

The plan, front elevation and side elevation can be drawn on squared paper:

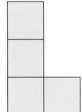

Plan from **A**

Front elevation from **B**

Side elevation from **C**

1 For each of the given cuboids, draw the following on squared paper.

i The plan   **ii** The front elevation   **iii** The side elevation

a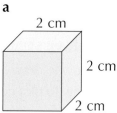

b

c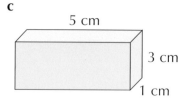

2 Copy each of the following 3-D shapes onto an isometric grid.

a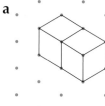

b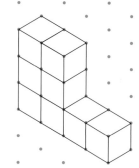

c

d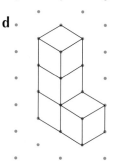

e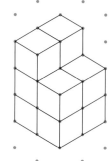

f

For each one, draw the following on squared paper.

i The plan   **ii** The front elevation   **iii** The side elevation

3 The plan, front elevation and side elevation of a 3-D solid made up of cubes, are shown below. Draw the solid on an isometric grid.

Plan

Front elevation

Side elevation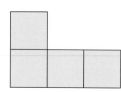

4 Make a 3-D solid from multi-link cubes. On centimetre-squared paper draw its plan, front elevation and side elevation and show these to a partner. Ask your partner to construct the solid using multi-link cubes. Compare the two solids made.

6

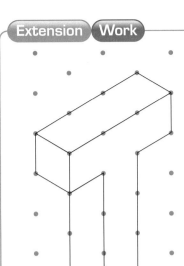

The letter 'T' is drawn on an isometric grid, as shown on the left.

1 Explain why only certain capital letters can be drawn easily on an isometric grid.

2 Draw the other capital letters that can be drawn on an isometric grid.

3 Design a poster, using any of these letters, to make a logo for a person who has these letters as their initials.

MTH
2-16c

Scale drawings

A **scale drawing** is a smaller drawing of an actual object. A scale must always be clearly given by the side of the scale drawing.

MTH
3-17b

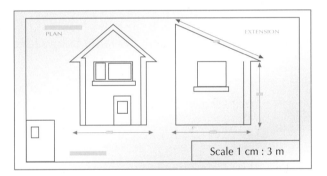

PLAN

EXTENSION

Scale 1 cm : 3 m

Example 15.2 ▷

This is a scale drawing of Rebecca's room.

- On the scale drawing, the length of the room is 5 cm, so the actual length of the room is 5 m.

- On the scale drawing, the width of the room is 3.5 cm, so the actual width of the room is 3.5 m.

- On the scale drawing, the width of the window is 2 cm, so the actual width of the window is 2 m.

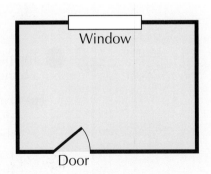

Window

Door

Scale: 1 cm to 1 m

Exercise 15B

1 The lines shown are drawn using a scale of 1 cm to 10 m. Write down the length each line represents.

a ▬▬▬▬

b ▬▬▬▬▬▬▬

c ▬▬▬▬▬

d ▬▬▬▬▬▬▬▬▬

e ▬▬▬▬▬▬▬▬

 2 The diagram shows a scale drawing for a school hall.

  a Find the actual length of the hall.
  b Find the actual width of the hall.
  c Find the actual distance between the opposite corners of the hall.

Scale: 1 cm to 5 m

 3 The diagram shown is Ryan's scale drawing for his Mathematics classroom. Nathan notices that Ryan has not put a scale on the drawing, but he knows that the length of the classroom is 8 m.

  a What scale has Ryan used?
  b What is the actual width of the classroom?
  c What is the actual area of the classroom?

4 Copy and complete the table below for a scale drawing in which the scale is 4 cm to 1 m.

	Actual length	Length on scale drawing
a	4 m	
b	1.5 m	
c	50 cm	
d		12 cm
e		10 cm
f		4.8 cm

 5 The plan shown is for a bungalow.

  a Find the actual dimensions of each of the following rooms:
  i the kitchen
  ii the bathroom
  iii bedroom 1
  iv bedroom 2
  b Calculate the actual area of the living room.

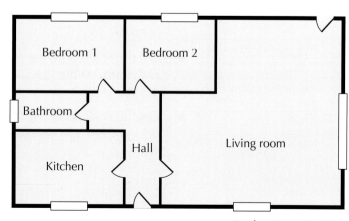

Scale: 1 cm to 2 m

MTH 3-17b

FM **6** The diagram shows the plan of a football pitch. It is not drawn to scale. Use the measurements on the diagram to make a scale drawing of the pitch. (Choose your own scale.)

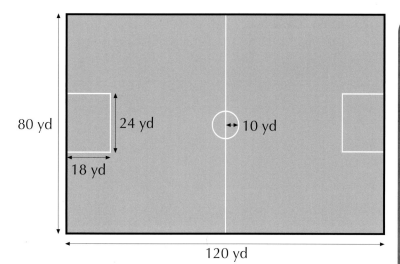

80 yd

24 yd

10 yd

18 yd

120 yd

MTH 3-17b

Extension Work

MTH 3-17b

1 On centimetre-squared paper, design a layout for a bedroom. Make cut-outs for any furniture you wish to have in the room. (Use a scale of 2 cm to 1 m.)

2 You will need a metrer ruler or a tape measure for this activity. Draw a plan of your classroom, including the desks and any other furniture in the room. Choose your own scale.

Coordinates in all four quadrants

MTH 4-18a

We use **coordinates** to locate a point on a grid.

The grid consists of two axes, called the **x-axis** and the **y-axis**. They are perpendicular to each other.

The two axes meet at a point called the **origin**, which is labelled O.

The point A on the grid is 4 units across and 3 units up.

We say that the coordinates of A are (4, 3), which is usually written as A(4, 3).

The first number, 4, is the *x*-coordinate of A and the second number, 3, is the *y*-coordinate of A. The *x*-coordinate is *always* written first.

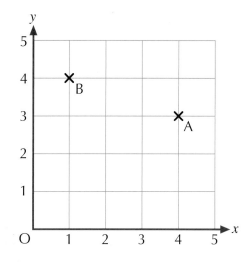

When plotting a point on a grid, a ✗ is usually used.

The coordinates of the origin are (0, 0) and the coordinates of the point B are (1, 4).

The grid system can be extended to negative numbers and points can be plotted in all **four quadrants**.

Example 15.3

The coordinates of the points on the grid are:

A(4, 2), B(–2, 3), C(–3, –1), D(1, –4)

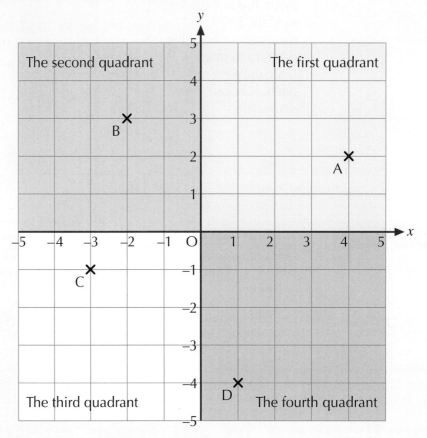

Exercise 15C

1 Write down the coordinates of the points P, Q, R, S and T.

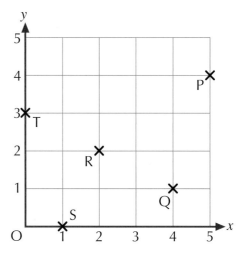

2 a Make a copy of the grid in Question 1. Then plot the points A(1, 1), B(1, 5) and C(4, 5).

b The three points are the vertices of a rectangle. Plot the point D to complete the rectangle.

c Write down the coordinates of D.

3 Write down the coordinates of the points A, B, C, D, E, F, G and H.

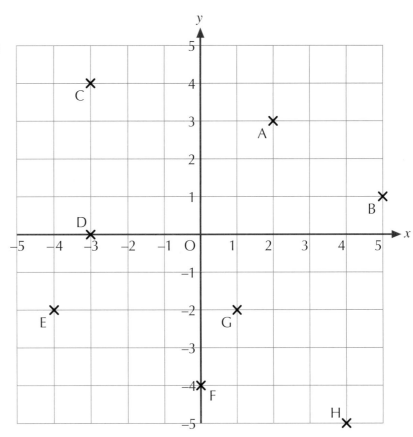

4 Make a copy of the grid in Question 3. Then plot the points A(–4, 3), B(–2, –2), C(0, 1), D(2, –2) and E(4, 3).

Extension **Work**

1 **a** Write down the coordinates of the points A, B, C, D, E and F.

b Using the grid to help, write down the coordinates of the mid-point of each of the following line segments.

   i AB   **ii** CD
   iii BE   **iv** EF

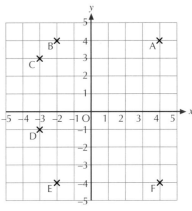

2 Copy the grid on the right and plot the points P, Q, R and S.

a Write down the coordinates of the points P, Q, R and S.

b Join the points to form the rectangle PQRS. Using the grid to help, write down the coordinates of the mid-point of each of the following lines.

   i PQ   **ii** QR
   iii PS   **iv** SR

c Write down the coordinates of the mid-point of the diagonal PR.

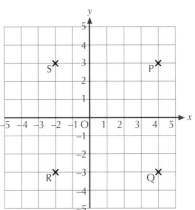

Constructing triangles

In Year 7, you learned how to construct triangles, using a ruler and a protractor, from given data. You constructed:

- A triangle given two sides and the included angle (SAS):

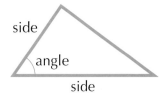

side
angle
side

- A triangle given two angles and the included side (ASA):

angle
angle
side

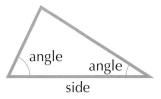

Example 15.4 shows you how to construct a triangle given three sides (SSS). You need a ruler and compasses for this construction.

Example 15.4

To construct the triangle PQR.

Draw a line QR 6 cm long. Set compasses to a radius of 4 cm and, with centre at Q, draw a large arc above QR.

Set compasses to a radius of 5 cm and, with the centre at R, draw a large arc to intersect the first arc. The intersection of the two arcs is P.

Join QP and RP to complete the triangle. Leave your construction lines on the diagram.

P
4 cm
5 cm
Q
6 cm
R

P
4 cm
5 cm
Q
6 cm
R

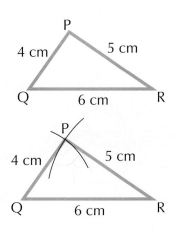

Exercise 15D

1 Construct each of the following triangles. (Remember: label all the sides and angles.)

a

5 cm
50°
6 cm

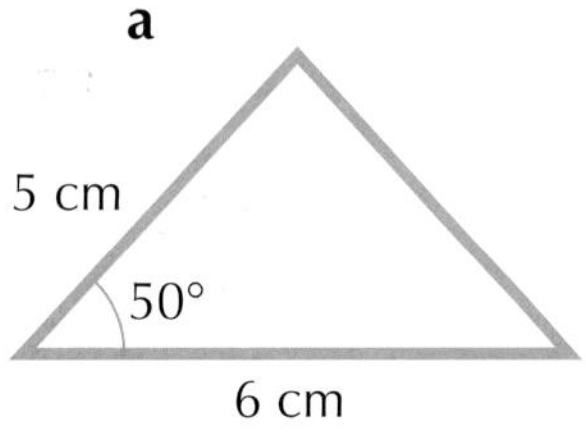

b

5 cm
45°
3 cm

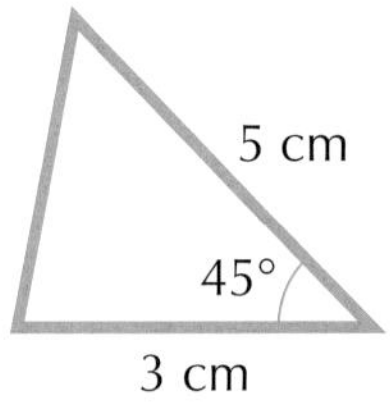

c

40°
60°
6 cm

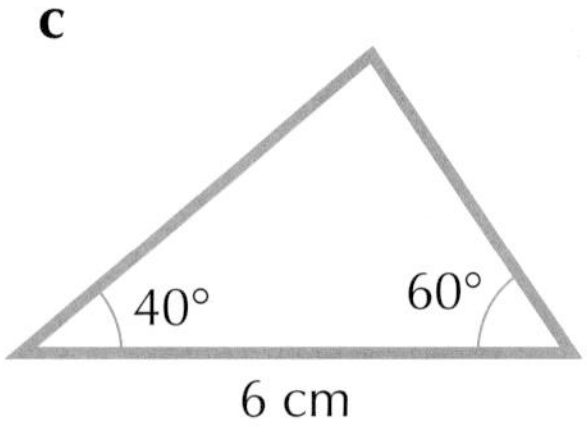

d

55°
70°
4 cm

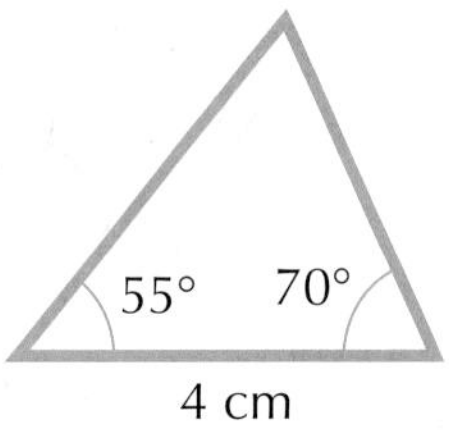

2 Construct each of the following triangles. (Remember: label all the lines.)

a

A
3 cm
4 cm
B
5 cm
C

b

D
6 cm
3 cm
E
6 cm
F

c

G
8 cm
3 cm
H
7 cm
I

d

J
6.5 cm
5.5 cm
K
8.5 cm
L

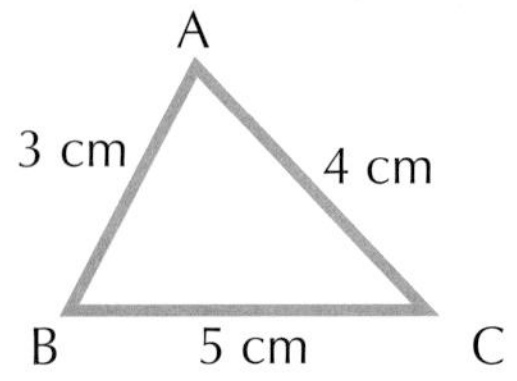

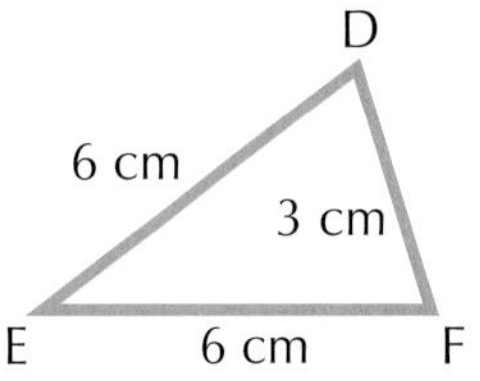

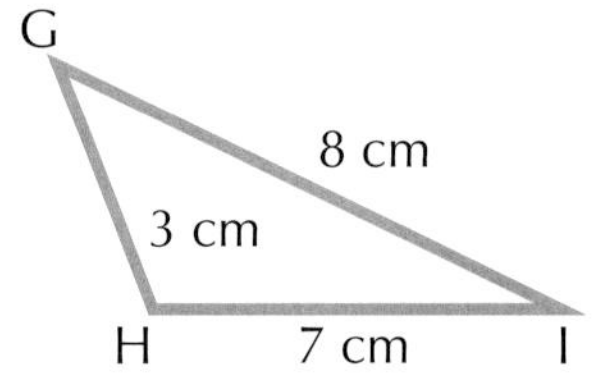

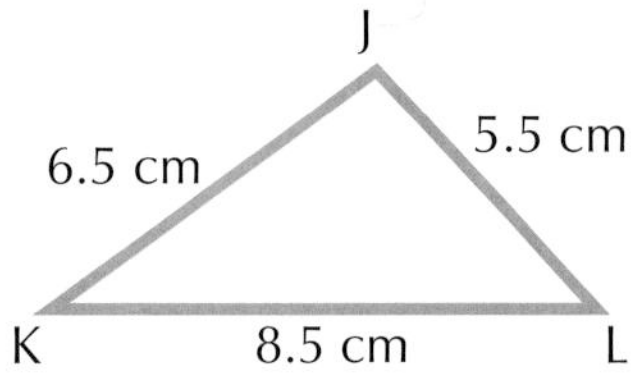

3 Construct the ΔXYZ with XY = 7 cm, XZ = 4 cm and YZ = 6 cm.

3-16a

4 Construct the ΔPQR with PQ = 5 cm, QR = 12 cm and PR = 13 cm. What type of triangle have you drawn?

5 Construct equilateral triangles with sides of the given length.

    a   3 cm   **b**   5 cm   **c**   4.5 cm

Extension **Work**

1 Construct the quadrilateral shown below using only a ruler and compasses.

MTH
3-16a

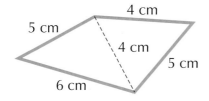

2 **a** Draw the net below accurately on card. Cut out the net to make a square-based pyramid. Make the square 4 cm by 4 cm, and each equilateral triangle 4 cm by 4 cm by 4 cm.

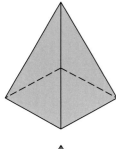

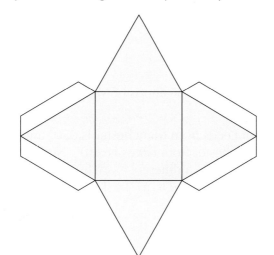

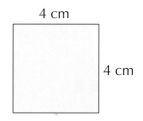

MTH
2-16b

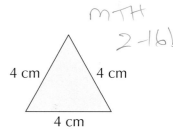

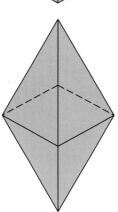

    b Construct two more square-based pyramids and paste their bases together to make an octahedron, like the one in the diagram.

Bearings

There are four main directions on a compass – north (N), south (S), east (E) and west (W). These directions are examples of **compass bearings**.

Bearings are mainly used for navigation purposes at sea, in the air and in sports such as orienteering. A bearing is measured in degrees (°) and the angle is always measured **clockwise** from the **north lines**. The symbol for due north is: N

You have probably seen this symbol on maps in Geography.

A bearing is always given using three digits and so is sometimes referred to as a three-figure bearing. For example, the bearing for the direction east is 090°.

Example 15.5 ▷ On the diagram, the three-figure bearing of B from A is 035° and the three-figure bearing of A from B is 215°.

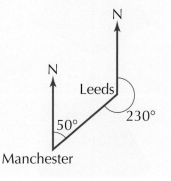

Example 15.6 ▷ The diagram shows the positions of Manchester and Leeds on a map.

The bearing of Leeds from Manchester is 050° and the bearing of Manchester from Leeds is 230°. Notice that the two bearings have a difference of 180°; such bearings are often referred to as 'back bearings'.

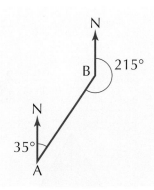

Exercise 15E

① Write down each of the following compass bearings as three-figure bearings.

a South   b West   c North-east   d South-west

② Write down the three-figure bearing of B from A for each of the following.

a

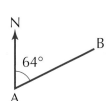

b

c

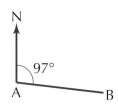

d

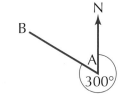

3 Find the three-figure bearing of X from Y for each of the following.

a

45°

b

160°

c
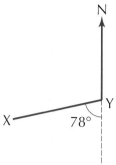
78°

d
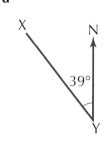
39°

4 Draw a rough sketch to show each of the bearings below. (Mark the angle on each sketch.)

    a From a ship A, the bearing of a lighthouse B is 030°.

    b From a town C, the bearing of town D is 138°

    c From a gate E, the bearing of a trigonometric point F is 220°.

    d From a control tower G, the bearing of an aircraft H is 333°.

5 The two diagrams show the positions of towns and cities in England.

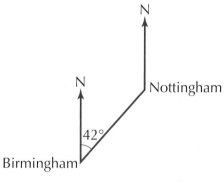

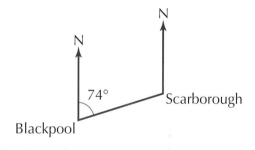

    Find the bearing of each of the following:

    a   **i**   Nottingham from Birmingham

         ii   Birmingham from Nottingham

    b   **i**   Scarborough from Blackpool

         ii   Blackpool from Scarborough

Extension Work

A liner travels from a port X on a bearing of 140° for 120 nautical miles to a port Y. It then travels from port Y on a bearing of 250° for a further 160 nautical miles to a port Z.

1 Make a scale drawing to show the journey of the liner (use a scale of 1 cm to 20 nautical miles).

2 Use your scale drawing to find:

    a the direct distance the liner travels from port Z to return to port X.

    b the bearing of port X from port Z.

A cube investigation

For this investigation you will need a collection of cubes and centimetre isometric dotted paper.

Two cubes can only be arranged in one way to make a solid shape, as shown.

Copy the diagram onto centimetre isometric dotted paper. The surface area of the solid is 10 cm².

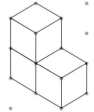

Three cubes can be arranged in two different ways, as shown.

Copy the diagrams onto centimetre isometric dotted paper. The surface area of both solids is 14 cm².

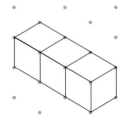

OR

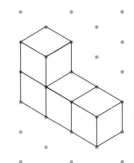

Here is an arrangement of four cubes:

The surface area of the solid is 18 cm².

Exercise 15F

1 How many different arrangements can you make using four cubes?

2 Draw all the different arrangements on centimetre isometric dotted paper.

3 What is the greatest surface area for the different solids you have made?

4 What is the least surface area for the different solids you have made?

5 Draw a table to show your results and write down anything you notice.

6 What do you think the greatest and least surface areas of a solid made from five cubes will be?

4 I can use coordinates in the first quadrant.

5 I can use coordinates in all four quadrants.

I can make a scale drawing.

I can use three-figure bearings.

I can draw simple plans and elevations.

I can find the surface area of a cuboid.

National Test questions

1 *2000 Paper 1*

Look at the shaded shape.

a Two statements below are correct. Write down the correct statements.

The shape is a quadrilateral.

The shape is a trapezium.

The shape is a pentagon.

MTH

3-17a The shape is a kite.

The shape is a parallelogram.

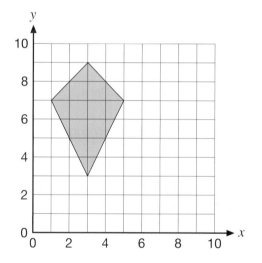

b What are the coordinates of points A and B?

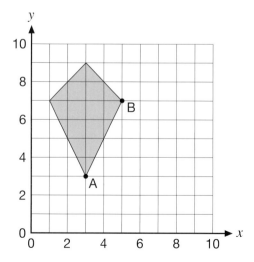

2 *2001 Paper 2*

A plan of a ferry crossing is shown.

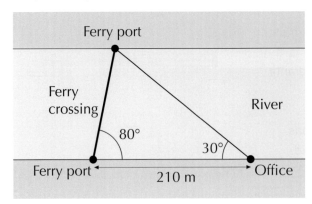

a Draw an accurate scale drawing of the ferry crossing (use a scale of 1 cm to 20 m).

b What is the length of the ferry crossing on your diagram?

c The scale is 1 cm to 20 m. Work out the length of the real ferry crossing. Show your working, and write the units with your answer.

3 *2005 3–5 Paper 2*

The scale drawing shows the positions of London and Paris.

a From London to Paris, the angle from north is angle a.

Measure accurately angle a.

b On the scale drawing, **1 cm represents 50 km.**

What is the distance, in km, from London to Paris?

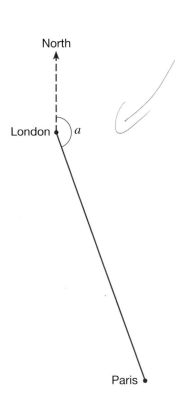

c A newspaper printed this information about London and Madrid:

From London to Madrid, the angle from north is **195° clockwise.**
Madrid is **1300 km** from London.

Show this information on a scale drawing.

The position of London is shown for you.

North

London

MTH
3–17b

4 *2003 3–5 Paper 1*

Use compasses to construct a triangle that has sides **8 cm**, **6 cm** and **7 cm**.

Leave in your construction lines.

MTH
3–16a

Photographs

FastPrint advertises the cost of photograph prints in their shop.

Print size	Price each	
3" × 2" (4)	£0.99	
	Quantity	**Price**
	1–99	£0.10 each
13 cm × 9 cm	100–249	£0.09 each
	250+	£0.08 each
	Quantity	**Price**
	1–49	£0.15 each
	50–99	£0.12 each
6" × 4"	100–249	£0.09 each
	250–499	£0.08 each
	500–750	£0.06 each
	751+	£0.05 each
7" × 5"	£0.29	
8" × 6"	£0.45	
10" × 8"	£1.20	
12" × 8"	£1.20	
45 cm × 30 cm	£6.99	

1 A school decides to use FastPrint to buy prints of a year group photograph. Pupils can choose the size of the prints they want. They can also choose to buy more than one size.

The school's order is as follows:

128	5" × 3½" prints
87	6" × 4" prints
75	10" × 8" prints
and 60	12" × 8" prints

What is the total cost of buying these prints?

2 **a** Find the area of each of the prints. (The units are square inches or sq in.)

b Which pairs of prints are twice the size in area?

 MNU 4-20a

3 Here are the sizes of three picture frames A, B and C.

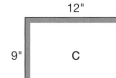

8" 8" 12"
6" A 5" B 9" C

a The 7" × 5" print will fit inside frame A. What will be the area of the outside border?

b Which of the prints will best fit inside the other two frames if a suitable border is to be left around the print?

5 EasyPrint also advertises the cost of photograph prints in their shop.

3" × 2" print	£0.25 each
6" × 4" print	£0.12 each
7" × 5" print	£0.20 each
8" × 6" print	£0.42 each
10" × 8" print	£1.20 each
12" × 8" print	£1.32 each

a If you order one of each print size from EasyPrint, which prints are cheaper than FastPrint?

b If you wanted to order 120 4" × 6" prints, which shop would you choose? How much would you save?

c How much more do you pay for a 10" × 8" print at FastPrint?

d What is the percentage increase in the price if you ordered 8" × 12" prints from EasyPrint rather than from FastPrint?

6 a The ratio of the length to the width can be written in the form n : 1 for each print size.

Copy and complete the table for each print at EasyPrint.

Print size	Ratio of length to width	Ratio in the form n : 1
3" × 2"	3 : 2	1.5 : 1
6" × 4"	6 : 4	
7" × 5"	7 : 5	
8" × 6"	8 : 6	1.33 : 1
10" × 8"		
12" × 8"		

b Any rectangle whose length and width are in the ratio 1.618 : 1 is known as a Golden Rectangle.

The Golden Rectangle is said to be one of the most visually pleasing rectangular shapes. Many artists and architects have used the shape within their work.

Which of the prints in the table are close to being golden rectangles?

4

12" × 8" 10" × 8"

8" × 6" 7" × 5" 6" × 4"

a Work out the ratio of the length to the width for each print.

Give your answers in their simplest form.

b The simplified ratio of the length to the width is the same for some of the prints. Which prints are they?

<table>
<tr><td>This chapter is going to show you</td></tr>
</table>

This chapter is going to show you

- How to calculate statistics from given data
- How to calculate a median for discrete data
- How to construct frequency diagrams for discrete data
- How to compare two distributions by using an average and the range
- How to compare theoretical probabilities with experimental probabilities

What you should already know

- How to construct frequency tables for discrete data
- How to find the mode and range for discrete data
- How to calculate the mean for discrete data
- How to construct simple bar charts

Frequency tables

There are three equal periods in an ice hockey game. Use the picture to work out the time on the clock at the end of each period.

END OF FIRST PERIOD
00.20

Example 16.1

The waiting times, in minutes, of people at a bus stop are shown below.

2, 5, 1, 8, 7, 6, 5, 1, 8, 7

2, 1, 0, 0, 2, 8, 7, 5, 6, 5

Construct a frequency table to represent the data.

The table can be set out either across the page in two rows or down the page in two columns. There were two people who waited 0 minutes, three people who waited for 1 minute, three people who waited for 2 minutes and so on.

Putting all this information in the table gives:

Waiting time (minutes)	0	1	2	3	4	5	6	7	8
Number of people	2	3	3	0	0	4	2	3	3

MTH
4-21a

Example 16.2 ▷ Use the data given in Example 16.1 to complete the table for grouped data.

Waiting time (minutes)	0–2	3–5	6–8
Number of people			

The data is now going to be grouped so that the people who waited 0, 1 or 2 minutes are counted together. Those who waited 3, 4 or 5 minutes are counted together. So are those who waited 6, 7 or 8 minutes.

The completed table gives:

Waiting time (minutes)	0–2	3–5	6–8
Number of people	8	4	8

Exercise 16A

1 The length of time 25 customers spend in a shop is recorded as shown.

Two more customers enter the shop. The first customer is in the shop for 5 minutes and the second customer is in the shop for 21 minutes.

Time (minutes)	Number of customers
0–10	12
11–20	7
21–30	6

Copy and update the table to include these two customers.

2 The heights (in centimetres) of 20 people are given below:

162, 153, 178, 165, 141, 173, 154, 150, 188, 187, 153, 164, 182, 163, 144, 176, 175, 164, 162, 177

a Copy and complete the frequency table.

Height (centimetres)	Tally	Number of people
140–159		
160–179		
180–200		

b Which class interval contains the most people?

3 The masses (in kilograms) of fish caught in one day by a fisherman are shown below:

1, 5, 3, 4, 6, 1, 2
4, 5, 1, 5, 4, 3, 3

a Copy and complete the frequency table.

Mass (kilograms)	Tally	Number of fish
0–2		
3–5		
6–8		

b Which class interval contains the least fish?

④ The temperature (in °C) of 16 towns in Britain is recorded on one day:

12, 10, 9, 13, 12, 14, 17, 16
18, 10, 12, 11, 15, 15, 12, 13

a Copy and complete the frequency table.

Temperature (°C)	Tally	Frequency
8–10		
11–13		
14–16		
17–19		

b Which class interval contained the most common temperature?

Extension Work

Record the number of pictures or diagrams on each page of this book.
Decide on suitable class intervals for the data to be collected together into a frequency table. Complete the table. Comment on your results.

The median

When dealing with data you often need to find an average. The mode, the median and the mean are all types of average.

This section explains how to find the median.

The median is the middle value for a set of values when they are put in numerical order.

Example 16.3 ▷ Here are the scores of nine players in a quiz. Find the median.

12, 11, 9, 14, 13, 9, 6, 17, 14

First, put the scores in order: 6, 9, 9, 11, 12, 13, 14, 14, 17.
The median is the number in the middle of the set. So, the median is 12.

Example 16.4 ▷ Below are the marks of twelve pupils in an English test.

17, 16, 19, 16, 15, 14, 18, 20, 14, 18, 17, 16

First, put the marks in order:

14, 14, 15, 16, 16, 16, 17, 17, 18, 18, 19, 20

There are two numbers in the middle of the set: 16 and 17. The median is the number in the middle of these two numbers. So, the median is 16.5.

Exercise 16B ① Find the median of each of the following sets of data.

a 4, 6, 3, 4, 5, 1, 8, 6, 6

b 21, 27, 22, 24, 27, 21, 23, 26, 25, 25, 24

c 7, 11, 6, 15, 12, 11, 10

d 102, 108, 106, 110, 98, 94, 109, 111, 105

2 Find the median of each of the following sets of data.

   a   14, 17, 15, 16, 18, 12

   b   3, 6, 4, 6, 3, 7, 0, 2, 6, 8

   c   84, 62, 73, 77

   d   112, 110, 109, 115, 113, 108

3 Find the median of each of the following sets of data.

   a   18 kg, 20 kg, 23 kg, 18 kg, 24 kg

   b   £1.50, £2.20, £1.78, £2.36, £1.47

   c   104 cm, 105 cm, 103 cm, 102 cm, 108 cm, 100 cm

   d   35 litres, 14 litres, 20 litres, 24 litres

4 **a**   Write down a list of five numbers which has a median of 10.

   b   Write down a list of seven numbers which has a median of 8.

   c   Write down a list of six numbers which has a median of 14.

   d   Write down a list of ten numbers which has a median of 12.

5 A group of swimmers are sponsored for swimming lengths of the pool.

Here is the number of lengths that each swimmer completes:

   17   12   23   8   7   17   18   22   30

Find the median number of lengths for this data.

6 Six pupils compare how much money they have brought to school.

Here are the amounts: £0, £2, £1.80, £0, £3, £3.60

Work out the median amount for these six pupils.

Extension **Work**

Ask people in your class to tell you the name of their favourite pop band or solo artist. Write down both their answer and the number of people in the band (one if it is a solo artist). When you have collected all your data, find the median number of people in the bands.

Drawing frequency diagrams

Look at the picture. How could you record the different ways in which pupils travel to school?

When data has been collected from a survey, it can then be displayed using different diagrams to make it easier to understand.

Bar charts can be used to show different categories, such as walking to school, using the school bus or going to school by taxi. This bar chart would have gaps between the bars.

Bar charts can also be used for grouped data. For example, when recording word lengths for 100 words, the number of letters per word can be grouped into categories, such as 1–3, 4–6, 7–9 and 10–12.

Bar-line graphs are used to show single values. A typical case would be, when rolling a dice 50 times, record the number of times that each score (1, 2, 3, 4, 5 or 6) is obtained.

Example 16.5

Construct a bar chart for the following data about the ways in which pupils travel to school.

How pupils travel to school	Number of pupils
Walk	4
Bus	5
Car	10
Cycle	6

It is important that the bar chart has a title and is labelled, as shown below.

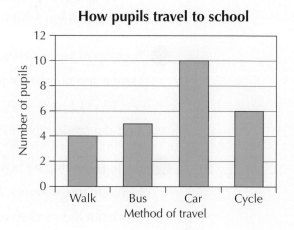

Example 16.6

A dice is rolled 50 times. Construct a bar-line graph to show the results.

Score on dice	Frequency
1	8
2	7
3	7
4	9
5	11
6	8

The length of each bar represents each frequency. Do not join the tops of the bars.

Score on a dice rolled 50 times

Exercise 16C

1 **a** Use the data in the frequency table to draw a bar chart to show the birthday season of a class of Year 8 pupils.

Birthday	Frequency
Spring	3
Summer	6
Autumn	8
Winter	7

b Use the data in the frequency table to draw a bar chart to show the favourite field event of competitors.

Field event	Frequency
Javelin	12
Discus	6
Shot	8
Hammer	9

c Use the data in the frequency table to draw a bar-line graph to show the scores out of 5 in a test.

Score in test	Frequency
0	9
1	12
2	6
3	3
4	7
5	1

d Use the data in the frequency table to draw a bar chart to show the number of words in 50 sentences.

Number of words	Frequency
0–10	8
11–20	12
21–30	25
31–40	5

MTH
4-21a

FM **2** The dual bar graph shows the mean monthly temperature for two cities.

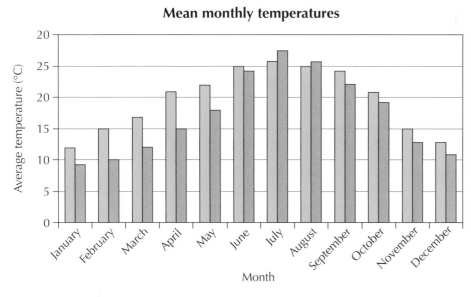

Mean monthly temperatures

City A
City B

a Which city has the highest mean monthly temperature?

b Which city has the lowest mean monthly temperature?

c How many months of the year is the temperature higher in City A than City B?

d What is the difference in mean temperature between the two cities in February?

MNU
4-20a

Extension Work

Use a travel brochure to compare the temperatures of two European resorts. Make a poster to advertise one resort as being better than the other.

Comparing data

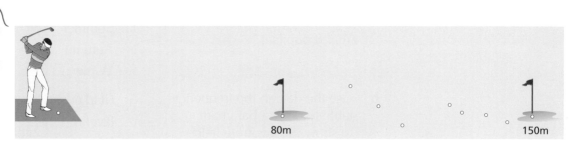

80m   150m

Look at the picture. What is the range of the golfer's shots?

Example 16.7 ▷ The table shows the mean and range of basketball scores for two teams:

Compare the mean and range. What do they tell you?

	Team A	Team B
Mean	75	84
Range	20	10

The mean tells you that the average score for Team B is higher than that for Team A. So Team B has higher scores generally.

The range is the difference in their lowest and highest scores. As this is higher for Team A, there is a greater variation in Team A's scores. That is, Team A is less consistent than Team B.

Exercise 16D

(1) The temperature of melting ice is 0 °C and the temperature of boiling water is 100 °C. What is the range of the two temperatures?

(2) The times of four pupils in a 100-metre race are recorded as:

14.2 s, 13.8 s, 15.1 s, 17.3 s

Write down the range of the times.

(3) A factory worker records the start and finish times of a series of jobs as shown below.

Job number	1	2	3	4	5
Start time	9.00 am	9.20 am	9.50 am	10.10 am	10.20 am
Finish time	9.15 am	9.45 am	10.06 am	10.18 am	10.37 am

Work out the range of the time taken for each job.

(4) The minimum and maximum temperatures are recorded for four counties in England in April as below.

County	Northumberland	Leicestershire	Oxfordshire	Surrey
Minimum	2 °C	4 °C	4 °C	4.5 °C
Maximum	12 °C	15 °C	16.5 °C	17.5 °C

a Find the range of the temperatures for each county.

b Comment on any differences you notice.

5 The table shows the mean and range of a set of test scores for Jon and Matt.

	Jon	Matt
Mean	64	71
Range	35	23

    a Compare the means of the scores, stating who was better.

    b Compare the ranges, stating who was more consistent.

6 The table shows the medians and the ranges of the scores of Kyle and Lisa after playing on a computer game.

	Kyle	Lisa
Median	875	1500
Range	200	650

    a Compare the medians of their scores, stating who you think is the better player.

    b Compare the ranges, stating who is more consistent.

7 The table shows the mode and range of shoe sizes for men and women in a high-street shop.

	Men	Women
Mode	9	6
Range	8	7

    Compare the modes and the ranges. What do they tell you?

8 Belinda bought three bottles of face wash. The total price was £18 and the range was £2.50. The cheapest bottle cost £4.50.

    a What was the cost of the most expensive bottle?

    b What was the cost of the other bottle?

Extension Work

Use an atlas or another data source (the Internet or a software program) to compare the population and area of China with the population and area of the United States of America.

Which average to use?

Look at the queue of people. Why is it impossible to find the most common height?

The table on the next page will help you decide which type of average to use for a set of data.

	Advantages	Disadvantages	Example
Mean	Uses all the values. The most widely used average.	May not be representative when the data contains an extreme value.	1, 1, 1, 2, 4, 15 Mean $= \dfrac{1 + 1 + 1 + 2 + 4 + 15}{6} = 4$ which is a higher value than most of the data.
Median	Uses only the middle value, so it is a better average to use when the data contains extreme values.	Not all values are used, so could be misleading.	1, 1, 3, 5, 10, 15, 20 Median = 4th value = 5 Note that the median is close to the values 1, 1 and 3 but further from the values 10, 15 and 20.
Mode	Most frequently occurring value. Can be used for non-numerical data.	When the mode is an extreme value, it is misleading to use it as an average. May not exist.	Weekly wages of a boss and his four staff: £150, £150, £150, £150, £1000. Mode is £150 but mean is £320.
Range	Measures how spread out the values are.	Uses the two most extreme values.	1, 2, 5, 7, 9, 40. Range 40 − 1 = 39 Without the last value (40), the range would be only 8.

5

Exercise 16E

1 The time (in seconds) to complete a short task is recorded for each of 15 pupils:

10, 10, 10, 10, 11, 11, 12, 12, 12, 13, 14, 15, 15, 16, 17

The values are then grouped into a frequency table.

a Write down the mode.

b The median is 13. Explain why the median is more useful than the mode in this case.

Time (Seconds)	Frequency
10	4
11	2
12	3
13	1
14	1
15	2
16	1
17	1

2 Look at each set of data and the average which has been calculated. Give one reason why the average stated may not be the best average to use.

a	3, 3, 5, 7, 8, 10	Mode = 3
b	0, 1, 2, 2, 8, 14, 16	Mode = 2
c	1, 4, 7, 8, 20, 21, 32	Median = 8
d	2, 3, 6, 7, 10, 10, 10	Mode = 10
e	2, 2, 2, 2, 14, 16, 28	Median = 2
f	0, 1, 4, 6, 9, 100	Mean = 20

3 Look at each set of data and calculate the two averages at their side. State which average, if any, is best suited to that particular set.

a 1, 2, 4, 7, 12, 100   median and mean
b 9, 10, 10, 10, 91   mode and mean
c 1, 100, 101, 102, 106   median and mean
d 1, 3, 5, 6, 7, 8   median and mean
e 1, 1, 1, 7, 10, 10, 10   median and mode
f 2, 5, 8, 10, 15   median or mean

Extension Work

Collect the attendances at English Premiership football matches over one weekend. Calculate the range of this set of data.

Repeat this exercise for the Scottish Premier division.

Compare the differences in the distributions of the data. Explain why the range is probably more suitable for the English division than the Scottish division.

Repeat the calculations but ignore the largest attendance in each division. What effect does this have on your answers?

Experimental and theoretical probability

Look at the picture. Would you say that there is an even chance of the jigsaw pieces coming out of the box face up, or do more pieces come out face down every time?

Example 16.8

Design and carry out an experiment to test whether drawing pins usually land with the pin pointing up or the pin pointing down.

Count out 50 drawing pins, then drop them onto a table.

Record the number with the pin pointing up and the number with the pin pointing down.

Suppose that 30 point up and 20 point down.

We could then say that the experimental probability of a pin pointing up is:

$$\frac{30}{50} = \frac{3}{5} = 0.6$$

Exercise 16F

1 Darren read that when people are asked to think a number between 1 and 10, (inclusive), they will pick 3 or 7 more often than any other numbers.

He tested this out by asking 20 people. Below are his results:

9, 1, 5, 7, 4, 5, 1, 3, 8, 7, 3, 2, 2, 1, 4, 5, 8, 7, 3, 4

a What was Darren's experimental probability that people would give him the number 3 or 7?

b Compare this result with the theoretical probability, which is 0.2.

c You may wish to carry out your own experiment, to see if you agree with Darren.

2 a Carry out an experiment with an ordinary dice by recording the number of times that it lands on 6 after 30 throws.

b Compare your results with the theoretical probability of a fair dice, which is $\frac{1}{6} = 0.167$.

3 Some pupils threw three fair dice.

They recorded how many times the numbers on the dice were the same.

Name	Number of throws	Results		
		All different	Two the same	All the same
Morgan	40	26	12	2
Sue	140	81	56	3
Zenta	20	10	10	0
Ali	100	54	42	4

a Write the name of the pupil whose data are most likely to give the best estimate of the probability of getting each result. Explain your answer.

b This table show the pupils' results collected together:

Number of throws	Results		
	All different	Two the same	All the same
300	171	120	9

Use this data to estimate the probability of throwing numbers that are all different.

4 The theoretical probability that a coin lands on its Head is $\frac{1}{2}$.

Toss a coin 40 times and record the results. State whether you think that your coin is fair.

Extension Work

1 Roll two dice 50 times, recording the total sum of the dice.

a How many times did you roll a 5 or 6?

b What was your experimental probability of rolling a total of 5 or 6?

c Compare this probability with the theoretical probability of 0.25.

2 Repeat Question 1, but roll 100 times.

3 Is the 100-roll experiment closer to the theoretical 0.25 than the 50-roll experiment?

4
I can collect data and record it in a frequency table.

I can understand the meaning of the mode and median, and how to use them.

I can construct and interpret bar charts.

5
I can understand and use the mean of data.

I know how to find probabilities based on equally likely outcomes and experimental evidence, as appropriate.

I know that different outcomes may result from repeating an experiment.

National Test questions

1   *2000 Paper 1*

   a   The diagram shows spinner A and spinner B.

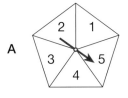

Which spinner gives you the best chance to get 1?

    Spinner A   Spinner B   Doesn't matter

Explain why you chose your answer.

   b   Here are two different spinners. The spinners are the same shape but different sizes.

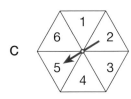
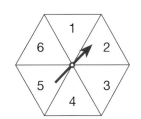

Which spinner gives you the best chance to get 3?

    Spinner A   Spinner B   Doesn't matter

Explain why you chose your answer.

M N U

3 - 22 a

c Each section of spinner E is the same size. Copy spinner E and fill in numbers so that both of these statements are true.

It is equally likely that you will spin 3 or 2.

It is more likely that you will spin 4 than 2.

MNU 3-22a.

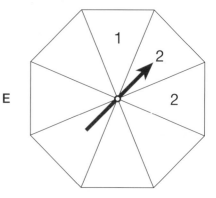

E

2 *2000 Paper 2*

a Paula played four games in a competition.

In three games, Paula scored 8 points each time. In the other game she scored no points.

What was Paula's mean score over the four games?

b Jessie only played two games.

Her mean score was 3 points. Her range was 4 points.

What points did Jessie score in her two games?

c Ali played three games.

His mean score was also 3 points. His range was also 4 points.

What points might Ali have scored in his three games? Show your working.

MTH 4-20b

3 *2006 3–5 Paper 2*

Wine gums are sweets that are made in different colours.

Pupils tested whether people can taste the difference between black wine gums and other wine gums.

The percentage bar charts show three pupils' results.

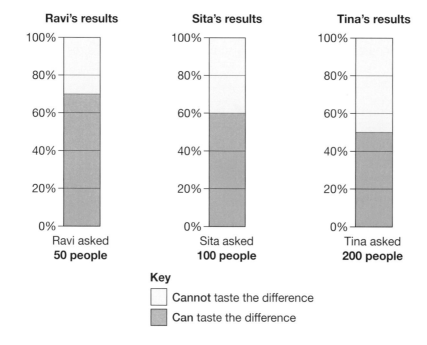

Ravi's results

Ravi asked **50 people**

Sita's results

Sita asked **100 people**

Tina's results

Tina asked **200 people**

Key

☐ **Cannot** taste the difference

▨ **Can** taste the difference

a Copy and complete this table.

	Number of people who were tested	Number of people who **can** taste the difference	Number of people who **cannot** taste the difference
Ravi	50		
Sita	100		
Tina	200		

b Explain why **Tina's** results are likely to be **more reliable** than Ravi's or Sita's.

MTH 4-20b

Questionnaire

Cris created a questionnaire for her Year 8 classmates. She went round asking 41 boys and 39 girls the following questions.

a   What is your favourite band or artist?   **b**   How many CDs do you possess?

c   Which is your favourite Wii sporting game?

This is a summary of her results.

Boy/Girl	Music	CDs	Wii Game	Boy/Girl	Music	CDs	Wii Game
Boy	Fall out Boy	12	Bowling	Girl	Kate Nash	17	Bowling
Girl	Arctic Monkeys	17	Bowling	Boy	Foo Fighters	32	Golf
Boy	Panic! at Disco	27	Boxing	Girl	Arctic Monkeys	43	Bowling
Girl	Kate Nash	34	Bowling	Girl	Spice Girls	26	Golf
Girl	Fall out Boy	32	Bowling	Boy	Kate Nash	32	Boxing
Boy	Foo Fighters	29	Boxing	Boy	Foo Fighters	44	Boxing
Boy	Arctic Monkeys	43	Golf	Boy	Arctic Monkeys	53	Boxing
Boy	Foo Fighters	41	Boxing	Girl	Kate Nash	45	Bowling
Girl	Arctic Monkeys	23	Bowling	Girl	Foo Fighters	36	Bowling
Girl	Arctic Monkeys	16	Golf	Boy	Fall out Boy	28	Boxing
Boy	Foo Fighters	26	Boxing	Boy	Arctic Monkeys	16	Tennis
Girl	Fall out Boy	37	Bowling	Girl	Foo Fighters	19	Tennis
Girl	Foo Fighters	24	Bowling	Boy	Panic! at Disco	20	Golf
Boy	Arctic Monkeys	16	Golf	Girl	Fall out Boy	31	Bowling
Boy	Fall out Boy	33	Boxing	Girl	Fall out Boy	40	Bowling
Girl	Kate Nash	45	Bowling	Boy	Arctic Monkeys	43	Bowling
Boy	Foo Fighters	52	Tennis	Girl	Panic! at Disco	55	Golf
Girl	Foo Fighters	37	Tennis	Girl	Foo Fighters	23	Bowling
Girl	Kate Nash	13	Bowling	Boy	Kate Nash	27	Baseball
Girl	Panic! at Disco	31	Bowling	Boy	Arctic Monkeys	35	Boxing
Boy	Kate Nash	50	Golf	Girl	Kate Nash	31	Golf
Boy	Arctic Monkeys	43	Bowling	Boy	Foo Fighters	28	Bowling
Boy	Foo Fighters	25	Boxing	Boy	Panic! at Disco	46	Boxing
Girl	Arctic Monkeys	30	Bowling	Boy	Fall out Boy	34	Boxing
Boy	Fall out Boy	17	Bowling	Girl	Arctic Monkeys	26	Bowling
Girl	Kate Nash	29	Tennis	Boy	Fall out Boy	18	Bowling
Girl	Spice Girls	31	Golf	Girl	Foo Fighters	22	Tennis
Girl	Arctic Monkeys	48	Bowling	Girl	Foo Fighters	40	Boxing
Boy	Foo Fighters	38	Boxing	Boy	Arctic Monkeys	51	Golf
Boy	Panic! at Disco	21	Bowling	Boy	Arctic Monkeys	42	Golf
Boy	Fall out Boy	20	Tennis	Girl	Kate Nash	46	Tennis
Girl	Kate Nash	37	Golf	Girl	Kate Nash	34	Boxing
Boy	Foo Fighters	48	Boxing	Boy	Foo Fighters	50	Boxing
Boy	Foo Fighters	23	Golf	Girl	Arctic Monkeys	43	Bowling
Boy	Arctic Monkeys	19	Bowling	Boy	Foo Fighters	54	Baseball
Girl	Kate Nash	24	Bowling	Girl	Panic! at Disco	23	Bowling
Girl	Arctic Monkeys	52	Bowling	Boy	Foo Fighters	33	Boxing
Boy	Kate Nash	49	Tennis	Boy	Fall out Boy	41	Boxing
Boy	Foo Fighters	38	Golf	Girl	Fall out Boy	37	Bowling
Girl	Panic! at Disco	25	Bowling	Girl	Kate Nash	46	Tennis

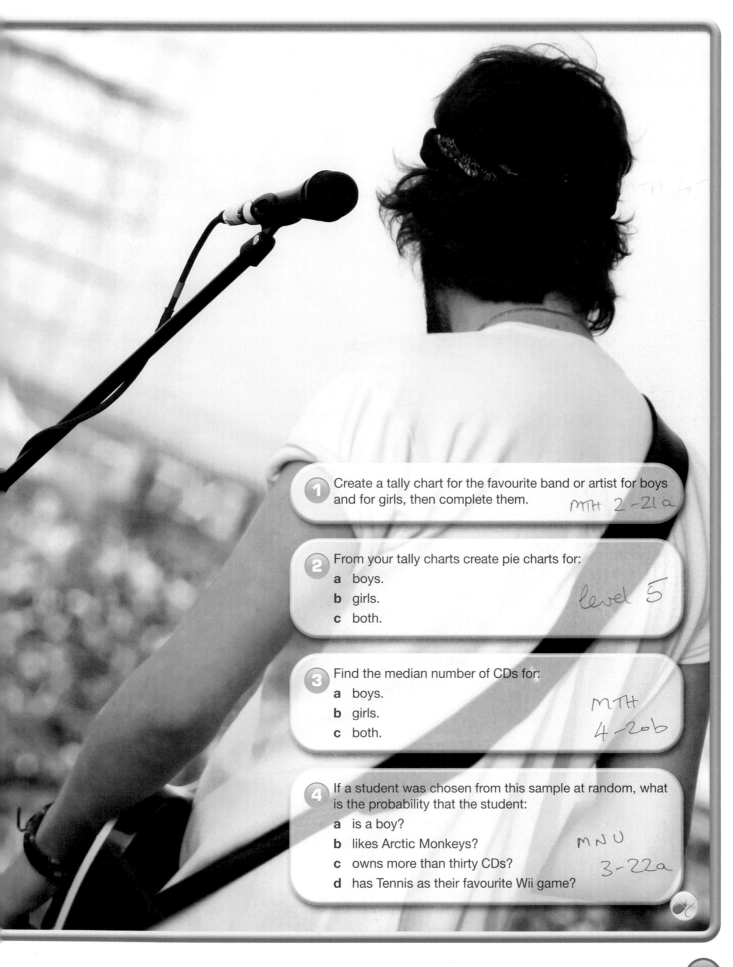

1. Create a tally chart for the favourite band or artist for boys and for girls, then complete them. *MTH 2-21a*

2. From your tally charts create pie charts for:
   a boys.
   b girls.
   c both.

   level 5

3. Find the median number of CDs for:
   a boys.
   b girls.
   c both.

   MTH 4-20b

4. If a student was chosen from this sample at random, what is the probability that the student:
   a is a boy?
   b likes Arctic Monkeys?
   c owns more than thirty CDs?
   d has Tennis as their favourite Wii game?

   MNU 3-22a

Index

William Collins' dream of knowledge for all began with the publication of his first book in 1819. A self-educated mill worker, he not only enriched millions of lives, but also founded a flourishing publishing house. Today, staying true to this spirit, Collins books are packed with inspiration, innovation and practical expertise. They place you at the centre of a world of possibility and give you exactly what you need to explore it.

Collins. Freedom to teach.

Published by Collins
An imprint of HarperCollins*Publishers*
77–85 Fulham Palace Road
Hammersmith
London
W6 8JB

Browse the complete Collins catalogue at
www.collinseducation.com

© HarperCollins*Publishers* Limited 2008

10 9 8 7 6

ISBN 978-0-00-726617-3

Keith Gordon, Kevin Evans, Brian Speed and Trevor Senior assert their moral rights to be identified as the authors of this work.

British Library Cataloguing in Publication Data
A Catalogue record for this publication is available from the British Library.

Commissioned by Melanie Hoffman and Katie Sergeant
Project managed by Priya Govindan
Edited by Brian Ashbury
Index by Michael Forder
Proofread by Marie Taylor
Design and typesetting by Jordan Publishing Design
Covers by Oculus Design and Communications
Covers managed by Laura Deacon
Illustrations by Nigel Jordan, Tony Wilkins and Barking Dog Art
Printed and bound by Printing Express, Hong Kong
Production by Simon Moore

Acknowledgments
The publishers thank the Qualifications and Curriculum Authority for granting permission to reproduce questions from past National Curriculum Test papers for Key Stage 3 Maths.

The publishers wish to thank the following for permission to reproduce photographs:

p.14–15 (main image) © Chris Schmidt / istockphoto.com, p.42–43 (main image) © Sergey Dubrovskiy / istockphoto.com, p.54–55 (main image) © Stephen Strathdee / istockphoto.com, p.54–55 (inset images) © Jovana Cetkovic and Lya Cattel / istockphoto.com, p.94–95 (main image) © Jeff Driver / istockphoto.com, p.108–109 (main image) © Angel Herrero de Frutos / istockphoto.com, p.108–109 (inset images) © Matt Baker, Jennifer Sheets, Milos Luzanin, Mark Evans / istockphoto.com, p.150–151 (main image) © istockphoto.com, p.162–163 (main image) © Chris Howes, Wild Places Photography / Alamy and (inset image) © istockphoto.com, p.176–177 (main image) © René Mansi / istockphoto.com, p.204–205 (main image) © Tetra Images / Alamy, p.220–221 (main image) © Jovana Cetkovic / istockphoto.com